Burying Lenin

Burying Lenin

The Revolution in Soviet Ideology and Foreign Policy

Steven Kull

Westview Press

BOULDER • SAN FRANCISCO • OXFORD

Copyright © 1992 by Westview Press, Inc.

Published in 1992 in the United States of America by Westview Press, Inc., 5500 Central Avenue, Boulder, Colorado 80301-2847, and in the United Kingdom by Westview Press, 36 Lonsdale Road, Summertown, Oxford OX2 7EW

Library of Congress Cataloging-in-Publication Data
Kull, Steven.
  Burying Lenin : the revolution in Soviet ideology and foreign
policy / by Steven Kull.
    p. cm.
  Includes index.
  ISBN 0-8133-1501-8 — ISBN 0-8133-1500-X (pbk.)
    1. Soviet Union—Politics and government—1985-   . 2. Soviet Union—
Foreign relations—1985-   . 3. Perestroika. I. Title.
DK288.K85 1992
327.47—dc20   91-45077
                                                                        CIP

Printed and bound in the United States of America

  The paper used in this publication meets the requirements
of the American National Standard for Permanence of Paper
for Printed Library Materials Z39.48-1984.

10   9   8   7   6   5   4   3   2   1

Contents

Foreword

A turning point for Russia occurred in 1917 when the Bolsheviks came to power, espousing the communist ideology of German social philosopher Karl Marx. The Russian communists turned Marxism-Leninism into a totalitarian system that eventually dominated a widespread empire and influenced the development of countries far from Soviet borders.

A second watershed was the fall of Marxism-Leninism in the Soviet Union in the late 1980s and early 1990s and with it the nearly bloodless dissolution of the Soviet empire.

Many causes have impelled this most recent change in the USSR. Economic difficulties and military confrontation with the West created pressure for change in Moscow. But the most important reason for the relatively peaceful nature of the change is that the revolution in the Soviet Union has been a revolution in thinking. A wholesale change in thinking among the Soviet professional, political, and intellectual elite enabled the changes to occur with very little bloodshed. This change brought new policies to fruition and gave them momentum over time.

Soviet President Mikhail Gorbachev had an instinct for change when he came to power in 1985. But it was the advisers, experts, and political figures around him who conceptualized the change and gave it content in various areas of political life. These individuals moved the change ahead, sometimes slowed it down, and reshaped it during the past six years.

Nowhere has this change in thinking been more evident and of more importance for the West than in the area of foreign and defense policy. New thinking loosened Soviet control over Eastern Europe and retracted Soviet influence in the developing world. Soviet military strength and the intention to use force has diminished to the point that the West has been able to dramatically reduce its defense effort and presence abroad.

But, as Steven Kull describes the evolution in Soviet thinking in this book, the change has not been instantaneous or simple. Different streams of thinking have persisted among the Soviet foreign policy elite and within the individuals responsible for making policy. Kull, Jennifer Lee, and I conducted extensive interviews with members of the Soviet foreign policy elite during the crucial 1988-1991 period when Soviet foreign policy altered dramatically. This was the period during which the Soviets pulled out of Afghanistan, the Brezhnev Doctrine was renounced, and the Berlin Wall fell.

We identified three distinct attitudes held by members of the Soviet foreign policymaking community during that critical, evolutionary period of time. They were: new thinking, the strong advocacy of a nonmilitary approach to foreign policy; traditional Marxist-Leninist thinking, which stressed the dangers of abandoning traditional policies and sought to slow down the change; and a third stream, great-power realism, which saw the objectives of Soviet policy as being the pursuit of classical geopolitical and economic interests, relatively free from either new or old ideologies.

The approach of this study was to press Soviet policymakers to find the limits of the changes in their thinking, then to push them to present their rationales for the remaining vestiges of traditional thinking. Through this process, the three streams of thinking (and the way they were often intertwined in the thinking of individual policymakers) emerged.

We saw the thinking of individuals evolve over the three-year period during which we conducted the interviews. For instance, we would interview people and find that they balked at some major change, such as the reunification of Germany. A few months later we would return and find that even that mental barrier had come down in the meantime. Perhaps most excitingly, we also saw Soviet policy change in response to the evolution in thinking. A change in the thinking of individual policymakers often found expression a few weeks or months later in a shift in the official Soviet position.

It was evident from the interviews that the change was quite wrenching for Soviet policymakers who had been schooled for their entire lives in Marxist-Leninist ideology. Giving up traditional ways of thinking was, as Kull points out, tantamount to giving up a religion for many of them, and it produced a great deal of tension. Sometimes their body language was extraordinary in the interviews. For example, there was the senior expert who literally twisted himself into a pretzel on his chair and hugged himself as he expressed his ambivalence about the changes in Soviet policy.

As interviewers, we were surprised when we encountered particularly passe expressions of traditional thinking, like the journalist who told us in 1988 that he still thought there would be justification for Soviet military intervention in, of all places, Yugoslavia. But we were impressed when an individual took the first cautious steps beyond the limits of official Soviet policy, supporting, for instance, German reunification.

Steven Kull's book is a portrait of a painful but exhilarating period of change seen from the most personal level of the individual Soviet policymaker. It provides not only a specific analysis of the evolution of Soviet new thinking about defense and foreign policy but more general insights into the process of changes in beliefs.

So much has happened since this process of development began in earnest in 1988: the attempted coup against Mikhail Gorbachev in August of 1991, the ensuing devolution of Soviet power to the republics, and the formation of the Commonwealth of Independent States. For example, the August 1991 coup attempt was a sign that traditional thinking, as described in this book, is not entirely dead.

Thus, the various streams of thought examined here will influence the foreign and defense policies of the Commonwealth and the various republics, and indeed, are already doing so.

For example, in Ukraine and in other nuclear republics, a tension is already visible between elements of new thinking and great-power realism in the way that these republics handle the presence of nuclear weapons on their territory. New thinking impelled leaders of Ukraine to renounce nuclear weapons in the fall of 1991 and to call for a nuclear-free zone in their republic. Very quickly, however, great-power instincts began to assert themselves. Ukrainian leaders began to see the value of nuclear weapons in conferring status and power on the republic, especially as Ukraine competes with Russia for influence. So in the winter of 1991, Ukrainian leaders began to back away from their nuclear-free pledge. In his speeches and statements, Ukrainian President Leonid Kravchuk has sometimes espoused the new thinking point of view, and at other times he has articulated the great-power position.

This obvious tension over nuclear weapons is but one example of the way in which the conflicts between the various streams of thinking portrayed in this book will persist and continue to influence policy as the Commonwealth of Independent States and the republics evolve further.

Gloria Duffy
Palo Alto, California

Preface

Shortly before this book went to press the Soviet Union officially dissolved. Thus, it may seem this book is of strictly historical interest. But, though the dissolution of the Soviet Union is a profound event, the change it marks may be less sharp and discontinuous than first meets the eye.

For decades, under the Soviet rubric, Russia has dominated its surrounding republics as well as Eastern Europe. Due to a number of profound changes Russia relinquished its hold over Eastern Europe and loosened its control over the non-Russian republics. Now, under the rubric of the Commonwealth of Independent States, Russia has further relinquished its control over the republics. At the same time, the Russian leaders are trying to salvage some degree of influence and to maintain a coherent foreign policy and military structure for the Commonwealth.

As of this writing this latter effort does not appear very promising. Ultimately, the Russian leaders may end up with their domain scaled back to include only Russia itself. However, even this would not signify that the former Soviet Union has become an entirely new animal. The Russian republic alone would still contain the majority of the population and the vast majority of the land mass, manufacturing capability, natural resources, and military capability of what once was the Soviet Union. In other words, the Russian bear may have lost some weight, may be sick, and may be more benign than before; but it will still be with us.

Of course, the real basis of continuity from the Soviet Union, to the Commonwealth of Independent States and, possibly, to a fully differentiated Russian nation, is the political culture of the Moscow-based elite. This elite has gone through a significant evolution. For some years there was a major factional conflict that climaxed in the abortive coup of August 1991. Since then old-school hardliners have been largely weeded out and new thinkers have gained a firmer hold. And of course, former Soviet President Mikhail Gorbachev has resigned. But for the most part, the personnel that makes up the foreign-policymaking elite has remained fairly constant. Many of the individuals who have taken over the foreign and defense policy functions of the Russian republic formerly worked for the Soviet government. For example, Andrei Kozyrev, presently the foreign minister of the Russian Republic, was formerly a high-level official in the Soviet Foreign Ministry.

Therefore, we can assume that the changes in the Moscow-based political culture instigated by Gorbachev's "new thinking" and described in this book will persevere in the future. When I have asked officials in the new Russian foreign-policymaking elite whether there are any significant differences between their orientation and that of new thinking they have insisted that there is one major difference—they intend to realize the principles of new thinking even more fully.

Nevertheless, many ambiguities still remain about the national identity of what was the Soviet Union. At times it seems that the Soviet Union is history and there are now 15 separate states. At other times it seems that the Moscow elite is simply trying to reincarnate as much as it can of the Soviet Union under the guise of the new Commonwealth of Independent States. On one hand, some of the former Soviet republics are developing their own armies. On the other, the once-Soviet army is still posted even in the Baltic States, which have not joined the Commonwealth, and Russia itself has no independent army nor does it plan to create one. Russian President Boris Yeltsin, objecting to Ukrainian claims on the Black Sea naval fleet, has both insisted that this fleet "cannot belong to any one republic" because it is the "indivisible" property of the Commonwealth of Independent States and that "the Black Sea fleet was, is, and will be Russia's."[1] Although Yeltsin has agreed to put all nuclear forces under the control of a "Combined Strategic Forces Command" for the Commonwealth, he has also insisted that he will have the decision on their use and has pressed for the elimination of all nuclear forces on non-Russian soil.

Perhaps by the time this book appears in print the situation will be clearer, but as of this writing it is difficult to find a word that refers to the political entity that was called the Soviet Union and is now being pulled in several directions at once. While all former Soviet republics have declared independence, eleven of them are both trying to assert their national sovereignty and joining in a looser version of the Soviet Union called the Commonwealth of Independent States. Russia is both championing the idea of the former Soviet republics' maintaining a unified military and foreign policy under the Commonwealth and, at the same time, trying to expropriate for Russia many of the international functions of the former Soviet Union. It is not yet clear what will be the institutional and linguistic successor to the Soviet Union. As a result, for lack of a better word, I have continued to use the noun "Soviet Union" and the adjective "Soviet" to describe this evolving political entity. I hereby apologize to the reader for any confusion this may create.

Finally, the processes that the Soviet Union has undergone over the last years have significance beyond the simple understanding of Soviets or

Russians. The transformation that we have seen from a resolutely totalitarian, expansionist, and renegade state to one that embraces principles of democracy, pluralism, disarmament, and international law is one that we should hope also to see occur elsewhere. The ideas and processes that have supported these changes should be of interest to us, as they pose fundamental questions about what kind of world we hope to create now that the long winter of the cold war has finally passed.

Steven Kull

Acknowledgments

Although I am listed as the sole author of this book, it is actually the fruit of a larger study that included two other researchers: Gloria Duffy and Jennifer Lee. They participated in approximately half of the interviews described in this book and played important roles in formulating the concepts expressed herein. A substantial portion of Chapter 8 is derived directly from research by Jennifer Lee. I am indebted to both of them for their knowledge of the Soviet Union, for their keen insights and for their great sense of humor—something that can be sorely needed when doing research in the Soviet Union.

In the course of carrying out this study we were the beneficiaries of a delightful measure of Soviet hospitality. On three of the four trips to Moscow we were the guests of the Institute for World Economy and International Relations (IMEMO) of the USSR Academy of Sciences—a veritable hothouse of new thinking. Sergei Blagavolin was our primary sponsor. His emphatic support for the original idea of the project was crucial to its inception. Throughout, he was unflaggingly helpful in providing us access to interviewees and offering us candid and penetrating perspectives on the unfolding events in the Soviet Union as well as being one of the warmest people I have ever met. Boris Messiya, also of IMEMO, was our constant companion and a true friend, patiently making arrangements for us as well as, in his wry and oblique fashion, offering us subtle insights into what was really going on. Both of them also spent short periods in residence at Global Outlook, gently looking over our shoulders.

On one of the trips I was the guest of the Institute of Social Sciences of the Central Committee of the Soviet Communist Party. Yuri Krasin, rector of the Institute, was my gracious host, and Yuri Lavrov succeeded in arranging crucial interviews. Andre Kokoshin also opened the doors of the Institute for the Study of the USA and Canada of the USSR Academy of Sciences, of which he is deputy director.

Perhaps above all, I thank the eighty Soviets who agreed to be interviewed for this study. Their openness and candor was a real testament to the reality of glasnost.

Several individuals were very helpful to me in the course of writing this book. Robert Legvold, Richard Smoke, and Vadim Udalov read the entire manuscript, offering invaluable comments. Others who read parts of the manuscript and/or were available to me to discuss key issues included

David Holloway, Ray Garthoff, and Stephen Shenfield. Throughout the writing of this book, R. Jeffrey Smith was a source of stimulating feedback and ideas as well as a close friend. Alexander George was a constant and guiding presence.

Several foundations played an absolutely critical role in supporting this project. The John D. and Catherine T. MacArthur Foundation was our primary benefactor. The Carnegie Corporation, the Alfred P. Sloan Foundation, Rockefeller Family and Associates, and the W. Alton Jones Foundation gave generously as well. For the first year of the study I was also the beneficiary of an award from the Social Science Research Council of an SSRC-MacArthur Foundation Fellowship in International Peace and Security.

The staff and interns at Global Outlook were an oh-so-necessary source of support. Larissa Thompson, Maren Leed, Kristen Hubbard, Don McClure, Sarah Lewis, Riaz Ahmed, Maria Reiling, Victoria Caron, and Leonid Zagalsky assisted in a variety of tasks, some interesting, some tedious. Nancy Doty and Ruth Shapiro kept the Global Outlook office on a steady course.

During the later stages of writing this book I was, for a period, a visiting scholar at the Center for International Security Studies at the University of Maryland. I benefited from the rich interaction with other scholars there.

Finally, I would like to thank my wife, Wendy Grace Kull, who was wonderfully supportive, and offered exceptional insights into Russian culture derived from her unique experiences.

S.K.

1

A Revolution of Ideas

When historians look back on the last half of the twentieth century, the event that will most likely stand out as the most significant is the collapse of Soviet Communism symbolized by the final demise of Vladimir Lenin. Though Lenin died in 1923 his image survived, peering out from millions of iconlike pictures, memorialized in countless statues—his stern visage perennially looking to a distant radiant future. After him a series of Soviet leaders came and went; all, however, eventually fell into disrepute. But Lenin remained, the ultimate father figure, lying in state in the mausoleum on Red Square—the spiritual center of Soviet society and much of the rest of the world.

In addition to being the leader of the revolution and the founder of the Party-state, Lenin formulated an ideology that, like a religion, fundamentally molded Soviet society and culture. His thinking prompted a highly centralized economic and bureaucratic system, an enormous military, and a posture of cultural isolation. He set in motion a messianic foreign policy that, at its zenith, directly influenced the societies of one-third of humanity. His polarized view of relations between the Soviet Union and the nonsocialist world became the defining feature of the post- World War II era.

Now, seemingly overnight, all this has changed. Shortly after Mikhail Gorbachev took the helm of the Soviet state he and his cohorts began to steer it away from Lenin's path, elaborating what was essentially a new ideology dubbed "new thinking." Contradicting the Marxist-Leninist view of social reality as most fundamentally conflictual, new thinking claims that the most fundamental reality is the underlying unity of the world. In contrast to the traditional emphasis on the interests of the proletariat, new thinking proposes a moral order based on all-human or universal values. Dismissing the belief that social evolution will inevitably lead all nations to socialism, new thinking claims that evolution is spawning more diverse social forms but at the same time pressing these diverse forms toward greater harmony and integration. New thinking rejects the notion that the Soviet Union should actively promote and protect socialist revolutions around the world. Instead, each country should be free to choose its own path of development without outside interference, the nature of its government to be dictated by the will of the governed. The keynote of international relations should not be class warfare, but compromise, cooperation, and adherence to international law.

Such ideas led in time to dramatic changes in Soviet international behavior. In Eastern Europe Soviet leaders accepted, and at times even encouraged, the overthrow of Communist Party governments, the removal of the Berlin Wall, the reunification of Germany, and the disbanding of the Warsaw Pact. In the Third World the Soviets withdrew from Afghanistan and, in most regions of conflict, have reduced or eliminated their aid to socialist factions. Instead, they have promoted the principle of "national reconciliation," which calls for feuding factions to accept the democratic electoral process as arbiter. They have adhered to the principle that the legitimacy of a government flows from the will of the governed, even to the extent of allowing their own republics to secede. In the United Nations they have pursued a newly cooperative posture and have even aligned themselves with the international coalition against their erstwhile ally Iraq. They have unilaterally reduced their bloated military and have vigorously pursued disarmament, repeatedly consenting to make the lion's share of cuts. And, throughout, they have repeated the refrain that it is time for the Soviet Union to come out of its isolation and rejoin the world community.

In the domestic realm, too—though the changes have been much more tentative and difficult—the Soviet Union has departed from Lenin. Gorbachev acknowledged the need for economic decentralization, market forces, and even private property. He supported the ideas of multiparty democracy, removed the Communist Party from its exclusive position of power and, ultimately, resigned as its secretary and suspended its activities. On prime-time U.S. television Gorbachev announced that, for the Soviet Union, communism has been a failure. However, it is only since Gorbachev's resignation and the dissolution of the Soviet Union that some of these departures from Leninist domestic politics have really begun to be instituted.

Finally, under the new regime the very image of Lenin has begun to expire. Throughout the Soviet Union likenesses of Lenin have been abused, besmirched, and exploded. The city of Leningrad has regained its prerevolutionary name St. Petersburg. And for Lenin's body, maintained for decades by formaldehyde, plans are being made to bury it in the ground, to finally go the way of flesh and obsolete ideas.

The Unique Revolution

Naturally, Westerners want to understand better how this historic change has occurred. The demise of this long-standing threat to Western security has profound implications. But there are also unique features of this revolution that give it particular import beyond its significance as a specific historical event.

The first feature is that this extraordinary event has occurred so peacefully. Historians would be hard put to find other examples of such a momentous event occurring without a war or at least large-scale civic violence and bloodshed. Throughout the world today are numerous hotspots boiling with the prospect of change. In our heavily armed age, with the horror of war amplified by the alchemy of high technology, the most pressing challenge is to find ways for such change to occur peacefully. The transformation of the Soviet Union offers a remarkable case study.

The second unique feature of the Soviet transformation is that not a single Westerner predicted its occurrence. Just a few years ago Westerners viewed the Soviet Communist Party as solid and intransigent—a permanent fixture on the world scene. Many Americans came to believe in the inevitable nature of East-West conflict with the same certainty as that of an orthodox Marxist. Any American who might have forecast recent events would have been dismissed as a hopeless dreamer.

Even as the change was occurring, many Westerners held to the idea that the change was not real, that the Soviets had a fixed and intractable nature that would soon reassert itself. With the slightest provocation, U.S. pundits announced the beginning of yet another Cold War.

Why was it so hard for us to see that this change was coming and to recognize it when it arrived? More than a simple oversight, this failure suggests a fundamental flaw in the way we analyze political processes and understand the potential for nations to change peacefully.

One reason that Americans may have overlooked the possibility for such revolutionary change in the Soviet Union is their tendency, when analyzing political events, to focus almost exclusively on objective factors. Although such objective factors, no doubt, played a role in the changes in the Soviet Union, the indications in these dimensions were not strong enough to suggest that something really revolutionary was in the offing.

For example, economic trends in the Soviet Union did not point clearly to a radical change. Though there has been a dramatic decline in the Soviet economy since the institution of new thinking, in the years that led up to new thinking (early to middle 1980s) there was no dramatic economic change. There was some flattening of economic growth, but no major decline of the type that occurred later. On the basis of this economic picture one might have expected to see in the middle 1980s some resistance to an expansion of Soviet commitments, but not necessarily the kind of major scaling back that did occur.

One could argue that with the correct economic information Western-ers could have predicted the changes that occurred. Perhaps the economic decline began much earlier than it was recognized in the West. Or perhaps the economic decline that came later was anticipated by the Soviet leader-ship and policies were adjusted in advance in this light. But even now there is no clear evidence that the Soviet economy went through some major decline before it was perceived in the West. And there is little indication that Soviet leaders anticipated the coming collapse or that the changes in their policies were driven by such anticipations.

Furthermore, even if Americans in the mid-1980s had had information that the Soviet economy was worse than it, in fact, was assumed to be or that the imminent decline was anticipated by the Soviet leadership, this would not necessarily mean that they could have predicted a scaling back of activism in Soviet foreign policy. The Soviet economy does not have some fixed limit on the amount of foreign policy activism it can support. Nations vary greatly in the percentage of their gross national product committed to military expenditures. In the 1970s the Soviet economy was smaller than it was in the 1980s and yet it supported a much more ambitious and expensive foreign policy.

This is not to say that economic factors did not play a role in the changes that occurred in the Soviet Union under Gorbachev. Indeed, as we shall see below, for many members of the Soviet elite, the failure of the Soviet Union to keep up with the West economically played an important role in under-mining their faith in Leninism and thus helped prompt an openness to new ways of thinking and a less activist foreign policy. But this was not the only possible response. In the face of economic stagnation the Soviet leadership could have decided, for example, to pursue a more activist foreign policy as a way to distract their public from problems at home. Apparently, economic factors need to be viewed in the context of the meaning assigned to them by the evolving political culture.

Another standard analysis of political events based on objective factors focuses on the relative power of various interest groups or bureaucracies. Here again, it is not surprising that this kind of analysis did not predict the changes that occurred. This analysis assumes that the behavior of individual leaders is largely determined by the institution within which they have a position, and thus the interests of maintaining the power of the institution prevail. Such thinking led, for example, to the oft-repeated assertion that Gorbachev was ultimately a member of the Communist Party and would never do anything to jeopardize the dominant position of the Party. Such an analysis would also apply to Eduard Shevardnadze, Alexander Yakovlev, and even Boris Yeltsin—all members of the Politburo when the radical changes in Soviet ideology were initiated. And yet all of these individuals did, in fact, play important roles in carrying forward a process that led to the ultimate demise of the Party. Also, this anomalous behavior was not limited to a few key individuals. It was the Party itself that annulled Article 6 of the USSR constitution, which established the dominant role of the Communist Party.

Of course,there is room within the bureaucratic perspective for the possibility that specific institutions will accommodate to pressure from competing institutions by relinquishing power. But in the mid to late 1980s there were no significant competing institutions in the USSR that one could see and evaluate through the bureaucratic lens. Though such institutions began to form at the beginning of the 1990s, during the critical years when the changes were being introduced the initiative came almost entirely from within the Party itself.

The Role of Ideas

The paucity of clear indications available through the more standard means of analysis leads us, then, to look to a realm in which there was, in fact, an abundance of signs foreshadowing the historic changes that occurred in the Soviet Union. This is the realm of ideas. As we shall see, almost immediately after Gorbachev came into office, within the Soviet elite there was an intense and high-profile reevaluation of the most fundamental features of Soviet ideology and foreign policy. More than a reevaluation of the means for pursuing established policy objectives, there was a reconsideration and radical reform of the objectives themselves and even of the entire legitimizing foundation of policy.

Such intellectual reevaluations are often dismissed by students of the political process as simply the result of superficial, and often retrospective, efforts to accommodate changes prompted by more objective factors. But in the case of the Soviet Union in the 1980s, apparently the changes in the realm of ideas predated and may even have prompted the objective changes that came later. The change in the activism of Soviet foreign policy appears to have been instigated less by a change in the economic ability to support such a policy than by a change in the attitude about suffering the economic expense (though, as we shall see, it appears that this change in attitude was influenced by the economic decline inasmuch as it contributed to a loss of faith in the prevailing ideology that prompted an activist policy). The collapse of the Communist Party appears to have been instigated more by intellectual ferment within the Party than by organized opposition outside of the Party.

The tendency to focus on objective factors is not surprising. The kind of changes that have occurred in the Soviet Union usually occur only in the aftermath of a war, a major economic breakdown, or a coup d'etat. But in this case, it appears that the changes in the Soviet Union were precipitated by a genuine ideological revolution, less like a conventional political revolution than a collective "aha" experience, a religious conversion, or (as we shall discuss below) a scientific revolution.

To some extent the potential for such an ideological revolution is specific to the Soviet Union. Because the Soviet political culture has never gone through the process of pluralization and secularization that began for Western culture in the Renaissance, ideology has continued to play a very central role. The Russian Orthodox Church was dominant until the 1917 revolution, and when Lenin instituted his particular brand of Marxism it took on many of the features and functions of a religion. More than a form of government, Marxism-Leninism offered a vision of the nature of all social life, even of reality, and a concept of legitimacy and meaning. It held out to the individual a path to self-transcendence through serving the revolution.

Furthermore, certain features of Russian culture have dovetailed with Marxist-Leninist ideology, giving it further strength. The Marxist vision of social relations as inherently conflictual corresponds to the centuries-old Russian experience of being perennially threatened and attacked by hostile forces from the West and the East. This feeling of insecurity, coupled with the Marxist-Leninist belief that the conflict with the capitalist world would ultimately be resolved through military confrontation, led the Soviet state to take a very suspicious attitude toward the outer world and to seek larger and larger military forces.

Marxism-Leninism also blended with a penchant for group narcissism—the shared sense that the Russian people are superior and have a unique role to play in the world. Lenin called for the Russian people to be the leaders of humanity, to messianically guide the world out of the chains of class oppression and into a classless and just society.

But, perhaps preeminently, Marxism-Leninism has appealed to the

Russians' deep-seated fear of chaos and their extraordinary willingness to submit to and have confidence in solutions based on centralized governmental control. This proclivity has led to a highly stratified and centrally controlled domestic structure as well as buttressing the belief that the solution to the problems of the entire world lie in the increasing power of a unified and centrally controlled Communist movement.

The convergence, then, of these preexisting Russian traits with a totalistic ideology served to create a self- confirming and powerful juggernaut. To students of the Soviet Union, this juggernaut has always seemed so tightly formed that its disintegration at the breathless rate we have seen over the past half-decade was inconceivable. And yet, because the fabric of Soviet culture has been so tightly woven it is also more possible for it to go through a sudden and radical shift, to make a quantum leap into a radically new ideology.

At the same time it is important not to overstress the unique character of Soviet political culture, to make it into something too exotic or assume that there are no broader lessons to be drawn from the Soviet experience. Even the pluralistic political culture of the United States rests on a bedrock of shared, though often implicit, ideological assumptions. This foundation also is not immune to destabilization. During the depression of the 1930s many Americans began to lose faith in the capitalist system and to turn to socialism and even communism as an alternative. The nation's troubled military involvement in Vietnam so rocked Americans' concept of their role in the world that it tore the fabric of U.S. political culture, prompting a challenge to a wide array of hitherto unquestioned assumptions. In the 1970s, when the Soviets made some minor advances in a few small countries in obscure corners of the Third World, many Americans worried greatly that the United States was losing the ideological battle. When the Japanese, in the 1980s, began making major economic gains, Americans began to doubt, and many still doubt, whether the United States still represents the wave of the future. If all these things were to have happened simultaneously (which approximates what happened in the Soviet Union in the 1980s), it is likely that the United States would also have been ripe for a major ideological revolution.

The Limits of the Change

As of this writing, the Soviet Union* is making important strides in the direction consistent with new thinking. This progress makes it easy to overlook the ways in which Soviet behavior has not changed. Despite their calls for disarmament, the Soviets still have the largest military in the world and continue to produce massive numbers of weapons. Despite their calls for all nations to withdraw their military forces from other nation's territories they still have hundreds of thousands of troops outside their own borders and a large navy that patrols areas far from their coastal waters. Despite their calls for eliminating the transfer of weapons to other countries, the Soviet Union is still one of the two largest weapons exporters and uses such transfers as a means of enhancing its geostrategic position. Despite their calls for reducing nuclear forces to the level of "reasonable sufficiency," and even after making the unilateral reductions announced in October 1991, they will still have an enormous nuclear arsenal with tens of thousands of highly capable nuclear warheads.

A number of questions arise: How much are these persisting behaviors simply vestiges of the past? Can we expect that they will change significantly in the future? To the extent that they persist, does this indicate the persistence of sub-rosa Leninist aspirations? Or are there other ideas and attitudes driving such behavior? Should we worry that such ideas and attitudes might reignite an expansionistic and ambitious foreign policy, for example, if the Soviet economy got back on its feet?

Finding out how Soviets rationalize such behavior may also give us insight into the potential international behavior of individual republics, especially the Russian republic, should they continue to move toward more independent foreign policies. The cultural proclivities that dovetailed with Leninism to form the Soviet juggernaut did not necessarily disappear when the Leninist framework collapsed. As we shall see, there are already signs that some of these ideas and attitudes are taking on new non-Leninist forms, forms that may shape the policies of the independent republics.

---

* As was discussed in the preface, I am continuing to use the term 'Soviet Union' because, as of this writing, it is not clear whether the former Soviet Union will evolve into a Commonwealth of Independent States with a coherent foreign and defense policy or if the republics will go their separate ways, thus making Russia the real successor to the Soviet Union.

Overview

This book seeks to explain both the roots of the changes in Soviet ideology and foreign policy associated with new thinking and the reasons for the persistence of Soviet behavior apparently at odds with the principles of new thinking. It examines the changes in Soviet ideology and foreign policy primarily as a function of the revolution of ideas in the Soviet political culture.

Two types of sources are used as windows on Soviet political culture. The first consists of material drawn from the Soviet public discourse—official statements by top government officials as well as articles and public statements by members of the general policymaking elite. The second consists of in-depth interviews carried out from October 1988 through May 1991 with eighty-two members of the elite who make foreign policy, including government officials in the Ministries of Foreign Affairs and Defense, officials in the institutions of the Central Committee of the Communist Party of the Soviet Union (CPSU), members of the military, journalists, and scholars in the various think tanks of the USSR Academy of Sciences. (For more detailed information on the nature of the public discourse materials analyzed, the individuals interviewed, and the interview process, see the appendix.)

Chapters 2 through 5 look at the revolution in Soviet ideology, examining various streams in the thinking of the Soviet policymaking community as well as new thinking. Chapters 6 and 7 explore how the changes in Soviet ideology have had an impact on Soviet behavior in the Third World and Europe. The final chapter considers how the changes in Soviet ideology converge with Western universalist concepts of world order and the prospects this convergence holds for the future.

2

Challenging Lenin

Although new thinkers have often tried to downplay the fact, the cornerstone of new thinking is its challenge to the orthodoxy of Lenin. Before new thinking there were some limited efforts to modify Lenin's Marxist framework. Joseph Stalin moderated some of its international aspirations. Nikita Khrushchev, in light of the effects of nuclear weapons, challenged the notion that a war with the capitalist West was necessarily inevitable. Leonid Brezhnev, for the same reasons, rejected the traditional certainty that, in the event of such a war, socialism would certainly prevail, saying that there could be no winners in a nuclear war. However, it is only with new thinking that Lenin has been challenged on such central questions as the ultimate direction of socioeconomic evolution.

Lenin stated unequivocally that this direction is toward the total victory of the proletariat over all other classes, leading to the institution of socialism throughout the world. Shortly after the 1917 revolution he wrote:

Our victory [will] be a victory only when our cause succeed[s] in the entire world, because we launched our action exclusively in the expectation of a world revolution....Our cause is an international cause, and so long as a revolution does not take place in all countries...our victory is only half a victory, or perhaps less.[1]

This outcome is not something that would only happen spontaneously. Rather Lenin saw the Communist Party as an active agent that would persist until "we have...conquered the whole world."[2]

In the last years of his life, Lenin did mellow a bit. He became more flexible and spoke less of the need to promote world revolution. Nevertheless, to the end of his life he was unwavering in his central belief that ultimately "the complete victory of socialism is fully and absolutely assured."[3]

In the ensuing decades since Lenin's death the central vision of the fundamental political and moral reality as the conflict between socialism and capitalism leading inevitably to the victory of socialism has, until recently, never been questioned. Even under Gorbachev, the Twenty-seventh Party Congress Programme in 1986 stated: "The present epoch...is an epoch of transition from capitalism to socialism and communism and of historical competition between the two world socio-political systems....The advance of humanity towards socialism and communism...is inevitable."[4] The program also stated: "History has entrusted the working class with the mission of the revolutionary transformation of the old society and the creation of the new one."[5]

The New Heresy

Nonetheless, in the first few years after Gorbachev ascended to the leadership of the Soviet Union all of these fundamental notions were called into question. The notion of the centrality and necessity of struggle between the social systems was directly challenged. In a historic speech to the Foreign Ministry in July 1988, then Foreign Minister Eduard Shevardnadze said flatly, "The struggle between two opposing systems is no longer a determining tendency of the present-day era."[6] Later he even called the idea of "world revolution" a "sincere illusion."[7] Poignantly, he even stressed the potential for truly amicable relations saying, "We do not want to fight, and love is still a remote possibility."[8]

In Gorbachev's speeches there was a complete absence of any reference to the ultimate victory of socialism. Instead, Gorbachev asserted that "the world is moving" not toward socialism but "to a pluralism which is natural for the new times." Rather than stressing the fundamental illegitimacy of capitalism in the conflict with socialism, he said that this newly embraced pluralism "presupposes equality and can only be realized on the basis of balanced interests."[9]

Among Soviet intellectuals with whom we spoke it was recognized that such statements did involve a real break from the past. As one policy analyst has noted:

> It's different because Gorbachev doesn't propose a single outcome at the end of a historical process. And [Marxist-Leninist] ideology assumes a predictable outcome at the end of a historical process....He doesn't say that at the end there will be a certain kind of system, a certain defined system in the end....He now seems to agree that "Yes!," capitalism has a future....He even agrees that we should let the Third World go the capitalist way. We shouldn't bother about any of our allies because they are going the capitalist way, because they should. It's normal....One could of course ask oneself whether Gorbachev believes that finally, in the very, very long term, in the final analysis, the world will move beyond capitalism by, say, the year 3000. But he never mentioned it in any speeches. He omits it completely....[It's] pluralism for good... a de facto break with this stage-by-stage outlook of historical development which Lenin had.

At times Gorbachev even portrayed the movement toward pluralism as something intrinsically positive: "The states and peoples of the Earth are very different, and it is actually good that they are so."[10] He said, "The increasing varieties of social development in different countries" calls for

> respect for other people's views and stands, tolerance, a preparedness to see phenomena that are different as not necessarily bad or hostile, and an ability to learn to live side by side while remaining different and not agreeing with one another on every issue....Thus, the question is of unity in diversity.[11]

Some Soviets we spoke with were quick to argue that this kind of thinking was not really so new, that the notion of living "side by side" originated in Lenin's concept of peaceful coexistence with capitalist states. However, for Lenin such a posture was meant as a temporary tactic, and he wrote that "it is inconceivable for the Soviet Republic to exist alongside of the imperialist states for any length of time. One or the other must triumph in the end."[12] Peaceful coexistence was necessary as a means of attaining a "respite" or "breathing spell" for socialism to build up its economic and military reserves and for the domestic forces of discontent to grow in the capitalist countries.

Such thinking persevered through the Brezhnev years. Brezhnev insisted that the peaceful coexistence of detente "creates favorable conditions for the struggle between the two systems and for altering the correlation of forces in favor of Socialism."[13]

Gorbachev, however, unabashedly rejected this notion, saying that it is "no longer possible to retain...the definition of peaceful coexistence of states with different social systems as a 'specific form of class struggle.'"[14] He traced the evolution of the idea of peaceful coexistence from being a temporary measure to being a permanent model for international relations.

> Naturally, there have been changes in Lenin's concept of peaceful coexistence....At first it was needed above all to create a modicum of external conditions for the construction of a new society in the country of the socialist revolution...[but it] subsequently became a condition for the survival of the entire human race, especially in the nuclear age. [15]

This last phrase points to the critical element that Gorbachev saw as prompting these fundamental departures from Lenin's central concern with the class struggle—the devastating potential for nuclear war. This threat was seen as generating a universal human interest in survival, an interest that transcends class interests. Gorbachev wrote:

> Since time immemorial, class interests were the cornerstone of both foreign and domestic policies....Acute clashes of these interests have led to armed conflicts and wars throughout history....But now, with the emergence of weapons of mass, that is universal destruction, there appeared an objective limit for class confrontation in the international arena: the threat of universal destruction. For the first time ever there emerged a real, not speculative and remote, common human interest—to save humanity from disaster.

New thinking flowed directly from this concern. Gorbachev explained: "The backbone of the new way of thinking is the recognition of the priority of human values, or, to be more precise, of humankind's survival.[16]

At times Gorbachev was quite direct in acknowledging that this emphasis on all-human values does conflict with traditional Marxism:

> It may seem strange to some people that the communists should place such a strong emphasis on human interests and values. Indeed a class-motivated approach to all phenomena of social life is the ABC of Marxism....Marxist philosophy was dominated—as regards the main questions of social life—by a class-motivated approach.

Nevertheless, he said:

> The vitality and creative potential of Marxism-Leninism by no means lies in the idea that every single line that its founders wrote is of absolute and everlasting significance. Many ideas, including major ideas that they put

forward under specific historical circumstances, belong to their own time. They have 'exhausted' their usefulness and receded into history.[17]

Boldly revising, Gorbachev said that given the new condition of nuclear vulnerability, the "primary thing that defines" international relations is no longer class conflict but "the immutable fact that whether we like one another or not we can survive or perish only together."[18] Therefore, "in the present situation it is especially important to not emulate medieval fanatics and not to spread ideological differences to inter-state relations."[19] Instead, international relations should be deideologized and "states belonging to different social systems can and must cooperate with one another in the name of peace."[20]

In this light Gorbachev challenged the legitimacy of any use of force. In his December 7, 1988, speech to the United Nations he said that

> force and the threat of force can no longer be, and should not be instruments of foreign policy. This applies in the first instance to nuclear weapons, but it goes further than that. Everyone, and the strongest in the first instance, is required to restrict himself, and to exclude totally the use of external force.

At the Twenty-seventh Party Congress he stressed the need to "shed once and for all, resolutely and irrevocably" ideas about "the acceptability and permissibility of wars and armed conflict."[21]

In this light Gorbachev also roundly promoted disarmament. The arms race was denounced as unwinnable and dangerous. Instead, all nations, though especially the superpowers, should engage in an arms control regime that would lower their respective military forces to the minimal level of sufficiency. Ultimately, nuclear weapons should be completely eliminated and nations should only have forces necessary for their territorial defense. Nations should also agree to refrain from transferring weaponry to other countries or even to factions fighting revolutionary wars.

Such thinking flies in the face of Leninist doctrine. Lenin clearly embraced the Marxist notion that violence and war are legitimate and necessary means for promoting the class struggle. Disarmament was seen as anathema. In a tract derisively titled "The 'Disarmament' Slogan," Lenin wrote:

> Socialists cannot be opposed to all war in general and still be socialists....To put "disarmament" in the programme is tantamount to making the general declaration: We are opposed to the use of arms. There is as little Marxism in this as there would be if we were to say: We are opposed to violence!...We

are living in a class society from which there is no way out.... [Disarmament] is tantamount to complete abandonment of the class struggle point of view, to renunciation of all thought of revolution.[22]

Gorbachev did not hesitate to tackle this issue directly. In his book *Perestroika* , published in 1987, he wrote:

> In developing our philosophy of peace, we have taken a new look at the interdependence of war and revolution. In the past, war often served to detonate revolution....But when the conditions radically changed so that the only result of nuclear war could be universal destruction, we drew a conclusion about the disappearance of the cause-and-effect relationship between war and revolution....At the 27th CPSU Congress we clearly "divorced" the revolution and war themes....[23]

As Shevardnadze said to the Supreme Soviet in late 1989, "In today's world many ideological goals are outweighed by threats to our civilization."[24]

After these challenges to Lenin that occurred in the first years of new thinking, Gorbachev and those around him refrained for some time from making new challenges. As part of his general move to the right in 1990-1991 Gorbachev even signed a decree banning any further removals of statues of Lenin and other monuments to the October revolution.

But in the months leading up to and following the summer 1991 coup, Gorbachev once again began to take important steps that further removed Leninism from its key position in Soviet political culture. In July 25, 1991, at a plenary session of the CPSU Central Committee he observed that "in the past, the Party recognized only Marxism-Leninism as the source of its inspiration." But now he has insisted that it is necessary to draw on a more diverse range of ideological sources.[25] After the coup, while he at first clung to the idea that the Party could be reformed, just days later he initiated the dissolution of the Party and resigned as its General Secretary. Finally on a U.S. television program, in response to a question about communism, he answered that the Soviet experience "has allowed us to say in a decisive fashion that the model has failed."[26]

The Process of Ideological Revolution

Naturally the question arises: How did this radical change occur? What was the process that led to this revolution in Soviet ideology? There is no real historical parallel for such a major political change to occur in a peaceful manner.

Perhaps the closest parallel can be found in the revolutions that have occurred in the field of science, revolutions that upset key elements in the prevailing view of reality. Such revolutions have been analyzed by Thomas Kuhn in his work, *The Structure of Scientific Revolutions.*[27] Briefly stated, Kuhn has found that scientific revolutions are preceded by the appearance of a number of anomalies that contradict the dominant scientific paradigm. Initially there are efforts to dismiss these anomalies as insignificant or to account for them by making slight modifications to the prevailing paradigm. With time, though, as the anomalies persist and grow, this dismissal becomes less and less tenable, until finally there is an effort to find a radically new paradigm.

This model did prove to be valuable in interpreting the Soviet ideological revolution. In the interviews we had the opportunity to ask Soviets what were the anomalies that gradually undermined their belief in the Marxist-Leninist framework. Two themes were recurrent: (1) the recognition of the condition of interdependence with and thus the need to cooperate with the West and (2) the failure of the socialist economies to compete with capitalism.

The most salient factor that prompted this growing awareness of interdependence was the insuperable ability of the West to inflict nuclear devastation on the Soviet Union. This undermined a key element in the Marxist-Leninist paradigm. Central to this paradigm has been the prospect of winning a war with the forces of capitalism. According to Marxism-Leninism, at some point the capitalist countries, suffering from increasing domestic dissatisfaction and unrest and threatened by the appeal of the political system offered by socialism, would desperately strike out militarily at socialist countries. A major war would ensue, but the socialist countries, due to their moral superiority, would prevail and socialism would be instituted on a global scale. The prospect of this apocalyptic climax has always played an important role in the Soviet stress on having a strong military.

Since the development of atomic and nuclear weapons there have been efforts to modify this element of Marxist-Leninist dogma in light of the potentially devastating effects of an all-out war. Khrushchev took the position in 1956 at the Twentieth Party Congress that although such a war with the capitalist West was still possible, it was not "fatalistically inevitable." There remained, however, ambiguity about whether, if such a war nonetheless occurred, the socialist forces would prevail. Within military circles there was an active debate. Those that argued against such a possibility stressed the destructive physical properties of nuclear weapons while those that held to the possibility of victory stressed socialism's ideological superiority.[28] In a famous 1977 speech in Tula, then General Secretary Brezhnev broke new ground when he declared the impossibility of winning a nuclear war. However, even then Brezhnev left some ambiguity by saying only that the imperialists could not hope to win a nuclear war. In 1981, though, at the Twenty-sixth Party Congress, he went a step further and stated unequivocally that no party could hope to win a nuclear war.

In the interviews, a number of Soviets explained that it took some years for this new perspective to take firm hold in the public consciousness. They cited several key factors that contributed to the gradual change. First, there was the increased tension in Soviet-American relations in the early 1980s that in the USSR, as in the United States, drew people's attention to the subject of nuclear war. Several Soviets interviewed referred to the impact of television programs sponsored by the International Physicians for the Prevention of Nuclear War, in which prominent physicians stated categorically that a nuclear war would be so devastating that they would have no means of effectively caring for the population. Others mentioned the results of a number of studies describing the probability of a nuclear war producing a nuclear winter. Above all, though, the accident at Chernobyl was cited as having had a major impact. Many Soviets saw in the release of radiation from the accident a tangible demonstration of the effects of nuclear weapons. This gave fresh impetus to the idea that a nuclear war would be unthinkable and that a new cooperative world order must be found that precluded the possibility of general war.

In the press Soviet leaders took pains to explain how the condition of mutual vulnerability necessitated an adaptation of Soviet ideology. Then Soviet Deputy Foreign Minister Anatoli Adamishin, for example, engaged in an imaginary dialogue with a Soviet citizen who asks: "How...are we to accept unconditionally the primacy of universal values when we have heard for so many years that it is a struggle between classes that is the main driving force of society at all stages in its development, and so on and so forth?" To which he answered:

> Obviously, the interests of people and their groups, parties and classes will clash within countries, and the interests of different countries will do so in the international arena....However, there have arisen objective limits beyond which a class of interests cannot extend....There is no escaping this objective reality. These limits have been set by the possibility, one which did not exist earlier, of physically destroying one another, and virtually the entire human race.[29]

For some respondents the state of mutual vulnerability derived from nuclear weapons was only one factor highlighting the fact that the Soviet Union was necessarily interdependent with the West and therefore must cooperate with the West. Another such factor was the existence of global environmental problems threatening life on the planet that can only be addressed through concerted efforts. As one respondent pointed out, "the biosphere does not recognize any ideological divisions."

Yet another factor was a growing perception of the interdependent nature of the world economy. Soviets recognized that the most prosperous nations were fully integrated in the worldwide flow of goods and services, referred to as "the international division of labor." The Soviet tendency to isolate itself economically, then, was seen as backward and problematic.

Finally, the threats from Third World sources— instability and especially terrorism—were seen as demonstrating that not all international problems were directly derived from the competition between the two world systems. Rather, such threats were seen as shared by both socialist and capitalist, and to deal effectively with them it was clear that countries from both systems would need to cooperate.

But of all the anomalies that challenged the prevailing Marxist-Leninist paradigm, the most compelling and most frequently cited was the failure of socialist economies to compete effectively with the West. Although socialist economies have for some time lagged behind the West, in the earlier part of the century socialists could find reassurance in the fact that their economies were, nonetheless, growing at a faster rate. More recently, though, these rates have slowed and many socialists have begun to doubt that socialist economies will in fact close the gap. A high-level official in the Information Department of the Central Committee whom we interviewed described a conscious effort to try to face this reality squarely:

> We must be objective. Maybe the most important decision for us was that we try to objectively see ourselves and the world around us....And how we can say that socialism will be victorious, will win, if our productivity is much lower than your productivity; if productivity in West Germany is much higher than productivity in East Germany; if the quality of production and the standards of living in South Korea is much better than in North Korea? You see? We see that in all these occasions, this competition between the two systems on the economic level—it is the decisive, the most significant level—this competition is not on our side.

The reason that this failure to compete economically was so crucial to Soviets is not simply that they desire a higher standard of living. The above-quoted Central Committee official recalled sadly, "Lenin said that the

system that has more production from an economic point of view will win."
Similarly the prominent academic Oleg Bogomolov said, "Lenin...said that
labor productivity was the crucial criterion of socialism. But today we see
that the West has been more successful precisely in this respect."[30] Therefore,
the fact that socialism is lagging behind called into question the entire
socialist paradigm and the belief that the world will ultimately move
toward socialism.

When we asked interviewees whether they still believed that the world
is ultimately moving toward socialism they almost invariably brushed off
the idea. For example, a political analyst at the influential Institute of the
World Economy and International Relations (IMEMO), stated: "We reject
the dogma that the proletariat should achieve socialism in the world....I
think that the Marxist theory that capitalism will be replaced by socialism
is wrong." A high-level Central Committee official said: "Personally I don't
believe in the triumph of socialism over capitalism because that is not our
aim now...,the majority of the country doesn't believe that this is our aim."
A Supreme Soviet delegate prosaically described the notion of a world
revolution as "a childhood dream that would never come true."

Other Soviets went so far as to say that not only is the evolution toward
socialism not proceeding, there are even movements in the opposite direction. Georgi Mirsky, a policy analyst at IMEMO, stated flatly in 1988 that:

> To affirm that the revolution is continuing is to make a misstatement....We
> must admit...as we take a realistic look at things at present there is not a
> single revolutionary process carrying the national liberation struggle
> further and deeper.

Instead he argued: "It is generally pro-bourgeois...mainly state-capitalist
systems that have become crystallized in capitalist-oriented countries."
And among Third World governments: "the overwhelming majority...are
by no means interested in the defeat of imperialism. They are fighting to win
a place in the sun within the world capitalist family."[31]

Kim Tsagalov, a prominent military academic, echoed similar thinking,
saying that the claim that Third World countries are naturally anticapitalist
"is largely invented." He spoke of the "ebb and flow in the world revolutionary wave" and said unhesitatingly that "the eighties showed that the
highest wave was over for both the world revolutionary process in general
and the socialist orientation in particular." He then went on to say that
capitalism, far from being on the wane, is on the rise:

The scientific and technological revolution, whose different effects are unforeseeable, enabled capitalism, especially in its citadel, to sharply enhance its survivability and to postpone its historically inevitable end indefinitely. In my view, all talk about a deepening general crisis of capitalism is now irrelevant. That's all there is to it. Capitalism has got its breath back and has rejuvenated itself as a result of technical and technological advances. It now reacts very flexibly also to social problems of bourgeois society.

He even went so far as to say that: "We can forecast in the group of socialist-oriented countries and in the Third World as a whole, growing trends toward a capitalist model of development."[32]

Some Soviets even argued that a key reason that developing countries are moving toward capitalism is that capitalist countries have fulfilled many of the ideals of socialism better than have the socialist countries, not only in the sense of economic productivity but also in the general quality of life for the working class. At the first Congress of People's Deputies in 1989 several deputies argued that socialist transformations have gone further in Western European countries than in the Soviet Union.[33] We were carrying out interviews in Moscow at that time and even people high in the party structure, though visibly shocked and disturbed by these comments, said that they had to agree that such ideas had some validity. One Central Committee official said sadly: "How can we talk about the competition and who will win in the twenty-first century if...capitalist countries, their road of development will lead to socialism of a higher level than ours?"

The irony of this situation has not gone unnoticed. Valentin Falin, then director of the International Department of the CPSU Central Committee commented: "It is a paradox that the CPSU introduced the idea of socialism in the world, but distorted it, while in other places in the capitalist world, it gained ground."[34]

Some Soviets have described the process of losing the socialist faith as an intellectual process. For example, the prominent academic Alexei Kiva has recounted his own experience of gradually losing confidence that socialism would help Third World countries out of their backwardness.

Is there conclusive evidence that the world is going over from capitalism to socialism? I doubt it....To shut our eyes to realities would mean showing the worst kind of opportunism....I am prepared as a Marxist to repeat in purely abstract theoretical terms our traditional affirmation that socialism will succeed capitalism in the same way as the latter succeeded feudalism. But as a scholar I am ready to qualify what I have just said, for I need incontrovertible proof which I do not see as yet....As for capitalism, it will certainly not be succeeded by the socialism we all know.[35]

For other Soviets, accepting the failure of socialism has been a very emotional process. Igor Yanin, of the CPSU Academy of Social Sciences wrote in 1989:

> We are now compelled to ponder over questions which not long ago it might have seemed sacrilegious even to raise. "Socialism as a social system has begun losing its appeal. There is a real threat of its being pushed to a secondary place in the world, with dramatic implications for the subsequent prospects of human progress," noted Vadim Medvedev....The above alarming statement by the party leads us to the simple but apparently inevitable conclusion that time is not on our side. We affirmed the reverse for so many years that this conclusion now hurts us almost physically...(To be precise, we have awakened social consciousness to what everybody knew, saw and sensed.)...We now know many bitter things about ourselves....We have arrived through suffering...at new political thinking....The only thing worrying and embarrassing us is: Why did this reversal have to be born so painfully, to be paid for with so much suffering? [36]

Vyacheslav Shostokovsky, former rector of the Moscow CPSU Committee High Party School, explained more recently:

> A country lives not only on its economy and institutions, but also on its mythology and founding fathers....It's a devastating thing for a society to discover that their greatest myths are based not on truth but propaganda and fantasy. But that is what we are experiencing now in the case of Lenin and the revolution.[37]

A prominent and senior member of the Supreme Soviet we interviewed said with resignation:

> We lost the economic and social and the technological edge with capitalism....nobody believes [that socialism will spread] in our country now....[The idea is] false that all the world and all countries would follow the same way....Before, we believed we had the best society in the world. Now the young generation believes they live in the worst society in the world.

For other Soviets, especially younger ones, the process of breaking with the dreams of the past has been full of anger that at times reaches a vitriolic pitch laced with heavy sarcasm. Marina Pavlova-Silvanskaya of the Institute of the Economy of the World Socialist System wrote in a 1988 article in *Sovetskaya Kultura* :

Right from childhood millions of people were told: "We are always correct in our daring designs...," we are unceremoniously remolding nature, we will alter our heritage beyond recognition, we will move mountains, we will reverse rivers. "Spiritually uplifting literature," propaganda drums constantly beating successes, education in the spirit of so-called historical optimism—all this created a particular social-emotional background: The confidence that everything is within our grasp once we have proclaimed our commitment to Marxism has generated a sense of being the chosen people, an irrepressible desire to show off to other peoples, to boast inexcusably, and to lecture them....The attitude that "there are no obstacles before us either at sea or on land" has ultimately produced the most abnormal of fruits, including a vast multitude of leaders at all levels, firmly convinced that everything is within their power provided they slam their fist on the table or shout louder into the telephone.[38]

The academic V.K. Chernyak, in a 1988 article in *Komsomolskaya Pravda*, wrote:

We have gotten used to phrases like: "We are mankind's vanguard"; "The future belongs to us"; "We will be victorious on a world historical scale." But have you tried to put yourself in the position of those who, in our opinion, are in the rear guard, to whom the future does not belong, and who, according to our viewpoint, are doomed to depart from the historical arena, doomed to perish? What must their attitude toward us be? When Khrushchev told representatives of capitalist countries "We will nail you into your coffin," he did not say anything unexpected; he only expressed in crude form the essence of the concept of class struggle in the international arena. It is no accident that people in the West have formed an impression of the USSR as being a country that seeks to conquer the world. Fear of the USSR undoubtedly played an important role in rallying the European capitalist states around the United States....Let us ask ourselves and reply honestly: Did our country not give other peoples reason to think of it as an enemy? If we find no such reasons, then why do we need the new thinking? In that case it should be possible to continue to live and work in the old way. Yet we ourselves admit that this is no longer possible. Thank God that as a result of changes in our domestic and foreign policy, new trends have emerged.[39]

3

New Thinking:
A New Ideology

The ideas that transformed Soviet policy were more than an effort to neutralize the more provocative features of Leninism. Implicitly and even explicitly Gorbachev and his cohorts elaborated an alternative view of the world that is highly coherent and can be aptly characterized as an alternative ideology. This new ideology is based on a universalist vision of the nature of reality and of the direction of sociopolitical evolution. From this vision flows the belief that legitimacy arises from the integrative process of evolution. Cooperation, even between classes, is seen as both laudatory and, given the universal nature of fundamental human values, possible.

The Universalist Vision

Though Gorbachev has rejected much of Marxism-Leninism, he has embraced the notion that a dialectical conflict is basic to the process of evolution. This conflict is seen as the natural result of the evolutionary differentiation of more diverse forms. However, rather than making this dialectical process the fundamental ontological principle, he has stressed that even more fundamental is the principle of the unity of the world. This underlying unity generates a natural movement toward greater integration.

Describing this dual process in socioeconomic evolution, in his speech to the United Nations in December 1988, Gorbachev said:

> The history of the past centuries and millennia has been a history of almost ubiquitous wars, and sometimes desperate battles, leading to mutual destruction. They occurred in the clash of social and political interests and national hostility, be it from ideological or religious incompatibility....However, parallel with the process of wars, hostility, and alienation of peoples and countries, another process, just as objectively

conditioned, was in motion and gaining force: The process of the emergence of a mutually connected and integral world.[1]
Gorbachev has also explained how this dual process is reflected in the present tension between socialism and capitalism:

> The coexistence on our planet of two social systems, each of which is living and developing according to its own laws, has long become a reality. But one must see the other reality as well. And that reality is that the interconnections and interdependence of countries and continents is becoming increasingly closer.[2]

To some extent this movement toward greater integration is seen as arising from the effect of conditions specific to the modern era, especially those engendered by technological development. Gorbachev has said that growing interdependence "is an inevitable condition of the development of the world economy, of scientific and technological progress, the acceleration of the exchange of information...in short the entire development of human civilization."[3]

Sometimes it is stressed that interdependence arises from increasingly shared environmental threats. As Shevardnadze has said: "Faced with the threat of environmental catastrophe, the dividing lines of the bipolar ideological world are receding. The biosphere recognizes no division into blocs, alliances or systems. All share the same climatic system and no one is in a position to build his own isolated and independent line of environmental defense."[4] Most frequently, though, it is stressed that the condition of mutual vulnerability engendered by nuclear weapons and the global consequences of a nuclear war have objectively created a more interdependent world.

More fundamental than these temporal features of the modern world, however, is the ontological reality of the unity of the world. Gorbachev has stressed that this unity underlies the apparent multiplicity of the world: "For all the contradictions of the present-day world, for all the diversity of social and political systems in it,...this world is nevertheless one whole."[5] He has used various analogies to underscore this underlying unity. Common are boat analogies: "We are all passengers aboard one ship..."[6] or "we are all in the same boat now."[7] Similarly, the Soviet Deputy Foreign Minister Vladimir Petrovsky used the image of the world as a "spaceship,"[8] reminiscent of R. Buckminster Fuller's concept of "spaceship Earth." Another analogy Gorbachev has used is that of a singular organism: "This worldwide organism may be contradictory and complex, but everything in it is linked by the same destiny."[9] Gorbachev has also compared humanity to a group of mountain climbers: "[t]he nations of the world resemble today a pack of mountaineers tied together by a climbing rope. They can either climb on together to the mountain peak or fall together into an abyss."[10] In a statement of the Congress of People's Deputies a familial analogy was used: "We are all children of Mother Earth and have a common destiny."[11]

Some new thinkers use near-mystical language to describe this singularity. Alexander Yakovlev, then a Politburo member and widely regarded as one of the original architects of new thinking, said that the countries of the world are "organically" connected so that "the results of their interaction are greater than the mere sum of their efforts." He even seemed to attribute to the world a nascent self-consciousness: "The world is becoming ever more aware of itself as a single organism."[12] Mikhail Kaloshin, an editor of the Foreign Ministry's journal *International Affairs* has written: "The Earth and civilization are an integral live, pulsating organism and humanity today is the collective mind of this organism."[13] Addressing the United Nations, Shevardnadze said that all nations "share a place where individual national efforts unite into a single energy field."[14] Gorbachev has called for the "formation of an integrated universal consciousness,"[15] something he has described as "a form of spiritual communion and rebirth for mankind."[16]

Most critical to this line of thought is the belief that humanity can actively reorient its awareness to the realization of the oneness of the world. Gorbachev has proclaimed that "mankind needs to rethink the values of its own existence, to transform the entire system of relationships in the world, economic, political, legal, and cultural, and first of all, to restructure its thinking in the realization that the world is one and interrelated."[17] In his December 7, 1988, speech to the United Nations he said that "we must search jointly for a way to achieve the supremacy of the common human idea over the countless multiplicity of centrifugal forces....Everyone should take part in moving toward more unity in the world."[18] Gorbachev has also called for such changes in the way humanity views its relation to nature saying that "[m]ankind is beginning to realize for the first time that it is a single entity, to see the indissolubility of interrelationship between man, society and nature, and to evaluate the consequences of its production activity and its political choices."[19]

Grasping the unity of the world is portrayed as a psychological process that requires a conscious effort. Adamishin has said: "Physicists....have long realized the unity not only of the world but of the entire universe. It is now politicians' turn." He complained that "the process of realizing our main unity—universal unity—is moving too slowly. Selfish economic and political ambitions and pretensions are hampering the efforts."[20]

To achieve this new awareness, according to new thinking, a key effort is neededto remove one's "ideological blinders,"[21] to "get away from that view of the world where we see everything in black and white"[22] and to develop "a new political intellect, which...destroy(s) the mutual `images of the enemy.'"[23] The idea that it is invalid to see the West as an enemy is a radical departure from the past. For decades the idea of the West as intrinsically imperialistic and aggressive—and therefore an enemy—has been a cornerstone of Soviet thinking. When the concept of the "enemy image" was first introduced it usually referred to specious Western tendencies to see the Soviet Union as a threat. But increasingly Soviets are stressing that it is also invalid for them to see the West as an enemy. In 1989 the Congress of People's Deputies issued this statement: "No force in the world really poses a threat to our security. We categorically deny the myth of a Soviet military threat...and we believe the time is ripe for burying its mirror reflection as well."[24] In a June 1990 interview Vadim Zagladin described the evolution of this process:

> Well, we saw the other side as evil incarnate and believed ourselves to be a source of nothing but good...Yes, we have had a one-sided view of the world. We regarded ourselves as being apart from the rest of the world, as it were. But now we see that we are part of this world and that we should live together with it, that there is not an empire of evil and an empire of good.[25]

Another key expansion of awareness, prescribed by new thinkers, is for peoples of various nations to expand their sense of identity to include a larger whole. Shevardnadze has said that the "the concepts `mine', `theirs', and `ours'" need to go through profound transformations based on "the recognition of the primacy of `ours.'"[26] He has called for a greater awareness that "this world (is) a single whole, that pain is indivisible, that there is no such thing as other people's trouble."[27] Yakovlev has said that with greater awareness of the world as a "single organism," "painful tension in one organ cannot fail to affect the others."[28]

Universal Values

In May 1989 the Soviet government declared that "in its foreign policy it proceeds from a vision of the world as a supreme value."[29] Closely allied to this "vision" is the concept of "universal values." As Adamishin has said, "For all the diversity of today's world...there exist universal values and common principles more important than all distinctions put together.[30] In new thinking these universal values are seen as creating the preeminent foundation of legitimacy.

The definition of universal values, though, is a bit fuzzy. There seem to be two definitions which, while not contradictory, are nonetheless distinct. Sometimes universal values are defined in terms of the interests of the larger whole of humanity over and above any component part. At other times they are defined as values that are universally held. However, as we shall see, these two are ultimately merged by the assertion that universally held values also happen to be ones that serve the larger whole.

The notion of universal values as those serving the interests of all of humanity emerged partly in contradistinction to the notion of class values. According to Lenin, all morality was to be entirely subordinated to the interests of the proletariat and of the class struggle. In the early to middle 1980s this principle began to be visibly challenged in the form of a debate among Soviet intellectuals about whether, given the destructive potential of nuclear war, "revolution" (i.e., class interests) or "peace" (universal values) should be the higher priority in Soviet foreign policy. With the rise of new thinking, this debate was firmly resolved as Shevardnadze in a key speech in June of 1988 proclaimed "the preservation of peace as the highest priority."[31]

Gradually this line of thinking was expanded beyond an interest in simply avoiding war. A general principle emerged that in every case the interests of the larger whole of humanity should take precedence over the "egoism"[32] of all sectarian interests, be they class, national, or religious. Universal interests came to be equated with morality itself and lead to a remarkably high-toned assertion that all foreign policy decisions should adhere closely to the highest moral principles.[33] Shevardnadze elaborated that the human race has to "establish a single axis of ethical coordinates and learn to subordinate its individual component parts and specific interests to the interests of the community of nations as a whole."[34]

Naturally it was recognized that a simple call to morality as the good of the whole hardly constituted a new idea. All ideologies claim to serve the good of the whole. And yet new thinkers reject the self-righteous and paternalistic posture that such ideologies, including Marxism-Leninism, tend to engender. When such ideologies shape a state's foreign policy it can easily lead to an effort to impose one's ideology, if necessary by force. To differentiate their emphasis on all-human values from such an ideological orientation, new thinkers have tried to emphasize that they are not proposing a set of fixed ideas but rather a kind of process. Petrovsky has said that "new thinking is not a doctrine but a method" and that "it would be a mistake to believe that universal answers can be found once and for all to every question that arises."[35] Shevardnadze has argued that universal values point to "dialogue in the name of unity."[36]

At the same time, though, new thinkers generally go further and insist that a dialectical effort to find agreement will necessarily produce fruit because at a deep level there are values common to all members of the human race—thus the second definition of universal values.

Such universal values are seen as being deep seated and ahistorical. Adamishin has written: "For all the diversity of today's world and the distinctive character of different countries, cultures, traditions, social systems, worldviews and political convictions, there exist universal values and common principles more important than all distinctions put together."[37] Yakovlev has said: "New political thinking is dictated by the centuries-old moral aspirations of people...which have existed over millenniums in all parts of the world...[and] which we call the universal human aspirations today."[38]

What then are these universal values in the sphere of international relations, values that are both universally held and serve the larger whole? These are sometimes listed as a series of virtues including "freedom, justice, tolerance, and pluralism in the defence of the principles of democracy."[39] Gorbachev has cited "trust" as a universal value.[40]   But there is also a conceptual framework that gives them a coherent theme: They are all seen as playing an essential role in creating a cooperative world order. Such a world order is seen as both reflective of the underlying unity of humanity and a necessary response to the contemporary threats to humanity's survival.

In stressing the value of achieving cooperation, even between nations of differing social systems, new thinkers frequently have recognized that this goal contradicts the traditional Leninist viewpoint that dialectical conflict is necessarily a preeminent feature of reality and especially in relations between nations with different class orientations. As a senior policy analyst we interviewed explained, Soviet new thinkers are discarding "some of the basic premises of our preceding theory about imperialism, about the inevitability of conflict and war." Shevardnadze has said, "We are moving away from the primitive beliefs about the allegedly congenital aggressiveness of human and state communities."[41] Gorbachev has written that socialism "must be freed from overtones of confrontational attitudes, of absolute, metaphysical confrontation between contemporary social systems."[42] Instead, "Life itself...require[s] a transition from confrontation to cooperation among peoples and states irrespective of their social system."[43]

This perspective does not rule out the reality of competition, especially between nations of differing social systems. However, it stresses that this competition both can and should be contained within a cooperative context.

Gorbachev has written: "Economic, political and ideological competition between capitalist and socialist countries is inevitable. However it can and must be kept within a framework...which necessarily envisages cooperation."[44]

The pursuit of a cooperative world order is not only seen as a necessary adaptation to a more dangerous world. It is also attributed with an intrinsic normative value, in some cases on the same plane as the traditional competitive effort to achieve world revolution. Shevardnadze has said that "cooperation for the salvation of civilization...this is the sacrosanct struggle. This is our world revolution." He also has recognized the discontinuity with traditional Marxism-Leninism, saying that the revolutionary struggle for cooperation "is not the world revolution that our predecessors spoke of....We must cooperate with everyone."[45]

To achieve this cooperative order new thinkers have outlined a number of key principles. A critical one is to abandon the maximalism of traditional Bolshevism and to embrace compromise. As a senior policy analyst explained to us, "new thinking is kind of a spirit of compromise."[46]

Closely related is the idea that one must take the other party's interests into account and then try to find some sense of fairness or a "balance of interests." Gorbachev has said, "big politics...cannot be built entirely on one's own interests, which are inevitably one-sided"[47] and Shevardnadze has spoken of the need, in negotiations, to "take as a basis an age old principle of...reciprocality."[48] As Victor Kremenyuk, a specialist on negotiation at the Moscow Institute for the Study of the USA and Canada, has written: "New political thinking implies...operating on the principles of equal benefit, reciprocal regard to the legitimate interests of the other side....Negotiations must establish a balance of interests, for without it no equitable and lasting agreement can be reached."[49]

A political analyst in one of our interviews explained further:

Respondent: Take again this example of regional conflicts. Now everything is judged by the balance of forces of conflicting parties and of their allies. If we move to the balance of interests, we try to objectively assess the real interests of the involved parties.

Interviewer: What do you mean "real"?

R: I mean real....The whole set of their geostrategic interests, their political interests, their economic interests. Without all these propagandistic and ideological dimensions or psychological dimensions that distorts enormously the regional interests of the parties. You have to understand why, just the "why" of the behavior of the other party. And trying to look at this behavior and this policy not through your own glasses but through the pure crystal of the objective situation in the world. Because now everything that is going on now in the world is seen through your national interests. But you've got to take into account the interests of the other side.

Another political analyst explained in more specific terms how this thinking would apply to what he called "the geopolitical differences" between the United States and the Soviet Union: "We are primarily a continental power and the U.S. is primarily a maritime state. We must take this into account... And of course it will not be some arithmetical approach, arithmetical equality. It will be the equality of the balance of interests." Or, as another interviewee said a bit more vividly, "a balance of interests means you don't push the other guy to the wall."

Such principles as balance and equality are seen not only as applying to the Soviet-American relationship. Gorbachev has written: "The only solid foundation for security is the recognition of all peoples and countries and of their equality in international affairs,"[50] and that this "principle of equal treatment" applies to "all countries regardless of their size, geographical position, or domestic conditions."[51] Soviet leaders have been surprisingly unequivocal in asserting that Soviet policy should absolutely adhere to this high-toned principle. Falin has categorically asserted that "we are prepared to be equal among equals in everything and everywhere."[52] Gorbachev has said: "We do not demand for ourselves either privileges or exemption from rules that are mandatory for all,"[53] and "the Soviet Union does not seek privileges or benefits for itself to the detriment of others and does not expect advantages at the expense of others."[54]

Gorbachev has even said that the Soviet Union is ready, along with other nations, to eliminate all its nuclear weapons so as to eliminate its special status as a nuclear power and thereby promote the equalization of all nations.[55] At the Twenty-seventh Party Congress he stated that "it is vital that all should feel equally secure."[56]

In line with this egalitarian thinking there is also an emphasis on all countries participating in the international decisionmaking process. As the late Marshall Sergei Akhromeyev, then an adviser to Gorbachev, explained, "each country has the right to participate as an equal with other countries in the discussion and resolution of *all* problems of international life"[57] (emphasis added). In this light, new thinkers have emphasized the need to build a broad-based consensus in international relations. In his December 7, 1988, speech to the United Nations Gorbachev said that "world progress is now possible only through the search for a consensus of all mankind."[58]

Another principle that flows from the value of equality is the notion of freedom of choice. This principle applies at the individual level in the form of human rights. It also applies to nations in their right to select their own form of government. Gorbachev has said:

> Freedom of choice is a universal principle to which there should be no exceptions....The failure to recognize this...is fraught with very dire consequences, consequences for world peace. Denying that right to peoples, no matter what the pretext, no matter what words are used to conceal it, means infringing upon even the unstable balance that it has been possible to achieve.[59]

The emphasis on equality and freedom, blended with the notion that legitimacy arises from the larger whole, points naturally to the value of democracy. New thinkers embrace democracy as a powerful universal ideal and the only viable social structure for creating stability. Yakovlev has observed that "democracy is today the slogan that imparts movement to the whole world, it is a condition for its survival and progress, a genuine path to the future....democratic orders...are the sole reliable base for the establishment of genuine social justice and freedom."[60] Petrovsky, in a speech to the UN, said: "Democracy is indivisible from the law."[61]

Furthermore there are indications that some Soviets recognize, as many Western political scientists have, that democratic institutions significantly reduce the probability that a country will initiate war. An article in the January 1988 issue of *Kommunist* notes that "bourgeois democracy serves as a definite barrier in the path of unleashing war....The history of the American intervention in Indochina clearly demonstrated this....The Pentagon now cannot fail to recognize the existence of limits placed on its actions by democratic institutions."[62] Andrei Kozyrev, formerly of the USSR Foreign Ministry, now foreign minister of the Russian Republic, wrote in 1990:

> The main thing is that the Western countries are pluralistic democracies. Their governments are under the control of legal public institutions, and this practically rules out the pursuance of an aggressive foreign policy. In the system of Western states...the problem of war has essentially been removed.[63]

And in the interviews numerous Soviets expressed hope that by bringing Soviet foreign policy under greater democratic control through oversight by the Supreme Soviet the Soviet Union would be less apt to launch such aggressive actions as in Afghanistan.

As we will see in greater detail in later chapters, the embrace of democratic processes as a supreme value has also had a significant impact on the Soviet approach to regional conflicts. The Soviets have departed from their traditional objective of simply promoting socialist factions. The fact that one side may be seeking to establish a socialist government is no longer seen as intrinsically giving that side preeminent legitimacy. Legitimacy can only be conferred by a democratic process that expresses the will of the whole of the people. Thus, to solve regional conflicts new thinking stresses the principle of "national reconciliation," which calls for feuding factions to cooperate in a democratic electoral process.

Interestingly, some Soviets have begun to view democratically elected governments as inherently legitimate. When the United States used limited air power to help Philippine President Corazon Aquino put down a rebellion, most Soviet commentaries were critical. However, Andrei Grachev, an aide to Gorbachev, said that he "understood" such a use of force, explaining that "democracy must be defended."[64]

New thinking also goes further than prescribing democracy as an intranational mechanism. A recurring refrain is that international relations, as well, must be "democratized." Gennadi Gerasimov, then Foreign Ministry spokesman, said that "the path to international security today lies through restructuring the whole system of international relations on a democratic basis that is common to all mankind."[65] The meaning of this notion is somewhat ambiguous. One could infer that it means establishing a democratic world government. And indeed there have been some efforts to develop some ideas along this line, the most prominent being an article by Georgi Shakhnazarov, an adviser to Gorbachev, titled, "Governability of the World."[66] On the whole, such ideas have not been given much serious attention, though a number of Soviets with whom we spoke did feel that there are such prospects in the long-term future.

Apparently a more limited interpretation of the idea of democratizing international relations is that nations should be responsive to world public opinion and, more importantly, to the opinions expressed by the UN General Assembly. For example, Shevardnadze, speaking to the Supreme Soviet in October 1989, said with a tone of moral outrage:

> When more than 100 UN members kept condemning our action for a number of years, did we need anything else to make us realize: We had placed ourselves in opposition to the world community, had violated norms of behavior, and gone against common human interests.[67]

Here again is the idea that the democratic process, by reflecting the larger whole (be it national or international) intrinsically confers legitimacy on certain positions.

But then new thinking also goes further, suggesting that, to democra-tize international relations, nations should be willing to subordinate some of their sovereignty to democratically derived international law and to the international institutional mechanisms of enforcement—in particular, the United Nations and its International Court of Justice. Concretely, this means countries should be willing to accept the compulsory jurisdiction of the International Court of Justice in a growing sphere of international issues. The steps the Soviets have so far made in this direction are still limited, but, as Petrovsky claimed at the United Nations, they arguably demonstrate "the Soviet Union's fundamental turn to the use of third-party arbitration." [68]

In a broader sense new thinkers see the integration of the world through the international rule of law as itself a universal value. Speaking at the United Nations Petrovsky said: "It is only law and order and self-restriction by international law that is capable of securing a positive evolution of the world." The United Nations, specifically, is seen as the key force for serving this evolution toward greater unity: "It is the United Nations alone that is capable of identifying and pooling, at a universal level, national aspirations, and uniting the disparate efforts into a single creative power."[69]

On a more philosophical note Shevardnadze, also in a UN speech, said: "Today the humane goal formulated by Kant two centuries ago has special relevance for us: 'The greatest challenge for the human race, which nature compels it to meet, is to attain a universal civic society based on the rule of law.'"[70]

Clearly, many of the values specified by new thinkers as universal values—equality, freedom, democracy, the rule of international law—are basically the same as Western liberal values. Sometimes Soviets seem to ignore the Western precedents for these ideas and act as if they were cut out of whole cloth by Soviet new thinkers. Some have tried to demonstrate that these ideas have precedents in Russian thinking going back before the revolution. Others, though, do recognize the Western roots of these ideas. Some go so far as to portray the values embraced by new thinking as basically signaling a return to European values. For example, Vyacheslav Dashichev of the Institute of Economics of the World Socialist System has said: "The USSR left European civilization about 60 years ago, the East European states 40 years ago, and now we return to the European cradle, to European civilization...to these basic human, I would say European val-

ues."[71]   Andrei Kolosovsky has spoken of "returning to the bosom" of
European civilization and has said that embracing universal values

> means that we are stating our readiness to accept anew the values of
> European civilization, many of which we vigorously rejected over the past
> 70 years, alluding to class interests.[72]

Others, though, stress that such similarities arise because socialism and
capitalism share common European roots. Fyodor Burlatsky, a prominent
intellectual and formerly a member of the Supreme Soviet, has explained
that

> for all the diversity of views, the bourgeois and socialist concepts go back
> to the same historical sources; they drew many ideas from the great
> thinkers of the age of the Enlightenment and the early bourgeois revolu-
> tions, from Voltaire and Rousseau, Montesqieu and Hugo Grotius, Jefferson
> and Paine.[73]

Vadim Medvedev, then a member of the Politburo responsible for ideology,
spoke of "return[ing] the country to the bosom of the world humanist
tradition."[74]

However, the most common means for accounting for the similarities
of new thinking and Western liberal values is to embrace the once heretical
idea that there is a growing "convergence" of socialist and bourgeois views.
For example, Dashichev has said: "The clear borders between socialism and
capitalism, in the old sense of the word, are disappearing. Convergence will
lead us to a new society."[75] Yakovlev commented: "Now for convergence.
I admit that my views have changed considerably in this respect since the
sixties. I think the convergence process is an objective one; it has been in
progress for a long time, and will increase."[76]

In our interviews it was quite common to hear such references to the
notion of convergence, in some cases coupled with an ironic comment about
how it used to be regarded as blasphemous. Even relatively conservative
members of the military spoke about it. For example, a colonel who had
previously praised Lenin in near-religious terms said that the world is not
ultimately moving toward socialism. Bringing his hands together in a
sweeping upward movement, he said that the world was moving toward a
"synthesis...of the best" in socialism and capitalism.

This idea of convergence and synthesis is attractive in a variety of ways.
It frames the Soviet movement toward capitalist values as being reciprocated
by the trend in capitalist countries, over the last decades, to incorporate
certain socialist ideas and gives a faint basis for still valuing the Soviet

socialist revolution. As Gorbachev said in a speech in Washington, D.C., in May of 1990:

> If there had not been our revolution and those societies which it engendered, then—despite everything that subsequently befell us, all the distortions and everything that we experienced, powerful and liberating stimuli were given to the world: equality of rights, justice, attention to the ordinary individual and his social protection!.... I shall tell you bluntly: If this had not occurred, capitalism would not have mobilized its resources. But a model arose and this was a spur. People had to think about how to oppose the model, how to prove that capitalism, too, could do something for people. That's precisely what happened. They said: Plans are nonsense, regulation is nonsense. But now people are regulating and planning everything. Only how? If they are doing it as we did, that is bad; but if special tasks are being tackled, if there is a regrouping of resources and so on, then our ideas have done some good.

The idea of convergence is also consistent with the new-thinking idea that out of the dialectical process universally accepted values will naturally emerge that reflect the underlying unity of humanity. In the same speech Gorbachev said, "So we are one civilization, with all our differences" and later that day he elaborated as follows:

> [T]he general idea which is capturing people's minds on the threshold of the 21st century is standing out ever more clearly. That is the idea of universal unity. Its practical implementation is an epoch-making task. The diverse nature of the world and the complexity of its problems are such that it can only be solved on the paths of synthesis, at all events by the mutual infusion of the aspirations, values, achievements, and hopes of different peoples. In a world of nuclear, ecological, and other threats global unification is the opportunity for the survival of mankind.[77]

The Legitimation of Self-interest

There are several paradoxical features of Soviet new thinking. One is in its description of the larger socioeconomic evolutionary process. This process is seen as both moving toward greater differentiation and pluralism, and toward greater unity and integration. Closely related is another paradox: Soviet new thinking exhorts humanity to achieve a higher moral level by acting in a manner consistent with values that serve the good of the whole of humankind; at the same time it rejects the notion of self-sacrifice for idealistic causes and has effectively rehabilitated the idea that self-interest is legitimate.

Some writers have challenged the whole phenomenon of revolutionary zeal. In a controversial article that appeared in 1989 Alexander Tsipko, then Central Committee official, called into question the revolutionariness of the original Bolsheviks. He asked, "Was everyone looking for the truth in Marxism and revolution" or were they driven simply by prideful impulses to be part of an elite vanguard and to avoid the "routine" of daily life? Tsipko disparaged the subordination of the value of personal relationships to the value of the revolutionary cause: "Even today many are convinced that one must love the laws of history more than one's own mother."[78]

In the realm of foreign policy this challenge to the notion of self-sacrifice has raised the question of whether the Soviet Union should make economic sacrifices to promote socialism in the world. New thinking has discouraged such efforts as part of the larger policy of "deideologizing" international relations. It has been proposed that national interests should become the highest priority in a nation's foreign policy.

New thinkers are explicit that such an orientation is something new for the Soviet Union. A foreign policy analyst we interviewed explained that in the past

> there was mainly the ideologically spelled-out interests like class interests, international interests, interests of supporting the fighting people, the struggling people....The category of national interest was simply excluded in foreign policy research for this country.

Dashichev has written that past Soviet policy was based on "the complete unification and merger of nation-state and ideological interests. We equated the two groups of interests. I think the consequences were disastrous."[79] Gennadi Yanayev, then vice president and later the leader of the abortive coup, denounced the past Soviet tendency to ignore its national interests and credited the new change in attitude for the fundamental reorientation that has occurred in Soviet foreign policy and in the larger world.

> [O]ur national interests...for several decades were sacrificed to a "bright future" and "historical expediency"—concepts deformed by ideological dogmas and confrontational stereotypes. This in turn contributed to our country's unnatural isolation in the world and held back integration trends, reproducing an atmosphere of hostility, suspicion, and mistrust. Strictly speaking, it was largely thanks to the political "rehabilitation" of our own national interests that prospects were opened up for the radical restructuring of the system of international relations on the basis of stability, security, and a balance of

interests, i.e., on the basis of panhuman interests.[80]

Such thinking flows partly from the assumption that ideological competition has become too dangerous in a nuclear-armed world. A greater emphasis on national interests is seen as an antidote to overzealous ideological tendencies and is most apt to lead to equilibrium in relations between states. For example, Igor Malashenko, then at the Central Committee's International Department (now a deputy spokesman for Gorbachev) wrote that "no matter how paradoxical it may seem, more consistent orientation by each member of the international community to the realization of its own national interests could become a first step foward achieving a "balance of interests" between nations."[81] Boris Pyadyshev, editor-in-chief of the Foreign Ministry's *International Affairs*, has written that to pursue an "integral and interdependent world" and "tranquility in relations between all states" the "important thing" for the Soviet Union is to maintain a clear "orientation to the national interest of the Soviet state."[82]

Others have put more stress on how the pursuit of national interest is intrinsically valid. In an article in *New Times*, Adamishin addressed the generic question of national self-sacrifice, asking rhetorically, "[S]hall we call for sacrifices today so that all may live better tomorrow?" And he answered "[E]xperience has categorically shown" that this question "must be answered in the negative....Our philosophers now openly characterize putting off man's well-being until some time in the future as sheer nonsense."

Adamishin then referred to potential challenges to such thinking from what he calls the "ideological approach" to foreign policy.

> I am aware that my putting priority on national interests gives rise to a great number of questions, not always ill-intentioned. Isn't this approach a pure manifestation of selfishness? How does it conform with lending a helping hand to one's ideological partners who are working for the building of a new society in their respective countries? Or what about giving aid to poor countries? In real life we meet such questions as these very frequently.

He responded by saying: "No one questions the principle that aid and support must be extended to others but it must be done within reasonable limits, without overdoing it. "But, he argued, the key question to be asked is, "What is the best way of promoting one's country?" And added, with a slightly defensive tone, "Almost every nation the world over is engaged in doing this, and there is no reason why we should despise it." [83]

Consistent with this new emphasis on national interests and the eschewal of self-sacrifice is widespread emphasis on the Soviet domestic economy as the main consideration in Soviet foreign policy. Shevardnadze said in 1989 that "the diplomatic service must turn more boldly to the problems of the economy....Our *main priority* is to provide conditions maximally favorable for perestroyka in the country.[84]

Bogomolov echoed a similar refrain, increasingly common among the Soviet elite:

> I think the economic evaluation of foreign policy should come to the fore. The task of foreign policy is not only to ensure the country's security, but also to facilitate its socioeconomic progress. Whether foreign policy helps to save resources for productive utilization - that is one of the main criteria in evaluating it.[85]

Other political analysts have sharply criticized past Soviet policy behavior for ignoring the relationship between economics and foreign policy. Academics Alexei Izyumov and Andrei Kortunov ridiculed in an article in *International Affairs* past Soviet tendencies to have "boasted...that it had no economic interests abroad, as if it were so rich that it need pay no attention to this sphere." They portrayed the Soviet Union as foolishly falling prey to insidious U.S. attempts to "get the Soviet Union involved in a broad-scale geopolitical rivalry" so as to "undermine its international positions." In its blindness, they pointed out, the Soviet Union ended up subsidizing other socialist countries, while the U.S. involvement in the Third World produces a net profit. The remedy that Izyumov and Kortunov proposed is quite forthright:

> We should display more selectivity in identifying our goals and commitments abroad. In particular, it would be expedient to gradually abandon our global rivalry with the USA and refrain from the costly support of unpopular regimes, political movements, parties...and bring [our] goals more into accord with our economic potential.[86]

This trend toward reducing the external activism of Soviet foreign policy has also been enhanced by growing Russian nationalism. In a 1989 interview with a prominent policy analyst he explained:

R : The public believes that there is no need for relations we had with Ethiopia or similar countries, the countries that demand help, and see nothing but their own narrow interests. Communist Russia, Communist Messianism has died...We don't have any economic foundation for messianic rule. Not only because of that. Because this idea has already become psychologically exhausting....[in the past] Russophiles and representatives of Russian messianism were united in one. But now there is a division. To make Russia a worthwhile country...they turn away from messianism.

I : Russophilism is turning away from messianism?

R : Yes.

I : Why do you think that has happened?

R : The experience of the twentieth century. The negative results of the Communist experiment in Russia. It was the Russian population that gained less.

I : The failure within domestically or the failure in terms of promoting it in the larger world?

R : Both. It's not just simply a negative reaction to failure. It's much clearer and deeper. There is an understanding that it shouldn't have been done at all. That it was immoral.

I : Immoral? Say more.

R : You shouldn't impose upon other people those norms of life that they don't need. And this kind of understanding is on the increase in society....We should have dealt with our own problems. We should have gained much more.

Consistent with, and perhaps one of the deeper causes of, the new stress on national interests and the domestic economy is a new emphasis on the legitimacy of personal gratification. Soviets have historically emphasized the value of individual self-sacrifice for collective goals. This Soviet commitment to the collectivist ethos has even taken on religious overtones complete with its own icons. Until recently a common sight in Soviet cities was posters and murals depicting muscular young men and women toiling side by side, their faces uplifted and glowing with the satisfaction of sublimating their personal interests to create a new Eden for all.

But now exhortations to make individual sacrifices for the collective good have all but disappeared. Gorbachev has even made the value of personal gratification one of the central tenets of his new thinking. Speaking in Poland in 1988 he explained "the purpose" of the changes he was trying to effect in the Soviet Union:

We want...to make sure that in a socialist society all people...live well and feel happy....The most important thing is for people in Soviet society...to feel good. That is the reason for the most important turnaround which we are both effecting through restructuring in the Soviet Union....The human dimension, the human criterion must be the main criterion for judging the achievements of socialism and, conversely, its losses. We are embarking on the humanization of society through restructuring and renewal. A man who feels good is capable of great things.[87]

Gorbachev has been quite explicit that this emphasis on personal gratification is a break from past attitudes. In a major article on socialism that appeared in November 1989 he wrote that the distortions originating with Stalin

> led to the loss of the main asset in the Marxist and Leninist concept of socialism: the concept of people as an end rather than a means. Instead of the idea of the free development of each individual as the condition for the free development of all there appeared an idea of people as "cogs" in the party and state machine....[88]

Such thinking was part of a general critique of the traditional Soviet attitudes toward the individual. Andrei Kozyrev, then a USSR Foreign Ministry official and now Foreign Minister of the Russian Republic, complained that the traditional Soviet system "has been suppressing the individual under the pretext of a class and ideological struggle in the international arena."[89] Such thinking has not been limited to the province of liberal intellectuals. Even military officers have expressed a change in attitude about self-sacrifice. For example, Colonel-General Nikolai Shlyaga, chief of the Soviet Army and Navy Main Political Directorate explained in a September 1990 *Pravda* article:

> new ideas are ripening. Inside the Main Political Directorate we are turning toward those human values which, to tell the truth, used to be proclaimed but in reality but were pushed into the background. The belief was: First the collective, then the individual. Today we are taking perhaps the most resolute step toward people....We recently invited the former leaders of major Army and Navy political organs, many of whom served at the front, in order to consult with them about reforming the political organs....Our honored veterans, as though by prior agreement, stated in unison: Whatever kind of reorganization you carry out, people must remain the focus of the attention of the future military-political organs.[90]

The psychologist Leonid Radzhikhovsky has analyzed how this attitude about sacrificing self-interests has had a distorting effect on the Soviets' motivation for work. He has written that in the past, "there took place (or rather was carried out deliberately) a substitution of normal, rational economic incentives." Instead, work became "a matter of honour, glory, valor and heroism." People are expected to "work in the knowledge that our theory is correct rather than out of consideration for lowly and petty personal gain." He has described the profound social consequences of this distortion as follows:

Our ideology and our social consciousness are a hodgepodge of the economy and religion, with the result we have neither religion in the traditional sense nor an economy in the normal sense of the word. Instead we have monsters—a "materialist religion," a "materialist mysticism," the cult of production.

Radzhikhovsky has particularly emphasized the deleterious effects of his distortion on economic production:

Yes, when people work to earn money to spend it today, they can manufacture Mercedes. When they work for the general welfare, for tomorrow, they manufacture Moskvich cars. Practice has demonstrated the worth of each economic model.... We no longer have any use for ideologically correct, but shoddy goods.[91]

These ideas echo statements made by Gorbachev that "we must...bring man back into socialist society and into material production, making him master there, and making him the main figure."[92] There seems to be an emerging consensus that only through mobilizing personal self-interest can the Soviet economy be jump-started out of its longstanding malaise. And there is a recognition that such a shift in attitude reverberates through to the foundations of Soviet ideology. As Len Karpinsky, a prominent intellectual, has written hopefully, "the grand experiment in earnest and selfless efforts to build socialism is behind us."[93]

4

The Resistance
To Giving Up Lenin

All Soviet citizens were born and bred in a political culture that revered Lenin and all that he stood for, so it is not surprising that there has been some resistance to simply writing him off. Perhaps most significantly, even Gorbachev seemed to have had some trouble letting go of Lenin. During the period when Gorbachev was formulating the key principles of new thinking that contradicted Lenin, Gorbachev simultanously tried to portray new thinking as continuous with Lenin. This equivocation, presumably, reflected a resistance in the larger Soviet society. Right up to the collapse of the coup in 1991 there were statements by prominent officials showing the persistence of Leninist thinking. And our interviews show that for many Soviets this process of ideological transformation has been marked by inner conflict and emotional pain.

Gorbachev's Equivocation

From the first formulations of new thinking Gorbachev tried to smooth over its discontinuities with Leninism. He attempted to present all the changes he was proposing as the logical outcome of the October Revolution. In his book *Perestroika*, published in 1987, he wrote: "We must impart new dynamism to the October Revolution's historical impulse and further advance all that was commenced by it in our society."[1] Later he said:

> The deep-seated meaning of restructuring is revival of the original aims of the October Revolution.... We understand that the vanguard role of the party can only be built on the basis of its profound and creative mastery of the great Marxist-Leninist dialectics.... We will not take a single step away from the socialist path.[2]

A Marxist interpretation of the socialist idea, he argued, "is the greatest social and spiritual value."[3]

Gorbachev portrayed Lenin in an unequivocally positive light with near religious overtones:

> The works of Lenin and his ideal of socialism remained for us an inexhaustible source of dialectical creative thought, theoretical wealth and political sagacity. His very image is an undying example of lofty moral strength, all-round spiritual culture and selfless devotion to the cause of the people and to socialism. Lenin lives in the minds and hearts of millions of people.[4]

He presented Lenin as the spiritual source of new thinking:

> We draw inspiration from Lenin. Turning to him and "reading" his works each time in a new way, one is struck by his ability to get at the root of things, to see the most intricate dialectics of world processes. Being the leader of the party of the proletariat, and theoretically and politically substantiating the latter's revolutionary tasks, Lenin could see further, he could go beyond their class-imposed limits. More than once he spoke about the priority of interests common to all humanity over class interests. It is only now we have come to comprehend the entire depth and significance of these ideas. It is they that are feeding our philosophy of international relations, and the new way of thinking.[5]

Gorbachev even tried to use Lenin to justify his new emphasis on personal gratification, not an easy task given Lenin's ascetic style and general emphasis on the need for self-sacrifice. He first said: "the purpose of what we are doing...in the Soviet Union...[is] to make sure that in a socialist society all people...live well and feel happy....The most important thing is for people.. to feel good." He, then, claimed this is a "return to Lenin's approach, which means fully bringing man back into socialist society...making him master there, and making him the main figure...." [6]

A common practice of Gorbachev and others was to take quotes from Lenin and stretch them in an effort to portray him as the original new thinker. One oft-used quote reads: "the essential principle of Marxism is that the interests of overall social development precede the interests of the proletariat."[7] It is true that in this quote Lenin is stressing that the proletariat should be willing to subordinate its immediate parochial interests to the long-term objective of social development. However, this by no means implies that the proletariat should abandon its confrontational approach and try instead to sustain a permanent equilibrium with capitalism in an increasingly pluralistic world. When Lenin called for the proletariat to subordinate its immediate interests, one of his concerns was that the proletariat will grow comfortable and give up the effort to promote revolution in the world—something Gorbachev, in effect, has proposed.

Another method Gorbachev used to obscure the discontinuities with Lenin was to suggest that the image of Lenin with which new thinking conflicts is, in fact, a false image generated by disreputable characters. New thinking was portrayed as growing from an effort to penetrate to the "original" Lenin.[8]

Even when Gorbachev was more candid about the discrepancies between new thinking and traditional Marxism-Leninism, he nonetheless tried to smooth them over by saying that it is only the time-specific concrete formulations of Marx and Lenin that are no longer valid in the new conditions. The underlying principles of Marxism-Leninism were presented as still fully applicable and "still need[ing] to be adequately implemented—in light, of course, of the new conditions."[9]

Naturally, the question arises as to why Gorbachev equivocated in this way, why he insisted on obfuscating the discontinuities between new thinking and Marxism-Leninism. Perhaps Gorbachev may have feared that to break the link with Lenin might provoke the party and the military to try to depose him.*

Gorbachev, by pretending that new thinking flows directly from Lenin, may also have been trying to accommodate major elements in Soviet society loyal to Lenin. Even though most Soviets may have been losing faith in the state religion established by Lenin, many may not have been ready to abandon him. Lenin was still seen as the Moses who led them onto the path out of backwardness and ultimately to superpower glory. Gorbachev had yet to prove himself as the new prophet to displace his forebear. Despite his successes in the foreign policy realm his domestic policy had largely worsened the daily life of Soviets. Furthermore, Gorbachev's visions of the Soviet role in the world were considerably less gratifying than those of Lenin. Soviets find compelling the messianic image of themselves as leading the world into the promised land of equality and justice. Without the political foundation to make an explicit break with Lenin, Gorbachev may have felt he had to inject a certain degree of obfuscation. He may have felt that the only way he could advance his new thinking was also to deny that anything really new was happening.

---

* When the coup finally occurred, it even appeared that Gorbachev's cautious strategy may be vindicated; after years of careful restraint it seemed that Gorbachev had finally gone too far and provoked the beast of the Right. But, paradoxically, in the end it was the Left that finally swallowed him.

Among Soviets intellectuals with whom we spoke from 1988 through early 1990, most held this view that Gorbachev was not really attached to socialism. By stressing the continuity with Lenin, Gorbachev, they argued, was simply trying to accommodate a need in the general public. Marxism-Leninism was still a "glue" that held Soviet society together and that "if we reject the past we delegitimize ourselves." Furthermore, it was explained, down the "scepter" of Marxism-Leninism, he would be vulnerable to the conservatives picking it up and using it to political advantage.

But beginning in mid-1990 some Soviet intellectuals with whom we spoke began to register some doubts about whether Gorbachev was, in fact, devoid of such traditional influences. Particularly disconcerting was Gorbachev's failure to follow through on his call for market reform in the Soviet economy. Though Gorbachev seemed to intellectually grasp the need for such a radical change, when the moment came to push through the new program he seemed to have a failure of nerve. Several Soviets with whom we spoke speculated that Gorbachev had reached a certain limit in his own personality.

In late 1990 Gorbachev also made a speech in which he dramatically revealed some of the depth of his feeling about retaining what he calls "the socialist choice." He affirmed that socialism is "my banner." With some defensiveness he said: "I've been told more than once that it is time to stop swearing allegiance to socialism. Why should I? Socialism is my deep conviction and I will promote it as long as I can work and talk." Then poignantly he tied his commitment to socialism to a strong familial feeling:

> Am I supposed to turn my back on my grandfather, who was committed to the (socialist) idea?...And I cannot go against my father who defended Kursk (in World War II), forded the Dnieper knee deep in blood and was wounded in Czechoslovakia. When cleansing myself of Stalinism and all other filth, should I renounce my grandfather and father and all they did?"[10]

One may wonder, too, whether for Gorbachev, as with many Soviets, such feelings of loyalty to the father also extend to Lenin.

Naturally it could still be argued that even such expressions of emotion were staged for political purposes, as a way of reassuring the hardliners. But this interpretation was undermined by Gorbachev's performance immediately after the coup failed. At that moment, with the threat from the hardliners evaporated, he had the opportunity to put himself forward unambiguously as the visionary reformer and to make a clean break from Lenin and the Party. But, instead, at his first press conference, even after the top echelons of the party had betrayed him, he reaffirmed his commitment to the Communist Party. Most significantly, he once again affirmed that he was a Socialist, praised the October Revolution, and respectfully quoted Lenin. It was only under pressure from Russian President Boris Yeltsin that he suspended the Communist Party several days later.

In his book *The August Coup*, published in the fall of 1991, he once again stated that he is "a confirmed supporter of the idea of socialism." He tried to distinguish the notion of socialism from Leninism by stressing that the idea of socialism appears in "many social and political movements" and even "draws strength from many achievements of Christianity." In a somewhat perplexing comment he wrote that to try to "expel socialism from the territory of Soviet Union" would be a "very dangerous Utopia." Nevertheless he explicitly refused to denounce the October Revolution, falling back on the hackneyed argument that it was simply Stalin who distorted "the ideas of October."[11]

These statements do not necessarily suggest that deep in his heart Gorbachev is really a dyed-in-the-wool Marxist-Leninist. Although it is probable that Gorbachev respects Lenin in some important ways, it is likely that Gorbachev has long recognized the important contradictions between his ideas and those of Lenin. Given the political risks he has taken by challenging Lenin, we may assume that Gorbachev has strong, self-conscious attitudes that Marxism-Leninism has seriously hampered the development of the Soviet Union.

At the same time there are features to Gorbachev's personality that would lead him to resist making a sharp break with Lenin. One of these is a strong tendency to believe that it is possible to make changes in a smooth, continuous fashion; he is noted for being a consensus seeker, even to a fault. Clearly he believed that it would be possible to displace Leninist thinking but to do so in a way that did not upset people's attachment (including perhaps his own) to the image of Lenin as something of a hero.

Gorbachev has also tended to believe that problems lend themselves to intellectual solutions. He seemed to think that he could maintain the continuity with Lenin by simply abstracting out of Lenin's thought what Gorbachev defined as the essence of the "socialist idea." This then could be the cornerstone of new thinking. However, to find this point of convergence with Lenin, Gorbachev had to reach to such an abstract level that there was not much substance to the link. Basically he tried to argue that new thinking was continuous with Lenin because it shared Lenin's humanistic concern for human welfare.

Apparently, this seemed intellectually satisfactory in Gorbachev's own mind and obviated, for him, the need to confront the painful question of whether Leninism was, in fact, a huge mistake. What Gorbachev overlooked was that Leninism was not simply a set of abstract ideas that could be intellectually manipulated, but was more fundamentally a political symbol and that to break with the ideas he would also have to break with the symbol.

In the end it seemed that even Gorbachev recognized that he had held too tightly to the Leninist tradition. In a televised session with reporters just days before his resignation in December 1991 he seemed to acknowledge that he had been too slow in breaking with the past. He hoped that perhaps it would be easier for his daughter's generation to make such a change. Then with a sad reflective tone he said, "It is not so easy to break oneself. The most difficult thing is to break oneself."[12]

The Public Discourse

In the public discourse the presence of traditional Leninist thinking has gone through cycles, waxing and waning according to the prevailing political winds.

In the 1988-1989 period, despite the emergence of new thinking, some Leninist thinking persevered, seemingly oblivious to the revisions of new thinking. References to "the historical inevitability of all nations arriving at socialism"[13] continued to appear. At CPSU-sponsored conferences there were still references to the Party's role in "leading society's movement toward the ultimate goal of communism."[14] And at the time of the 1989 anniversary of the October revolution the radio announcer rhapsodized:

> The revolution's lofty ideals have inspired and still inspire the peoples of our country to everything which is best, bright, and heroic—everything that has gone down in history as the continuation of Lenin's cause. On the path illumined by October the first socialist state in the world has achieved major accomplishments and has turned into a mighty power.[15]

Even the relatively new-thinking Vadim Medvedev, then responsible for ideology in the Party, persisted in the idea that socialism would ultimately prevail over capitalism: "History will decide which of the two systems is more progressive and durable. We are confident of the potential and prospects of socialism....Lenin is closer to us than ever before."[16] In Party academic writing, traditional thinking was thinly veiled by an effort to explain how the agenda of new thinking will actually serve zero-sum Leninist goals. Yuri Krasin, then pro-rector of the Central Committee Academy of Social Sciences, wrote:

> An assured peace and disarmament will...enable (socialism) to reveal more fully its advantages in the peaceful competition with the capitalist system. The struggle for peace does not certainly solve the "who will win" question in relations between contending social systems.... Without removing grounds for the class struggle, a non-violent world and peaceful coexistence influences its forms and help establish means for waging it....Marxists are firm in their belief that socialism will gain the upper hand in the peaceful competition....New political thinking does not imply giving up the socio-class goals of the struggle for social and national liberation.[17]

At the same time there were also more overt expressions of opposition to new thinking, steeped in Marxism-Leninism. The most prominent critic of new thinking was then Politburo member Igor Ligachev. Although he frequently claimed that he, in fact, embraced new thinking, he periodically made statements contradicting key principles. In contrast to the idea that the world is moving toward pluralism and diversity and ultimately toward an integration of capitalism and socialism, Ligachev stated: "ultimately there are only two paths—socialist and capitalist....I am an adherent of communist convictions and scientific socialism."[18]

Ligachev also directly contradicted the new thinking call for deideologizing international relations, saying in August 1988: "We proceed from the class nature of international relations. Any other formulation of the issue only introduces confusion into the thinking of Soviet people and our friends abroad."[19] Even the relatively moderate then Prime Minister Nikolai Ryzhkov, referring to the widespread loss of commitment to communism, bewailed "the deideologization of society," accusing officials in charge of ideology of making a "major miscalculation."[20]

Members of the military were especially reactive to new thinking. Military figures complained about the declining prestige of the military that followed from the new thinking analysis that criticizes nearly all postwar uses of Soviet military force and, in general, dismisses military force as declining in utility and questionable in its legitimacy. Army General Vladimir Lobov (later to become Chief of Staff) grumbled: "It has become almost 'fashionable' in some mass media to attack the honor of the military and the Soviet Army's history.... Certain ideologists are now trying to persuade public opinion that the socialist army is a 'social evil.'" Lobov reacted with indignation to efforts to demilitarize Soviet society:

How is it possible, for example, to cast doubt on the rituals of mounting honor guards at monuments and memorials, or the holding of military sports games? Why prevent children from playing with war toys or building model aircraft, ships, and tanks? Demagogical claims that all these rituals supposedly develop "bellicosity" in young souls introduce pacifistic ideas into young people's minds and create doubts about the need for universal military service and the very readiness to defend the fatherland.[21]

Many civilians also joined in defending the military against the criticism of new thinking. R.S. Bobovikov, a candidate member of the Central Committee at the April 25, 1989, Central Committee Plenum said:

Why...open a debate in the newspapers....It would be better to be more solicitous toward and increase the prestige of our existing Army....A tendentious approach leads to the collapse of the moral, ethical, and ideological values of socialism, and exerts a harmful influence on public opinion, especially on young people.[22]

At times the critique of the antimilitaristic strains in new thinking took on a very emotional coloring, particularly in relation to the question of Afghanistan. In a *Krasnaya Zvezda* review of a film on Afghanistan veterans (titled "Pain") V. Dashkevich, a member of the USSR Writers Union, complained that there is not enough appreciation of the worthy intentions of the intervention in Afghanistan: "The authors do not touch on the international and military aspects of the conflict, failing to bring the viewer closer to an answer to the question of what and whom Soviet soldiers died for in the far off mountains."

Dashkevich then criticized the role in the film of Ales Adamovich, a popular antimilitaristic spokesman, quoting an article in which he calls not for military patriotic education but "antimilitary patriotic education," and paraphrasing Adamovich derisively: "Talk of courage and heroism, of patriotic traditions, of internationalism, of combat experience in today's global thinking turns out to be superfluous. Moreover, they should engage in the absolute opposite." Finally he has warned: "Calling now for the immediate cessation of military-patriotic education in our country is a risky undertaking. One so wants to say: 'Careful! Paid for in blood....'"[23]

Other writers also objected to the new tendency to downplay the importance of sacrifice. Alexander Prokhanov, in an article in *Literaturnaya Rossiya*, defended the Afghan intervention, stressing the value of being willing to make sacrifices for ideological ends:

We have always helped the peoples of fraternal countries to preserve the revolution....And in order that the revolution survive, we had to relinquish some of our limited resources for the good of the world labor movement. They were not only ideological, financial, and economic resources but were, of course, military resources as well.

Prokhanov berated "the peaceminded youth—the rockers, the breakers, the punks" who are not "willing to sacrifice themselves" and extolled the Afghanistan veterans saying:

Ten or so years later, when many of them occupy executive positions in the economic, party, and ideological apparatus, they will be a consolidated force that is conscious of the idea of suffering, struggle and stoicism." Finally he declared: "Glory and honor to us that we have preserved great ethical ideas...the idea of sacrifice in the name of great, global goals.[24]

Not surprisingly, military figures also expressed alarm that the ideas about the unimportance of sacrifice were generating a growing antipathy toward military service. Then Defense Minister General Dimitri Yazov (later a leader of the coup) denounced "so-called 'ideas' about the inessentiality of military service."[25] An article in the military newspaper *Red Star* complained, with profound bewilderment, that "this year every other draftee failed to arrive on schedule at the draft commission. We had to resort to the militias' assistance." A colonel cited in the article observed that "the majority of young men" show "pacifist sentiments," describing a meeting of draftees in which "of 550 young men not one evinced a desire to serve in the army." He reported with utter dismay that the draftees also "express dissatisfaction with the excessively small money allowance...and suggest that servicemen's right to leave...and even to change their boots for...sneakers be enshrined in legislation."[26] Yazov expressed concern that Soviet boys, rather than playing with guns, are pretending to be businessmen.[27]

Through most of 1990 there was an observable decline in traditional Leninist rhetoric. This did not mean, though, there was a reduction of criticism of the policies that had been generated by new thinking. Some policies, especially those that led to the loss of dominance over Eastern Europe, were attacked vociferously. Occasionally these criticisms took on an ideological coloring. For example, at the Twenty-eighth Party Congress in July 1990 Major General Ivan Mikulin referred to the Soviet withdrawal of support for Communist governments in Eastern Europe as a "betrayal of the idea of proletarian internationalism"[28] and accused new-thinking Soviet diplomats of "looking at the world through rose-coloured glasses."[29]

But on the whole, in the public discourse, conservative forces refrained from a frontal ideological attack on new thinking.

An outstanding exception, though, was Nina Andreyeva. A teacher of chemistry, Andreyeva gained notoriety in March 1988 when *Sovyetskaya Rossiya* published a letter in which she lambasted the ideological revisionism then occurring, complaining that her students were experiencing "ideological confusion" and "loss of political bearings."[30] Later she formed the organization Unity: For Communism and Leninist Ideals and became a regular figure in the Soviet media. Never to be stifled, in an interview in August of 1990 she denounced the CPSU Central Committee for having "emasculated [Marxism-Leninism] of class, proletarian content," called for "the resignation of the Gorbachev-Yakovlev-Shevardnadze group," accused Gorbachev of "social democratism," and enunciated her favorite slogan—"socialism or death!"[31]

Beginning at the end of 1990 and lasting into the spring of 1991 there was a resurgence of conservative forces in the Soviet government. The conservative group of Supreme Soviet deputies Soyuz gained strength and the more liberal Interregional Group waned. Gorbachev, losing his nerve for serious economic reform, sensing a general fear of growing chaos, and under tremendous pressure from the military, moved to the right politically. Perhaps most dramatically, Shevardnadze, feeling abandoned by Gorbachev, resigned in December 1990, complaining of the activities of some of the military members of the Soyuz group and warning of the potential for a reversion to dictatorship.

Suddenly there was a renewal of traditional Leninist rhetoric and a series of direct ideological attacks on new thinking. Ivan Polozkov, first secretary of the Russian Communist Party, stated in January 1991:

> By differentiating between panhuman interests and class interests and by giving priority to planetwide values, we did a disservice to the socialist idea....The dialectical unity of class and panhuman interests was violated. Yet you and I know that no one ever expressed panhuman interests better than the working class. By forgetting this and drawing a veil over class contradictions, we basically robbed the party of a very important methodological tool and politically disarmed the broad masses of Communists.[32]

Yuri Belov, secretary of the Leningrad Oblast of the CPSU Central Committee, deploring what he called "anti-Lenin hysteria" and the "crazy multiparty system," complained:

> Panhuman values are generally seen outside the context of class interests, and instead of being given primacy they are regarded as absolutes. The

entirely justified emphasis on mankind's global problems overrules the problem of the conflict between labor and capital. Soon, the latter problem is entirely denied the right to exist. The new political thinking...boils down to the deideologization of East-West political relations. The Leninist dialectical unity of struggle in the ideological sphere...gives way to the virtually automatic unity of the two social systems.... The party has in effect been rolling back its ideological and theoretical opposition to capitalism.[33]

Particularly pugnacious was Nikolai Petrushenko, a delegate to the Supreme Soviet and one of the conservative colonels Shevardnadze referred to in his resignation speech. With a highly defensive tone Petrushenko wrote:

I am rebuked for being "aggressive" and "frenzied".... Only a blind and deaf person would not recognize now that in our society under the cover of sickly-sweet conversations about "consolidation" and "common human values," a very real ideological, political, and economic class struggle is going on....I myself prefer to pull together with the working people in the name of the defense of their vital interests. And I will not budge!"[34]

However, the most aggressive attack on the notion of panhuman values, and new thinking in general, came in an interview with Ligachev that occurred in February 1991. Although Ligachev had previously made efforts to create a modicum of continuity between his ideas and new thinking, and had been relatively quiet since he was removed from the Politburo in an interview in the summer of 1990, the kid gloves finally came off.

Ligachev: To rectify the mistakes committed in policy, we must revise individual theses and theoretical guidelines advanced in recent years. I have in mind the correlation of class interests and panhuman values, the postulates on the world's integrity and unity, the substitution of the "socialist idea" for the concept of socialism as a social system, and the allegation that during the last period of his life V.I. Lenin altered his viewpoint on socialism. Unless we rid ourselves of mistaken principles, we will continue to make serious miscalculations in policies....The class approach to assessing social phenomena has virtually been abandoned, and a realistic understanding of everything that is happening in society has been distorted....

Belan: You spoke of the class approach—is this not lip service to the old thinking, to traditional views?...

Ligachev : Pardon me, the class struggle is a cruel reality of our days. The process of society's stratification and the demarcation of political forces no longer along national lines...is taking place....Armed formations are being created, and people are being persecuted and killed. And local authorities certainly do not express the working people's interests....A class of exploiters, a class of operators in the shadow economy is coming into being deep within society....There are classes, they exist, they have their own interests, and they come into conflict before our eyes....The ignoring of class interests in theory and the substitution of panhuman values for them are also making themselves felt in political activity both inside the country and in the international arena. This tells in ...forgetting the class nature of international relations, and disparaging of international solidarity and internationalism....I want to emphasize that I am one of those who firmly believes that, ultimately, socialist ideas and the ideas of social justice will prevail. [35]

By the spring of 1991, as Gorbachev began to move away from the right and to mend fences with Boris Yeltsin, the political center of gravity began to shift. Leninist rhetoric and vitriolic criticism of new thinking once again subsided. Die-hard Leninists were forced into an increasingly defensive position.

At the CPSU Central Committee Plenum in July 1991, A.N. Ilin, second secretary of the Russian Communist Party, complained that, in the draft program, "ideas about the need to restore and develop the fundamental principles of the teaching of Marx, Engels and Lenin as the base of the contemporary concept of socialism and the CPSU's policy have groundlessly disappeared from the text." Countering Gorbachev's call for drawing on sources of thought other than Marxism-Leninism, Ilin insisted that "materialist dialectics—the living soul of Marxism—does not accept the mechanical admixture of different and, at times, mutually exclusive world outlook tenets."[36]

After the failure of the coup in August 1991, even such plaintive laments as these died out. Some fringe groups still cling to the old time religion. But, with the discrediting and suspension of the Communist Party in the aftermath of the coup, Leninist rhetoric has effectively faded from the dominant political discourse.

Inconsistency and Inner Conflict

It is easy to think that the discontinuities in Soviet ideology simply arose from the net effects of two conflicting groups within the foreign-policymaking elite, each with their own opinions. However, this is too simple a model. As in most societies, in the Soviet Union there were probably some true believers in one or another philosophy. However, most likely the largest portion of the population was influenced by both old and new thinking. To the extent that this was happening we may expect to find evidence of tensions, inconsistencies and, at times, even contradictions in the ideological perspectives of some individuals.

An example can be found in a 1988 article in the military newspaper *Krasnaya Zvezda* (Red Star) stirringly titled "Command of the Epoch," by Lieutenant Colonel V. Markushin. He set out to resolve the apparent inconsistency between the idea that the world is undergoing a "transition from capitalism to socialism" and that "these two opposite formations are obliged to get along together and cooperate." He asked whether "the idea of the priority of human values...negates...the thesis of the antagonistic nature of relations between capitalism and socialism." He answered, "No. This antagonism has existed and still exists. It is an objective law which exists independent of anyone's will." He then proceeded to, apparently, upbraid those who would support the pluralistic vision of the future, saying:

> The fact of the matter is that socialism is not an alternative to capitalism, is not just one of the roads along which mankind may travel or not. Socialism is a qualitatively new level of development in human society in compari-son with capitalism.

But then shortly after this insistence on the continuing validity of the notion of inevitable   confrontation between socialism and capitalism, he shifted his tone and seemed to complain about the persistence of this thinking in others. "The force of inertia in obsolete political thinking based on dangerous ideas of confrontation is strong....Progress toward a safe, stable world could advance further if it were not for the inertia of ideological...confrontation."[37]

A similar dynamic was evidenced in comments by Ivan Antonovich, pro-rector of the Central Committee's Academy of Social Sciences. He began by denouncing the competitive approach to relations with capital-ism: "In the past we spoke a great deal about an irreconcilable antagonism between capitalism and socialism. At present we look to a balance of interests, considering that it might serve to strengthen and safeguard peace." And yet, shortly after, he went on to say that the very fact that socialism is proposing this noncompetitive orientation demonstrates that it

will ultimately prevail: "The fact that socialism proposes this strategy to the
world is in itself eloquent because it not only shows to whom the future
belongs but prepares Communists for the new historical responsibility."[38]

Such dynamics also appeared in the interviews. One respondent, an
official in the Central Committee who dealt directly with ideology, first
explained how the Soviet Union has fully abandoned the notion that
socialism will ultimately prevail. Then, as if to demonstrate the point more
convincingly, he quoted Lenin to the effect that only through having
superior productive capabilities will one or the other system triumph. We
pointed out that this sounded like he was suggesting that the competition
should simply move out of the military realm into the economic, but that the
idea that socialism would ultimately prevail still stood. However, he
emphatically denied this implication.

In some cases interview respondents embraced new thinking in an
unambiguous fashion, even recognizing the discontinuity with traditional
Marxism-Leninism, but nevertheless resisted making this discontinuity too
explicit. For example, in an interview two young political analysts spoke
about how the world is moving toward greater pluralism. When we asked
how this fits into the framework of Marxism-Leninism one of them said in
a slightly hushed conspiratorial tone, "It doesn't." But then he and his
cohort became a bit uncomfortable with this candor and began to emphasize
how Lenin emphasized the notion of peaceful coexistence in his later years.
We then asked whether Lenin had ever given up the idea that socialism
would ultimately prevail. At this point they both held up their palms and
said, "Don't push us, don't push us."

One of the more poignant examples of the struggle between old and
new thinking was in an interview with a colonel from one of the military
academies. I was the first American he had ever spoken with and he seemed
quite eager to have the interview and to explain his views to me. He arrived,
visibly nervous, bringing me a gift of a Soviet officer's hat and shoulder
boards.

In the interview he tried hard to tie together his support for new
thinking and his loyalty to Lenin. The colonel revered Lenin as nearly a
demigod. He explained that "We personify Lenin with the truth....He is a
symbol of truth." At one point he expressed his bewilderment at the fact that
Shakespeare was a better writer than Lenin but concluded that this must be
because Shakespeare, too, was "close to the essence of things." But when
asked whether the world is moving toward socialism, as Lenin predicted,
he recognized that capitalism was doing better than socialism.

I :   Do you see that the world is ultimately moving toward socialism?

R : There is a problem here. Socialism declared excellent slogans, excellent mottos....Socialism is supposed to bring up the technologically developed personality. Did we achieve this? History and reality show that capitalism achieved more in this field than socialism. It's a pity, but these are our realities. That's why we are restructuring things from an economic point of view, from a political point of view, but not ideology.

However, despite this affirmation that ideology was not being restructured he made the previously heretical argument that the world is not moving toward socialism but convergence with capitalism.

I : So do you still feel that the world is ultimately moving towards socialism?
R : If we can take these three formations—slavery, feudalism, and capitalism—yes. The world passed through these three stages. The next stage will be a convergence.
I : There won't be socialism or capitalism, there will be a structure that contains them both?
R : Yes.
I : That's interesting.
R : Very interesting.

He then tried to argue that this movement toward convergence is consistent with Lenin because Lenin embraced the notion of peaceful coexistence. In this way he argued that the Soviet Union should try to promote socialism in the world and that, through convergence, capitalism will become socialism and thus socialism will ultimately prevail.

I : Isn't this different from what Lenin said? And Marx?
R : We go back to this principle of convergence. The principle of peaceful coexistence is one of the principles set by Lenin....
I : If the world is moving towards this convergence, and in certain ways capitalism is more effective in developing this new kind of technological man, why does the Soviet Union continue to support socialist factions more than other factions?
R : That's the notion of ideology. We follow the principle of "Proletariats of all countries, unite!" We shouldn't leave our friends in trouble in this time. So the principles of ideology continue, we abide by these principles.
I : Of supporting socialist countries?
R : Yes....We would follow the principles which allow Marxist-Leninist

ideology everywhere. This is a real principle, and one of our main principles. In the economic field, we are going on the wave of convergence....Using Lenin's policy of peaceful coexistence, we would develop economically in such a way that we would be the first and the United States would be the second. And we would have no idea about Japan....There is a saying, "Where they have trade, there is no place for war." It's better to trade than war. These are words by Lenin. Peaceful coexistence. What was capitalism? Capitalism has developed so that imperialism is almost socialism. All economic bases of capitalism lead to socialism. This is economic reality.

Some respondents had a visible struggle between new and old thinking, leading them to change their positions several times during the course of the interview and even, over time, between interviews. For example, one respondent, a senior journalist we interviewed in late 1988, first embraced some of the principles of new thinking, talking about how the fact of interdependence meant that scientists should work out new foundations for international relations. But then minutes later he began to criticize some aspects of new thinking. He complained that the Soviet Union was making too many concessions in arms control treaties and rejected the notion that the threat from the West had declined and that international relations could be deideologized:

> I don't quite agree with what Shevardnadze said outlining the main directions we have to go. He was too rosy, too optimistic.... We have to be more realistic in this respect. This is a revolutionary approach to deemphasize the class divisions. Deemphasize ideology... it's some kind of wishful thinking.

We then discussed Eastern Europe. Ignoring the new- thinking principle of nonintervention, the journalist took a very strong Brezhnev-era style position, saying:

> Well I hope there will be no repetition of 1956, 1968, but if, for instance, the situation in Poland gets out of hand then we will be faced with a difficult decision about what to do. Naturally, '56 was a very painful decision but the result of the whole was positive, for Hungary, not for us but for Hungary. Now if the Poles cannot settle their domestic difficulties maybe some of them will be happy if we'll help them through some radical surgical operations. We shall not be happy at all, but even in Yugoslavia nowadays, in some quarters they call on us to intervene.

When we probed further, though, he shifted his position several times. We asked, "Are these operations being considered now?" He answered "Well, of course, we have to consider all options, the worst, the best, naturally. But the worst scenario is something not so bad actually." A bit later, though, he changed his tune, saying: "Well, nowadays I think really it is unthinkable that we shall use force outside like we did in '56 or '68. Really, it is unthinkable."

But then in the next sentence he shifted again, saying, "What we should do in an emergency I do not know." We asked what an emergency would be. He said: "Well, say if the opposition forces in Poland take arms and start shooting people, that's an emergency. Then we shall have to think whether to come to the aid of the government if the government asks us for military help or not." But then again he changed his tune saying, "But, really, it's not a possibility. I draw a very imaginary, a very unreal picture."

We then discussed the possibility of reducing Warsaw Pact forces in conjunction with NATO reductions. The journalist was in favor of such ideas. We asked whether this reduction wouldn't interfere with the Soviet ability to deal with "emergencies" in Eastern Europe. He said it would, but was nonetheless unequivocal, saying, "We are prepared for the complete withdrawal of forces. American forces out of Western Europe, our forces out of Eastern Europe." But then a prankish twinkle came into his eyes and he said, "But we can easily suggest this knowing that the United States will not even agree to discuss this, so for us this is a very safe proposal." We then asked whether it might be possible for the Soviet Union to reduce its forces in Eastern Europe on a unilateral basis. To our surprise he said:

> Oh yes, I think if we did as we did in the past in the '50s, I think now we see those unilateral steps that Khrushchev took in a favorable light. We want some of our generals, not to mention civil servants, to recognize that we have too many tanks and it is unnecessary now in our armed forces.

We spoke with him again the following year. Interestingly, right at the beginning of the interview he spoke in an animated way about the changes going on in Soviet society and in his thinking, saying that "the great dam broke" and "the ancient stables have to be cleaned." Still, his ambivalence continued to show. When we asked whether this reevaluation was a good thing he answered, "No, it was necessary. Not good or bad, but it was necessary." Nonetheless, on closer questioning on such issues as intervention in Eastern Europe, his position had become firmer that the Soviet Union would not intervene under any circumstances.

The Experience of Change

It goes without saying that such a fundamental change as the transition
to new thinking is a personally difficult process. In the 1988-1989 period a
number of prominent Soviets described this difficulty. Political observer
Pavel Kuznetsov explained: "There's been a painful process underway here
of a reassessment of social values, overseas commitments, and domestic
and foreign policy priorities."[39] Oleg Bykov of IMEMO said "the birth of
the new thinking is accompanied by torment." [40] Akhromeyev said that
"new thinking is not penetrating army and navy life easily."[41] And even
Shevardnadze revealed that, though he is not a conservative, the changes of
new thinking elicit "inner conflict" in him.[42]

In the interviews and in some published material there are fascinating
accounts of the subjective process of transiting from old to new thinking. For
example, a policy analyst from IMEMO explained:

> It's clear that after many decades of our strategy of development, it's
> impossible to free yourself from the old prejudices at once. I can give you
> a personal example. When I study some of the problems of the Third
> World, from time to time I catch myself with the thought that I am thinking
> in an old way. And it's quite possible that what I've told you is a mixture
> of old thinking and new thinking. Probably the younger generation will be
> freed from all this, will get away from all this. The new leadership that is
> in power worked under Khrushchev, Brezhnev, and Stalin. So it just took
> a toll on them. No one can get rid of the education and upbringing he got
> in previous years. That's why I think the development for restructuring is
> too slow.

Others described the process of change in more collective terms but
their language revealed emotions they presumably felt in a personal way.
A policy analyst at IMEMO, full of the bewilderment of insight, told us that
with the notion of class struggle: "We were trying to impose our outlook on
you. Of course, it was not right and was even laughable. This way of looking
at the world brought everything into a tunnel."

Sometimes in the interviews respondents' body language revealed
their conflict. In an interview with a high-level Foreign Ministry official we
asked whether the West was now perceived as threatening and imperialis-
tic. He was quite unequivocal in saying that it was not. We then asked
whether this contradicted Lenin's concept of the nature of capitalist states.
He first avoided the question. When we pressed he became visibly uncom-

resting on top of his left and nervously began to lightly slap his left arm with his right hand. After once more trying to avoid the question, he said:

We base our negotiations on the idea that the military threat from the West is disappearing now. And we don't have the philosophical image of the enemy anymore. Of course, it is quite impossible to change yourself in one day, to change the way of thinking. My generation, I am almost 60 now, was raised on certain notions. For some of us it's easy to overcome this idea, but it is hard for somebody else.

He then described his personal experience, saying that in the past he would periodically have thoughts that deviated from the orthodox line. As he said this he began to raise his left arm in an outward moving arc. But, he said, then an internal censor would come—at which point his right arm took hold of his errant left and began to pull it back down to the table—and guide him away from having such thoughts. In the present, though, he said he feels completely free to think all kinds of thoughts—blithely throwing both palms upward.

Another insight into the process of adaptation to the changes of new thinking can be found in the way Soviets cope with objections and resistance to new thinking. It has become quite common for government officials to articulate some of these objections and then to answer to them. These imaginary exchanges can be seen as reflecting dialogues within individuals as well as between them. For example, Vadim Zagladin has written that the notion of the primacy of universal interests over class interests

has prompted a good many questions and even reproaches: "How can you talk about universal human interests if the world is divided into opposing systems and its capitalist part into hostile social classes?"
But the human race has objectively always been a single whole. Objectively it has always had and will have common interests irrespective of class divisions. Yes, the interests of the classes—in our days the capitalists and the working class—are antagonistic. But are theirs only antagonistic interests? A dogmatic mind will shudder at the very question. But a dialectical mind will admit the legitimacy of the question.[43]

Zagladin's imaginary dialogue then continued as he suggested the need for a "peaceful resolution" between capitalism and socialism:

This often prompts the following objections: "What about the current objectives of the proletariat as a social class? Can we call on the worker to join the capitalist in the struggle for survival if the very capitalist oppresses and exploits him? Doesn't the thesis about the primacy of the universal human interests amount to renouncing the struggle for the class interests of the working people?" No, it doesn't....Today even for the working class the struggle for universal human interests is the struggle for its class interests. Peace and disarmament mean not only survival, but the solution of the current social problems and political rights for the working people today.[44]

So what were the roots of the resistance that were apparently addressed in such dialogues? Some of the comments made in the interviews lend insight. Perhaps most penetrating was an analysis of the collective Soviet psyche by a young political analyst. He first described how deep the messianic urge is in the Soviet people:

> I think for the public here as for the public in the United States it was very important to feel that this country is more than a country, that it has some, you know, that it has some mission in the world. And you know we lived with such an idea for a very long time. Even before the revolution...the idea that Russia has something to say, has something to give to humanity, it has to lead other nations. It is a very strong movement in the public consciousness here.

But, he explained, now Gorbachev is trying to draw the Soviet Union back from these grandiose self-images. "Politically," he said, "it's a very smart move because it makes you feel more flexible." Nevertheless, "psychologically, people can be very unhappy about feeling that all the sacrifices they made and all the suffering they came through and all the problems they had to solve" were to no real avail. "It calls attention to the fact that the country with all this suffering and all these tortures of its history, the country didn't achieve too much, didn't accomplish too much and it is still lagging behind and it has nothing to say to humankind. It has to study, to learn, rather than to teach."

He also argued that the new emphasis on personal gratification and economic interests will not simply displace traditional ideological zeal:

> There is a difference between American and Soviet society. American society traditionally was oriented on consumption....For this society, consumption was for a long time neglected and was even derogatory. You know, people are thinking about spiritual, about sacrifices, about tributes you have to pay to the state and society. And you know your consumption or pleasure, something like that, there was some derogatory meaning. That is why it is not easy to change it.

In this context, he explained, Soviets feel "they are losing their sense of identity; what we are, where we are going." And he emphasized that "even some economic progress, a rise in the level of consumption" would not solve this problem.

In some of the other interviews there were clear signs of some of these feelings. For example, a senior political observer interviewed complained that many Soviets now think that we give too much aid [to socialist countries]. They're mistaken.. ..We are a great country. I mean we have responsibility that we cannot just throw away....Yes, maybe we shall have to tighten our belts. Well, it happened so often in all our history and then we were much poorer. He then proceeded to lament the loss of ideological fervor among Soviets, even expressing some nostalgia for the period of Stalin and discomfort about the fact that it is presently coming under such attack:

R : When I was a schoolboy, the international outlook was better developed and people lived harder. There was an internationalist mind. Now we are more materialistic, I would say especially among the young people.They expect, they want more. They are not so content with what they have as I was....I had a sort of vision, a goal as a schoolboy, something to believe in....[Now] life is...unfortunately, less idealistic in the sense that I had a sort of vision, a goal, as a schoolboy, something to believe in. And now we demolish so much of everything that we had in the past, we criticize so much of what we had in the past.

I : Can you say more about what those goals were that you had as a young person?

R : Well, just simple. Stalin was a great leader. He symbolized the best....Perestroika is very popular, but there will be a reaction to look at our past in a more balanced way, this will happen sure. So far it's natural, natural that being so idealistic, so superficial and mistaken about our past we discard everything.

Some Soviets ostensibly accept as inevitable the decline in the Soviet Union's ideological activism in the world, but the sadness in their tone betrays their ambivalence about it. For example, an influential policy analyst interviewed explained that the Soviet policy has to respond to the fact Soviet "consumers are frantic." We asked whether this meant a reduction of subsidies to socialist countries.

R : It's painful but I think it's in the cards. We'll have to. Anyway, we cannot afford the same level of giveaways, to put it crudely.

I : Is there any nervousness about the political consequences of this?

R : Sure! But the way things are in the Soviet Union, of course we'll have
to.

When we asked a foreign ministry official whether he thought that,
with the noninterventionist Soviet policy in Eastern Europe, the potential
movement toward the neutralization of Europe was a positive trend, he
answered grimly: "It is an existing trend. Trying to brake the trend is no use.
And if anybody has any bitter feelings about it, they should hide them—or
better—get rid of them."

5

The New
Great-Power Thinking

One of the purposes of this study is to examine not only the roots of the change in Soviet ideology and foreign policy but also the roots of the persistence of traditional Soviet behavior. Most significant is Soviet behavior that has been proscribed by new thinking: the maintenance of the largest military in the world, sizable numbers of foreign-based troops, a vast and widely dispersed navy, a huge program of weapons transfers, and an enormous nuclear arsenal.

It is easy to assume that the persistence of such behavior reflects the persistence of Leninism. And, indeed, as the previous chapter illustrated, Leninism has continued to have some influence on the Soviet foreign-policy elite. This influence, though, should not be overestimated. In recent years it has declined sharply.

Even the August 1991 coup leaders refrained from invoking Leninism as a basis for their legitimacy. In their first news conference they tried instead to borrow the legitimacy of none other than Gorbachev himself—the very one they had placed under house arrest in the Crimea. They insisted that they had no intention of changing any of the policies instituted by Gorbachev, only that the new committee would engage in "more thinking" and be "more organized."

And since the failure of the coup Leninist language has all but disappeared from the Soviet political discourse. Nevertheless, there continue to be aspects of Soviet foreign policy that are not consistent with new thinking. This suggests that there may be factors other than new thinking and Leninism influencing Soviet foreign policy.

This is not really surprising. Though Leninism as an ideology is clearly dying in the Soviet Union the feelings and attitudes that originally sustained Leninism are not necessarily dying as well. As was discussed above, a complex of Russian traits dovetailed with Leninism to create the juggernaut of Soviet Communism. These traits include the tendency to view the world as inherently conflictual and, thus, to feel threatened or attacked, and to put great stock in military power. Another is a group narcissism that leads to a great concern for national status and prestige.

As Leninism has declined it appears that these traits have taken on a new form of expression. Even when Soviets apparently eschew Marxism-Leninism they do not necessarily embrace new thinking. Rather some Soviets appear to take a third position: a position based on a model of international relations similar to Western realist theories. According to this new Soviet realist perspective, competition is a natural and inevitable feature of state behavior and great powers naturally play a special, privileged role in international relations. Such thinking leads to the view that it is appropriate for the Soviet Union to seek to maintain its great-power status, if necessary, through competitive behavior.*

Originally we found such great-power thinking almost exclusively among Westernized intellectuals who would be characterized as liberals within the contemporary Soviet political landscape. In most of these cases, this stream of thinking has been heavily infused with new thinking to the extent that a cooperative relationship with the West was seen as a desirable, if difficult, outcome. On the question of maintaining the independence of the republics there was a preference for maintaining a strong Union so as to maintain the Soviet Union as a great power, but there was also an attitude that the center must accommodate the demands of the republics for greater autonomy.

More recently, in the years 1990-1991, this kind of thinking also began to appear at the conservative end of the Soviet political spectrum. In this case there has been greater suspicion of cooperation with the West, a more hardline approach to negotiations with the West, a strong concern for the loss of Soviet status, and a supreme concern for maintaining a strong Union.

As the liberal substream appeared first and is much more developed conceptually, it will be presented first.

---

*This perspective needs to be distinguished from an aspect of new thinking that is also sometimes labeled "realist." As discussed in Chapter 2, many new thinkers, as well as the "realists" being discussed here, stress the importance of putting aside grand ideological aspirations and focusing instead on national interests. The difference is that new thinking claims that when nations focus on their national interests they will naturally find a certain equilibrium, because, at a fundamental level, nations' interests are interdependent and therefore ultimately convergent. According to the realist perspective, national interests are fundamentally polarized and thus competition is inevitable, though it may be possible, through adroit diplomacy, to achieve some degree of cooperation.

The Inevitability of Competition

Perhaps because most of the liberal proponents of great-power thinking come from the milieu of new thinking, they would generally try to downplay the difference between the two perspectives. Some, however, explicitly made the distinction. For example, a political analyst we interviewed described two different dominant viewpoints among Soviets. From both perspectives, ideology is of "second- or third-rate importance" and mainly contrived for "domestic consumption." Nevertheless he identified some key differences, particularly in relation to such questions as the necessity of competition between the superpowers. The first perspective—the more standard new-thinking perspective—he explained, is held by

> people who stand for a very, very different scene, a principally different type of relationship between our countries as our final goal....(According to them) we really don't have any significant differences or controversies between our countries. All the controversies that we have, or the majority of them, are simply remnants of the Cold War period....The people who are for the most profound changes, they argue [that] both of our countries really can cooperate and nothing can be regarded as a very serious obstacle in this way. All the problems that we have now...can be negotiated if we find adequate mechanisms for negotiations.

The second perspective he portrayed, while not a Marxist-Leninist dialectical perspective, nonetheless stresses the inevitability of competition:

> Look, we are rivals, historical rivals....You cannot negate the political realities, this is the objective result of history that the Soviet Union and the United States have become two major powers of the world after the Second World War and even if we have some agreements which would regulate somehow our rivalry, that would not exclude the rivalry from the relationship completely. There will be some other causes for further rivalry. Even if Russia was non-Communist, say Czarist Russia or something like that, we still would have this type of relationship with the United States. So we shouldn't just devise any false hopes or false morals. And let's be realistic and think about a relationship with some kind of regulated rivalry.

Such realist thinking also came up when we asked Soviets to explain the notion of the balance of interests. A common argument among new thinkers is that the balance of interests needs to replace the balance of power in structuring international relations. Similarly new thinkers see deterrence as a very problematic concept and that international relations need to be ordered instead by normative structures. According to the new realist perspective, though, the balance of power and the dynamics of deterrence play an integral role in establishing the balance of interests. For example, an official in the Foreign Ministry explained:

> We cannot achieve the balance of interests other than through a balance of power.....Given the conflicting interests of the sides, the balance of them can be achieved only through the hope that we can return to the concept of deterrence. Deterrence is based on the balance of power. So it seems to me that there is no way for achieving a balance of interests [other] than through deterrence, a relation based on deterrence, deterrence is based on strength....Based on that, we can move toward the balance of interest.

He wrote off "idealistic approaches" to the balance of interests that rely purely on normative principles.

> Well, there can be some idealistic approaches that we should impose a balance of interests, certain interests of one party are counterbalanced by certain concessions by the opposite party and so on. But this will not be a stable solution. A stable solution can be achieved only with a balance of power.

He viewed the competition for power as largely unavoidable. He explained: "Because of fluctuations, the weaker side will do its best to become stronger, and when it becomes strong, the opposite side will do its best to become stronger and when it becomes strong, the opposite side will feel itself weaker." And only through this competition playing itself out can the level of destructiveness reach a point where both sides are deterred and stability is reached:

> and this (competition) will go on until they reach a point of deterrence beyond which further getting stronger becomes senseless. That is the situation with the superpowers right now....It seems that unless every possibility of negative development is exhausted, mankind cannot move to the possibility of positive development. Deterrence is a negative development. Balance of power is a negative development. Balance of interests is a positive development, but their interaction is that the first should go before the second.

Such thinking can also be found in some published Soviet literature. Genrikh Troffimenko, a senior policy analyst at the Moscow Institute for the Study of the USA and Canada, has written that although "in principle" such thinking can have a "higher" connotation, "as a rule the balance of interests reflects the existing balance of power."[1] Dashichev has claimed that even Lenin understood the need for a balance of power to create equilibrium between states.[2] V. Mikhaylov, a prominent nuclear weapons scientist, deputy USSR minister of nuclear power generation and the nuclear industry and a self-described "hawk," has written:

> It is hard and painful to be a realist. But throughout our long history, communities of people united to form states have fought one another, by military, political, or economic means, for living space, spheres of influence, and simply a place in the sun. The forms of the struggle have changed, but the essence remains the same to this day. All the same I do not think mankind is doomed. I agree with Margaret Thatcher: We can all be saved only by nuclear parity, mutual deterrence in nuclear expansion.[3]

This realist tone can also be heard in the description of the change in Soviet foreign policy away from its traditional ideological orientation. For example, Alexei Pushkov, then a consultant to the International Department of the Central Committee, has written that Soviet-American "rivalry is increasingly being regarded not as ideological but as state rivalry, i.e., a totally different phenomenon."[4] In an interview, Georgi Pryakhin, then deputy chief of the CPSU Central Committee Ideology Department, concurred that Soviet foreign policy is becoming "more a superpower's policy than an ideological policy."[5]

Even the greater openness to Western realist thinking has become increasingly explicit. In November 1988 the academic Alexander Chubaryan called for a more open attitude to the notion of the balance of power, asking rhetorically: "Do we have a right to completely discount something like the traditions and logic of European balance."[6]

This suggestion has increasingly been heeded. In the June 1990 issue of the Foreign Ministry's *International Affairs*, Vadim Udalov, a first secretary in the Foreign Ministry, published a remarkable article that enthusiastically embraced the utility of realist thinking.

> In the past, ideologized labels beyond which our serious researchers could not venture prevented them from, among other things, giving due credit to certain ideas of the theory of "political realism."...It is obvious that such a vision has never been and could not be alien to our outlook. Suffice it to recall that one of the main merits of Soviet foreign policy has always been seen in strengthening the positions and influence of socialism, i.e., socialist countries, primarily the Soviet Union itself. Today, when we maintain that in the nuclear age force must not be used as a political instrument, we insist on the unacceptability of precise recourse to military power as a means of

pressure while accepting and even welcoming the exertion of influence as such in certain situations, meaning its civilized forms. Anyone who views today's world realistically is bound to recognize that all countries still see their paramount foreign policy task as building up or at least preventing any decline in their international influence....The fundamental, all-pervasive foreign policy interest of any state is to build up its influence (power).[7]

In July 1990 Igor Malashenko published a piece, also in *International Affairs*, titled "Russia: The Earth's Heartland," in which he explained that the competition between East and West is not fundamentally derived from ideology but from the geopolitical realities flowing from the fact that the Soviet Union stretches across the Eurasian heartland.

> The confrontation of the continental power which controls the heart of Eurasia and the coalition opposing it is by no means confined, geopolitically, to a contest between East and West, socialism and capitalism...but is an element of genuinely global politics. Properly speaking, the very terms "East" and "West" also reflect in a way, if inadequately, the fact that it is not only ideological rivalry or even a clash of social-political systems but also a "deideologized" geopolitical confrontation....The international order based on a balance of forces in Europe crumbled during the war, and a power vacuum arose on the European continent, in which the interests of the two mightiest powers, the Soviet Union and the United States, that became geopolitical rivals, were bound to clash. The USSR and the US have become the main poles of the international system, and relations between them the main axis of world politics....In those circumstances, ideological opposition was largely no more than a "transformed" geopolitical confrontation.[8]

Also, in August 1990 Vladimir Razuvayev cited Hans Morgenthau's concept of 'national interest' and said approvingly that an

> indication that national priorities are starting to dominate our foreign policy is the emergence of new terms in the Soviet foreign political vocabulary. Some people speak about "buffer zones" and "strongholds." Others use the word "geopolitics," this time without the attached adjectives "bourgeois" and "pseudoscientific."...The essence of the demands made on Soviet foreign policy is to bring it in conformity with the national interests of the Soviet Union.[9]

Such realist thinking has also entered into Soviets' analysis of Soviet behavior. Contrary to the traditional interpretation of Soviet behavior as being strictly motivated by ideals in contrast to the West's reprehensible striving for power, the prominent journalist Alexander Bovin, on a television talk show, approvingly portrayed the Soviet Union as behaving like a traditional great power. "We, too, pursue a policy of force toward the United States—nor can we fail to. We are a great power. If, let us say, attempts are made to frighten us by a show of force, then we are compelled to do so."[10]

Some Soviet analysts have also spoken freely about the need to maintain their status and prestige as a great power. There seemed to be a strong consensus that, in the past, military might was the key measure of a nation's status. In the current era, however, they believed that there was a dramatic change occurring in favor of economic power as the critical index. This generated a concern that the Soviet Union, despite its military might, was losing its great-power status in light of its economic weakness. Igor Malashenko has written:

> Considerations of status and prestige obviously loom large in the policy of any nuclear power.... Our nuclear might was seen during the recent period of stagnation as well-nigh the basic token of our status as a "superpower"....[But now] we can preserve the status of a truly great power only by jerking socioeconomic development out of its inertia.[11]

Vladimir Petrovsky commented shortly before the August 1991 coup that

> new superpower criteria are emerging and the importance of "military muscle" is gradually declining....The people's economic prosperity and the equality of life in all its diversity are coming to the foreground. We must capture this trend and move in the same direction as the rest of the world. Our influence will depend on the solution of domestic economic and political problems. [12]

The Special Position of Great Powers

Contrary to the oft-stated new-thinking principle that all nations should be regarded equally, the new great-power thinking says that the Soviet Union, like the United States, should have a special role in the world commensurate with its position as a great power. In a Soviet-conducted poll of 110 Soviet foreign-policy experts, 59 percent held the new-thinking view that "the USSR and the USA must possess the same rights as all other members of world community," but 32 percent agreed that "the USSR and the USA must possess peculiar rights in accordance with their peculiar status in world community."[13]

Comments made by political analysts in the press imply a special global role for the Soviet Union. Bovin has said that "the Soviet Union is a superpower with global interests. This is true now and this will remain so in the future."[14] The political observer Nikolai Shishlin has commented that "the Soviet Union is indeed a great power conscious of its responsibility for the destiny of the world, for the destiny of present-day development, conscious of its responsibility for everything taking place."[15]

Such thinking came up in the interviews as well. One political analyst referred to the "global responsibility of the Soviet Union...for the situation, well, everywhere in the world." As he had previously made some comments about the equality of all nations, we pointed out that this notion of global responsibility implied a certain inequality. He replied, "Yes, but it only emphasizes the scope of responsibility." We then pointed out: "On the one hand there is responsibility. On the other there is privilege, power." He then laughed and said: "Yes, we know. We know that. Those who have more responsibility, they will have more, so to say, more pleasures, but at the same time more headaches."

Sometimes these ideas came out indirectly and in a somewhat defensive fashion. For example, in an interview with a Soviet Foreign Ministry official we asked him to define the practical implication of the ideas of democratizing international relations and treating all nations as equal. He answered that they mean "the willingness to listen to the opinions of others. Rejection of force as a means of settling international disputes. More attention to the United Nations where others can have a voice."

But then, recognizing that this did not necessarily imply equality of all nations, the official said, "Of course, different countries have different weight internationally depending on a variety of things." But he insisted somewhat defensively, "We are on a much more equal basis than we used to be." When we pressed for more definition of the meaning of equality he reacted with some irritation, "You know, you can take any statement and make it an absolute and take it too far." He then shifted his emphasis to the idea of democratizing international relations and even seemed to abandon the idea of establishing equality between nations.

> We are trying to be more respectful....To me it is a manifestation of ourselves trying to act more democratic in international relations. I don't see any connection between that kind of an attitude and any kind of desire to say from now on everybody is equal.

This great-power thinking came up in numerous interviews when we asked whether the permanent members of the UN Security Council should have the special powers derived from having a veto. Virtually every individual we asked affirmed the desire to maintain the veto power even if the other permanent members would be willing to relinquish it. We pointed out that this position seemed to conflict with the new-thinking notions that all nations should be treated as equal, that no nation should have special privileges, and that international relations should be democratized. When respondents tried to explain this discrepancy, most frequently they would stress that the permanent members have a special role to play in managing the international order. Others recognized that the Soviet Union used the veto power to pursue its interests but this was, nonetheless, seen as a natural and unobjectionable feature of the world order. As one diplomat explained: "In the real world there are certain interests which we, the Soviet Union and the United States, are trying to guard, and at this point we both are permanent members and our friends think that [it's] the best way for us."

In some cases this great-power orientation even extended to the idea that the Soviet Union and the United States should seek to maintain their existing spheres of influence. Sometimes this was equated with the idea of maintaining the balance of interests. For example, in one of the interviews we referred to the new-thinking idea that the superpowers should mutually withdraw their military forces from the rest of the world.

Respondent: There were ideas of some withdrawal from some areas so as to curb confrontation. But I think the idea of the balance of interests somehow excludes or somehow puts an end to the total discussion. It's not a problem of withdrawal; it's a problem of alignment of interests....

Interviewer: So the concept of balance of interest is really a concept of realignment within the status quo, not a concept of retraction.

R : Yes, mainly within the framework of the status quo. But, of course, with the very strong input of the ideas of limiting to some very minimum possible the military component....Whether we like it or not we have...some kind of world order. It's imperfect, of course....But this is something we have done, a part of reality. So I think the best way to go further would be to find ways to not destroy that order.

I : And is that order based on the U.S.-Soviet maintenance of the current spheres of influence? Is that what you're saying?

R : Yes, yes.

Similar ideas have even appeared in the Foreign Ministry's journal *International Affairs*. Andrei Kozyrev (then in the Soviet Foreign Ministry and now foreign minister of Russia) and Andrei Shumikhin (of the Institute for the Study of the USA and Canada) wrote in March 1989:

It would be reasonable to recognize the status quo which has taken shape towards the end of the 20th Century concerning the spheres of the economic, military, political and ideological influence of the USA and the USSR, capitalism and socialism. Attempts by either side to change it, to undermine it by direct or covert actions are fraught with serious dangers and are by and large counterproductive.... In a certain sense, Soviet-American relations in the Third World can be based on the principle of "correct reciprocity" meaning that each power consciously renounces actions that may...impinge upon the traditional geopolitical interests of the opposite side.[16]

This theme of superpower cooperation within the status quo has also been extended to include the suggestion that the superpowers should cooperate to preserve their superpower status in the face of numerous current challenges. For example, a policy analyst we interviewed said:

Now the United States and the Soviet Union are still superpowers, but how long will we be superpowers given the background of competition from China, from Japan, from the European Economic Community? Maybe we don't have that much time. It's when we have that much time as superpowers, maybe we could do something creative, something positive... Maybe we could contribute to some positive development in the world, acting from our superpower position. And in this way, maybe we can prolong to our satisfaction our superpower status by acting positive....Maybe in the process of doing something positive for mankind, we would keep our superpower status or status of a leader of conflicting systems for a longer time because the systems would not be conflicting... coming together for a noble task, and this way we would create our—I say, if not superpower status, then our prestige, our leading role, and so on.

Often this kind of thinking has a high moral tone to it. For example, the academic Vitaliy Goldansky has said

if one wants to make surer progress in international politics...it makes sense to follow the premise that USSR-U.S. relations are of special value....The USSR and the United States can assume the role of helmsmen in the rough sea of world politics. I think everyone will benefit from this. [17]

Similarly Gorbachev, reporting to the Supreme Soviet on his meeting with U.S. President George Bush in June 1990, praised the idea that the superpowers should "conduct affairs...as great powers bearing a special responsibility towards the world and endowed with the capabilities to realize this responsibility they bear."[18]

Others, with the same moral tone, have specified how the superpowers should exercise their special role. For example, a Central Committee official explained to us how the United States and the Soviet Union should deal with such areas of conflict as Angola and Afghanistan: "Our role as a Great Power, for example, must be to be the mediator in these types of conflicts. Because these conflicts are one of the potential sources of additional confrontation among our countries and among the blocs."

The political observer P. Vorobyev has even counseled that failure of the USSR and the United States to take such an activist role in the Mideast was partly to blame for Iraq's invasion of Kuwait. In an August 1990 article he explained that the rivalry between Mideast powers had been

> exacerbated by the withdrawal of the major powers, above all the USSR and the United States, from direct involvement in the region's affairs....You get the impression that in elaborating a new line in regional affairs—a line which is undoubtedly correct, more well-considered and reasonable—the USSR and the United States failed to give enough consideration to the "regional superpower" factor. We can now see that the candidates for this role have taken the stage.[19]

At other times, though, this kind of thinking takes on a more openly self-interested and even chauvinistic tone. For example, Viktor Girshfeld, a former military officer who writes on foreign affairs, made a proposal to the "Great World Powers wishing to keep their place under the sun." He suggested that to maintain their superpower status they should quietly establish a system of condominium whereby they will each continue to maintain a military presence in their respective regions of the world. This presence, he argued, will serve "as a barrier to the outbreak of conflict among the aborigines." [20]

Conflict with New Thinking

Though most Soviets who articulate this new realist perspective insist that it is part of new thinking, there are occasions when Soviets do encounter some of the contradictions between the two perspectives. As they try to resolve these contradictions they sometimes sound a bit muddled and confused.

For example, the academic Yelena Arefyeva, in a July 1989 article in *Izvestiya* tried to address what she calls "the gulf that has formed between declarations of a departure from ideology in interstate relations" and the fact that the Soviet Union still gives aid, differentially, to socialist states. Consistent with new thinking, she argued that foreign aid can be reduced, especially ideologically oriented aid, saying that "there are reserves for reducing the volume of concessionary credits and the nonrepayable transfer of resources. These include, first, ideologically determined assistance...."

However, as she considered further the implications of this reduction in aid she shifted her position in favor of maintaining it. But the reasons she gave for maintaining foreign aid were not based on ideological considerations but rather on the idea that the Soviet Union must uphold its position as a great power.

> However difficult our economic position is now, we are still a great power. Membership of this 'club' imposes on us a duty to participate in the resolution of global problems....We should participate autonomously and through international organizations in the transfer of resources to the liberated states on aid terms.

To maintain the Soviet Union's great-power status, not for ideological reasons, Arefyeva also insisted that "for quite a long time to come we will have to fulfill commitments we adopted earlier" to give aid to socialist states. Furthermore, she explained that new aid-related obligations "will arise in connection with our awareness of our new role in international affairs." Therefore, she warned, "One cannot really count on a very large saving of resources."[21]

Similar conflicts have appeared in comments made by Alexander Bessmertnykh, then deputy foreign minister and later foreign minister, in a published roundtable discussion. Consistent with the new thinking emphasis on national interests he seemed to reject the notion of taking on the burdens of being a great power:

> Speaking of the "burden of a great power," isn't it too heavy for us? I suppose being a great power is very burdensome. I mean primarily the degree of responsibility which a great power is compelled to assume...for the evolution of the situation on the planet.

But then, immediately afterwards, he insisted that the Soviet Union, as a great power, should take on such responsibilities: "For a great power to set aside its burden is to renounce part of its great responsibility. This would hardly be right."

Apparently aware of the potential contradiction in his comments Bessmertnykh then tried to find a middle position, asking rhetorically whether there is anything "in our activity on the world scene that we could renounce." He criticized the ideological conception of Soviet interests that prompted the Soviet Union to have "too broad an interpretation" of its "national interest" and to become involved in the external world without due regard for the limits of its economy. He declared, "this is something we can renounce in some cases." But then he also seemed to abandon the idea that the Soviet Union should maintain its active involvement in the world to uphold its role as a great power. Instead he reverted to the new-thinking idea that Soviet external involvement should be constrained by a more limited definition of Soviet national interests.

> We have no need for excessive involvement in regions where no direct interest of ours is at stake and where involvement is onerous both politically and economically. And so, being at the stage of new thinking, we see one of our tasks in framing our policy pragmatically.

And he called for discarding "plans which are exaggerated and exceed our possibilities" and "increase the burden of military spending." [22]

During the course of some of our interviews respondents came to realize the underlying conflict between realist thinking and new thinking. In an interview with a political analyst who specializes in European affairs, we were speaking about the Soviet withdrawal from Eastern Europe. It was evident from his tone of voice that he was not really happy about this withdrawal though he repeated the new-thinking argument that such a withdrawal is advisable because the Soviet Union could not really afford such a dispersed military presence. When I asked him why the Soviet Union had previously maintained such presence there, he made a rhythmic expanding movement with his hands and gave the realist explanation, "That is simply what great powers do. They try to expand." I then asked him whether it had been a mistake for the Soviet Union to try to expand in this way. Without hesitation he said "no" and explained that the Soviet Union had, by its military presence there, gained greater influence. When I asked why that was important, he repeated that "this is what great powers do."

I then asked him to explain again why it was now important for the Soviet Union to withdraw from Eastern Europe. Once again without hesitation he explained that by expanding this way the Soviet Union had exhausted itself economically and had so damaged its economy that it would probably lag behind the West for quite some time. But when I asked, again, whether this means that it was a mistake for the Soviet Union to have extended itself in this way in the first place he repeated that it was not and gave the same realist explanation.

I then pointed out that he was arguing that it was not a mistake for the Soviet Union to expand into Eastern Europe because this had given it greater influence, even though the Soviet Union must now give up this presence and influence and on top of that must suffer the economic setback that resulted from the effort. This stopped him short. He sat quietly for a while, turning to look out of the window, his eyes resting on a distant horizon. Then, with a deep sigh, he said, "Maybe it was a mistake."

The Role of Cooperation

Though the great-power stream of thinking can be clearly distinguished from standard new thinking, it would be misleading to imply that great-power thinking has not been heavily infused with new thinking. Indeed all of the Soviets who presented the great-power line of thought would, and often did, characterize themselves as new thinkers.

This characterization is not entirely unjustified. Of all the Soviets interviewed not one of them could be characterized as expressing an unalloyed version of realist or balance-of-power thought. Though they held to the view that competition for power inevitably plays a key role in state behavior, they also insisted that cooperation was a distinct possibility and, indeed, a desirable one. Though they stressed that relative military force played a key role in determining the shape of the international order, they also stressed that it is desirable and possible for this order to be increasingly conditioned by normative concepts and international law. They saw the reality of mutual vulnerability between the great powers as playing a critical role in creating the necessary objective conditions for the evolution in a normative direction. Though they deemed it as inevitable that great powers would seek to maintain their status and prestige, they also seemed to think that it was possible, through the conscious efforts of their leaders, for great powers in the contemporary era to seek status in more constructive and less dangerous realms than military competition.

Therefore, the goals of the great-power line of thought are essentially convergent with those of new thinking. The critical difference between the two streams of thought centers on the question of whether the Soviet Union should unilaterally take significant steps beyond the existing order. As we will see in greater detail in the following chapters, the pure new-thinking stream presses for the Soviet Union to take the lead in changing the world order by unilaterally changing its behavior in accord with the precepts of new thinking. Great-power thought is more inclined to stress the importance of starting with what is sometimes called the "existing realities." Although it supports change in the cooperative directions outlined by new thinking, there is also a strong concern that taking unilateral steps might be viewed by the rest of the world as accepting the idea that the Soviet Union is no longer a superpower. Therefore, there is an emphasis on the need for all steps toward greater cooperation to be reciprocal with other nations, especially the United States.

The net effect of this position, in many cases, is that the great-power orientation ultimately becomes aligned with the more conservative position of those who are still influenced by Leninist thought. The Leninist stream resists cooperation with the West because it is seen, correctly, as part of giving up the dialectical class struggle. The great-power stream resists unilateral cooperative steps out of concern for the loss of Soviet power and stature. The critical difference between Leninist thinking and the great-power orientation is that the latter is fundamentally aligned with new thinking in that it ultimately does seek to achieve a cooperative world order. As we shall see, though, the impact of this stream of thinking on Soviet policy varies with each issue, largely according to the response of the United States.

Conservative Great-Power Thinking

Over the last several years as the Soviet political spectrum has divided itself into "liberal" and "conservative" poles, the latter has generally been associated with a continued adherence to traditional Marxism-Leninism. More recently, though, a new strain of conservatism has appeared that embraces deideologization of Soviet foreign policy but nonetheless clings to the idea that the Soviet Union should maintain itself as a great power on the world scene.

The contrast between these two elements in conservative thinking is well characterized by the differences between the two famous colonels that were the leaders of the Soyuz faction of hardline delegates to the Supreme Soviet and were the target of Shevardnadze's resignation speech. One of these colonels, Nikolai Petrushenko, seems to be a classical orthodox Marxist-Leninist. His criticisms of Gorbachev's foreign policy have been laced with traditional Marxist-Leninist jargon.

The other, Viktor Alksnis, seems to reject the ideological approach. He has said, "We must put aside all ideological conflicts about capitalism and socialism,"[23] has complained how others "relapse into the old ways of thinking," and has used the term "Bolshevik" as an epithet. He is openly anti-Stalinist and even makes implicitly critical comments about Lenin, such as comparing Yeltsin's willingness to let the republics secede with Lenin's signing of the "degrading Brest peace" by which Lenin surrendered the Baltics and other republics.[24]

Alksnis has claimed that he is not fundamentally opposed to some of the main changes in Soviet foreign policy. He even claims to accept in principle the withdrawal of Soviet troops from Eastern Europe. His complaints have centered, instead, on how rapidly troops were being withdrawn, thus forcing them to live in uncomfortable and humiliating "tent cities."[25]

Overall, what most concerns Alksnis is that the Soviet Union is losing its great-power stature. He has accused Gorbachev of helping to "eliminate the Soviet Union as superpower in the world arena." The West, Alksnis has said, "now thinks it can talk down to us. They used to think of the Soviet Union as Upper Volta with missiles. Now they just think of us as Upper Volta. No one fears us." He has ridiculed new thinking, saying that the Soviet Union has been reduced to a weakling like Cupid, "armed, naked and trying to impose our love on everyone." "Andropov," he has claimed, "was a realist. Gorbachev is a romantic."[26]

Such great-power thinking has also appeared in the Soviet press. The political observer Stanislav Kondrashov has written:

> The rhetoric about panhuman values was not always adequate to the task of the practical defense of the national interest....Not only in the eyes of some of the military, but in...our forced departure from East Europe and our necessary abandonment of empire (you cannot force someone to be nice) was a disorderly retreat, if not a humiliating flight, in which there was not even time to prepare housing for the troops.[27]

And in the military newspaper *Krasnaya Zvezda* (Red Star) Alexander Golts has written:

> It is clear now that the period of arms reduction has not been put to proper use. We are losing international authority more rapidly than we are destroying our missiles. Moreover, we are turning from being a subject in international relations, from being a country that used to shape the world political process, into being their object.[28]

Not surprisingly, such sentiments also appeared after the United States-led alliance attacked Iraq in January 1991. B. I. Oleynik, deputy chairman of the USSR Supreme Soviet of Nationalities, in a speech to the Central Committee, grumbled that the Soviet Union had effectively ceded a special role to the United States in maintaining world order. He complained how Americans "standing comfortably with one boot in Grenada's face and the other in Panama's, lecture us like professors on these same panhuman values (meaning the illegitimacy of intervention)." He then expresses his discomfort with the idea that the Soviet Union seems to submit to the normative constraints of such principles while accepting the United States as a policeman that is not so constrained:

> [D]oes a different principle apply here: "What Jupiter is allowed to do, the bull is not allowed to do"? Yet this kind of selectiveness indicates that we have given our a priori consent for a special role, Jupiter's role, to be played by one side, whose actions, whatever they may be, are not subject to analysis by the bulls ambling amenably to the slaughter—and some people are trying hard to drive our country into that herd![29]

It is not the arena of international relations, though, but rather that of interrepublican relations that has most vividly stimulated such conservative great-power thinking. Describing the differences between the liberal group of Supreme Soviet delegates known as the Interregional Group and the conservative Soyuz faction, M. Loginov in an article in the *Literaturnaya Gazeta* explained:

> [T]he Interregionals are supranationalists. For them freedom and democracy are higher than Russia, higher than the Union. [But for the Soyuz group] the USSR is recognized as the absolute value....The main thing...is a united and indivisible state. Everything must be done to preserve it.[30]

Vyacheslav Shostokovsky, former rector of the Communists' High Party School and now a leader of the new liberal Republican Party, explained in early 1991 that such feelings are also quite strong in the general population. He said that the large majority that supported the referendum decision in favor of maintaining the Union were not acting on the basis of socialist idealism but rather great-power romanticism:

> [P]eople were voting for a romantic vision of the 'great power,' the 'multinational empire' that is so hard to part with....People long ago gave up the myths of communism and socialism and all the rest. It is much harder to give up the mythic idea of Russia—great, horizonless Russia.[31]

Not surprisingly, Gorbachev, in February 1991, when trying to drum up support for the referendum on keeping the Union together, did not use Marxist-Leninist language. Rather he pitched his argument to great-power sentiments, warning that any devolution of the Union would undermine the Soviet Union's status in the world: "The Soviet Union, not without reason is called a superpower. Its policies have an influence on all the processes that happen in the world. Huge efforts have gone into acquiring such influence. But it can all be squandered very quickly."[32] Also, in the draft of the new Union Treaty the terms "socialism" or "communism" were never even mentioned.

This concern for preserving the Soviet Union as a great power for a period converged with certain elements of the newly revitalized Russian nationalism. Although most Russian nationalists have tended to align themselves with separatist political trends, others have supported maintaining the Soviet Union as an expression of the Russian empire. David Remnick of the *Washington Post* reports how, as even the Russian Orthodox church joined this cause, it brought together some curious bedfellows:

> For decades, Communists waged open war on the Orthodox church and its priests. But with the virtual death of ideology and militant atheism, the army and the church, especially its most obedient, conservative patriarchs, are joined in the common cause of empire. For them the weakening of Russia, both as a state and as an idea, is unacceptable.
>
> A few weeks ago, at the Red Army Theater in Moscow, priests and army officers took the stage and announced their unity. They spoke not of Lenin or Gorbachev, but rather Alexander Nevsky, Dimitri Donskoi, and other warrior-priests of Russian history and legend. With a row of war-won medals dangling from his cassock, a priest blessed the huge audience of young soldiers, saying: "God is our general!"
>
> "It doesn't matter if one soldier carries a Communist Party card and another carries a crucifix!" said one speaker, writer Yulia Sokolova. "The church and the army are one for Russia!"...The military speakers, for their part, spoke of their emotional connection not to the Bolshevik Revolution, but rather to the Russian motherland. [33]

As mentioned, when the leaders of the abortive coup attempt tried to legitimate their efforts, they did not try to draw on Leninism, but also tried to appeal to great-power sentiments. In their "Address to the Soviet People" of August 20, 1991, they stated:

> We are addressing you at a grave and critical hour for the destinies of the fatherland and our peoples!...The deepening destabilization of the political and economic situation in the Soviet Union is undermining our positions in the world....Only yesterday, a Soviet citizen traveling abroad felt himself the dignified citizen of an influential and respected state. Now he is frequently a second-class foreigner, and his treatment bears the hallmarks of either scorn or compassion. Soviet people's pride and honor must be restored in full....[Our policies] will enable [the Soviet Union] to take its fitting place in the world community of nations.....We have never been ashamed of our patriotic sentiments and deem it natural and legitimate to bring up the present and future generations of our great power's citizens in this spirit. [34]

Despite the common threads running through them it is important to note the differences between the conservative and liberal substreams of the great-power orientation. Many proponents of the liberal great-power line would be horrified to hear that they were viewed as in any way being in bed with the likes of Viktor Alksnis, old-school Great Russia chauvinists, or, above all, the leaders of the abortive coup. Likewise many conservatives would find it hard to see their kinship with "pointy-headed" intellectuals who use Western theoretical concepts to explain that Soviet behavior is competitive not because of some unique and laudable feature of the Soviet Union, but because that is just how nations are.

Nevertheless, there are signs that these disparate trends do converge around a number of shared principles. In particular, there seems to be agreement that the Soviet Union should seek to maintain its great-power status even if this requires a certain amount of competitive behavior (some of which may even be proscribed by new thinking).

From the Western point of view the most important question is how these converging trends will view the prospect for cooperation with the West to reduce the risks and costs of competition and even to reduce the competition per se. It is too early to say how much this stream of thinking will promote such cooperation, but it is safe to say that this stream is much more likely to promote cooperation than the more traditional stream. As was discussed above the liberal substream has been heavily infused with new thinking to the extent that it views cooperation, although difficult to achieve, as desirable. The conservative substream, even though it does not necessarily embrace cooperation as intrinsically worthwhile, is nonetheless much less ambitious in its long-term goals than traditional Leninism and is relieved of the view that competition with the West should be the essential foundation of Soviet foreign policy.

Finally, there is the question of how much this kind of great-power thinking will influence the new Russian foreign-policymakers. Although it is too early to come to a definitive conclusion, it does appear that such thinking is playing a significant role. The new Russian leaders have made it clear that they have not become so embroiled in their domestic problems that they have lost all concern with their global position as a great power. The Russian foreign minister Andrei Kozyrev, shortly before the final demise of the Soviet Union in December 1991, affirmed that

Russia will remain a great power. It may not be a superpower, but it will be a great military power and part of the global strategic balance... Russia will be the continuation of the Soviet Union in the field of nuclear weapons.[35]

Boris Yeltsin in a December 12, 1991, speech to the Russian parliament explained that the initiative for establishing the Commonwealth of Independent States was prompted by a concern that an independent nuclear-armed Ukraine would be a "serious violation of the geopolitical balance."[36] And the Russian Federation demanded and succeeded in acquiring the Soviet permanent seat on the UN Security Council.

6

The Third World

In this chapter we will examine the effect of the various streams of thought so far explored on Soviet policy and behavior in the Third World. We will review first the new-thinking principles concerning the Third World and then look at how actual Soviet behavior has and has not conformed to the precepts of new thinking. Finally we concentrate on the rationales that Soviets give for behavior not consistent with new thinking.

New Thinking About the Third World

Central to the new-thinking approach to the Third World is an effort to remove the ideological element in Soviet policy. As Shevardnadze stated in 1988 "the Soviet Union supports a deideologization of international relations and the exclusion of an overwhelming component of ideological differences from foreign policy and diplomacy."[1]

Such thinking has led to a renunciation of the traditional Soviet effort to promote socialism in the Third World as well as to approach it as an arena of polarized competition with the capitalist West. Instead, new thinking proposes a pluralistic and cooperative order based on the freedom of nations to choose their social system and the prohibition of intervention by foreign powers. To realize this order, new thinking calls for the elimination of arms transfers, especially to conflicting ideological factions; resolution of regional conflicts through a process of national reconciliation; and the reduction and ultimate elimination of the superpower's military presence.

Renouncing Ideological Activism

Perhaps most dramatic in the new approach to the Third World is the renunciation of an activist policy seeking to expand socialism, stressing instead the principle of nonintervention. Speaking in Havana in April 1989, Gorbachev said:

[N]ot infrequently [regional conflicts] result from outside interference and attempts to prevent nations from making their independent choice. Attempts are made to justify actions of this kind by...invocations of some political or ideological values....And so I would like to state clearly that we are resolutely opposed to any theories and doctrines justifying the export of revolution or counter-revolution, all forms of foreign interference in the affairs of sovereign states.[2]

These principles led to widespread criticism of past Soviet behavior in the Third World. Most prominent is criticism of the intervention in Afghanistan. In a stunning speech to the Supreme Soviet in October 1989 Shevardnadze said that in the Afghanistan intervention "we violated norms of proper behavior..., went against general human values..., [and] committed the most serious violations of our own legislation, our party and civilian norms." [3]

The following December Aleksandr Dzasokhov, then chairman of the Supreme Soviet Committee on International Relations, reported to the Congress of People's Deputies on a study carried out by the committee on the decision to intervene in Afghanistan. He denounced the intervention, saying, "We set ourselves against the majority of the world community and against the norms of conduct, which should be accepted and observed in international relations," attributing the decision to "the excessive ideologization of Soviet foreign policy." The decision to send in troops was also seen as wrongly made by the Communist Party apparatus rather than the Supreme Soviet. "New thinking," he concluded, "intends excluding the possibility of any repetition of anything like the 1979 action."[4]

Among academics such criticism has frequently extended to the entire Soviet effort to promote socialism in the Third World. For example, D. Volskiy has mockingly used ideological cliches from the past and portrayed Soviet-supported factions as hopelessly vain, inept, and no better than their non-socialist predecessors:

It has happened more than once...that, once in power, the "national-patriotic forces" have conducted themselves like feudal or even pre-feudal lords; that the "important national economic projects" created with a wave of their hands...were needed simply to gratify their vanity; and that the country that had embarked on a path of "progressive transformations" has reached economic catastrophe....[5]

Other academics have denounced all efforts to promote ideology, placing Soviet efforts on a par with other political and religious movements. N. Simoniya, of IMEMO, has written:

Indeed, the entire history of mankind from the ancient past to the present day provides us with examples of successful and unsuccessful attempts on the part of various religious and political trends to conquer the minds and hearts of the largest possible number of followers throughout the world, resorting to the aid of the cross, the sword, and ideological propaganda for this purpose....We also went through a period of illusions and attempts to present one political form of the revolutionary process—socialist orientation—as almost a universal model for the transition to socialism in the countries of the three continents.[6]

In some cases, criticism of Soviet intervention in the Third World has even been buttressed by a traditional Marxist analysis. According to Marx, societies must go through a progressive evolution from feudalism through capitalism and only then to socialism. Soviet activism in the Third World has sometimes been portrayed as a spurious attempt to force this evolutionary process in an unnatural way. For example, Dashichev has said:

Revolution cannot be imported; it must arise from inside. In Afghanistan we had no conditions for such development....It was a great mistake to think that a feudal or pre-feudal society with illiteracy and a lack of economic development was ready for socialism....We made the same mistake in Africa. [7]

At least as common, though, are brazen challenges to the Marxist-Leninist framework itself. In particular, there has been a rejection of the classical notion of a world revolution. Bovin has stated bluntly: "The world revolution is not on the agenda. Therefore, the thesis of the Soviet Union's support for the world revolution has become useless."[8]

A general from one of the military academies whom we interviewed explained that the risks of military confrontation simply made the goal of world revolution too dangerous:

Our ideological conception about victory in the revolution and using any means to achieve victory in the revolution...this concept of helping meant using force to help revolutions in other countries. But the level of weapons and the level of risk is very high...[and] the old principles won't work.

Other interviewees emphasized that Soviets have actually lost interest in world revolution because the effort to promote it is too demanding. A policy analyst commented that "our country does not want any kind of world revolution right now, of course.... Right now nobody talks about it" because, he explained, the Soviet Union "doesn't want to strain." An official from the Central Committee Information Department told us that the

Soviets would "applaud" if the U.S. succeeded in pulling Cuba out of the Soviet orbit, primarily because it would relieve them of the burden of these "huge sums of money involved" in their economic subsidization. An individual who works for one of the publications of the Foreign Ministry said, with tired disinterest, about the competition for the Third World: "You know, if you're asking my opinion, I don't care. There's no problem with me if you want Angola, if you want Ethiopia, I'm telling you, 'That's your problem.'"

Just as the concept of world revolution has lost currency, so has the Marxist-Leninist idea of national liberation. Originally this concept was more broadly defined to mean the process of liberating nations from any social structures, especially colonialism, that inhibited the natural process of social evolution. It was assumed, though, that such unfettered development would lead naturally to socialism. Therefore, in the postwar era the concept of promoting national liberation came to mean more specifically the promotion of socialist forces in the world.

With the principle of nonintervention enshrined as central to new thinking, however, this concept of promoting such national liberation has taken a severe drubbing. As one Foreign Ministry official said to us, new thinking specifically abjures "interference into the Third World" and embraces "freedom of choice, not support for wars of national liberation." Another policy analyst, recognizing that "there were actions in the past that would help the socialist forces to win in some regions," said that now "the Soviet Union doesn't pose itself the aim of expanding socialism everywhere....The Soviet state in its practical actions will not try to expand socialism to Bolivia, Argentina, etc."

Furthermore, numerous Soviets even reject, with just a few exceptions, the utility of the concept of national liberation in the present-day context. As one policy analyst explained:

National Liberation Movements in the true sense of the word are in South Africa, in Palestine, maybe some other areas of the world. But as regards the National Liberation Movement as such, the big movement, which had as its aim the overthrow of the colonial rule, is a matter of the past now. It's all over. Because the task of achieving National Liberation has been achieved now. And what we used to call National Liberation Movement, you know, it was kind of tantamount to the Third World, developing countries, it automatically meant: National Liberation Movement.

So nobody even bothers to think...what is the purpose of the National Liberation Movement, how can you explain it? What nation is going to be liberated from whom? Ones that have the sovereignty, they have a lot of problems of their own....And if we put this aim before them that until you

overcome your backwardness, you must wage struggle for national liberation, what kind of national liberation is it? What is the purpose of applying
the term to India for instance? Or to Egypt? Or to Morocco?...As for me, I
don't apply the term National Liberation Movement, or National Liberation revolution to the situations which exist now in most of the countries
in the Third World.

We pursued this question in an interview with an official in the
Information Department of the Central Committee:

Interviewer: Is this a widespread view, that the notion of national liberation
is no longer applicable? What about El Salvador? What about the
Philippines? Are these no longer seen as national liberation struggles?
Respondent: You see we don't use this terminology in our political literature
during the last some years. Maybe it is right because this term "national
liberation movement"—it is in the retrostyle maybe.
I : Retrostyle?
R : Retrostyle, yes. And, of course, maybe it was good in the sixties. And
it was the struggle for independence of the French and England colonies
in Africa and so on. But now all these countries are free. And what it is
in El Salvador, for myself we can't use this terminology "national
liberation movement" to deal with the situation in El Salvador. It's
another situation...the nature of this government is anti-democratic.
And for this reason these forces are fighting it... But I am not sure that
all these forces are taking part in this military activity in the country—
they are only progressive forces...[but] it's not our affair to deal with
such movements as in El Salvador, for example. Because we have our
own problems. It's not our problem to support them.

Another official within the Central Committee Information Department
similarly seemed to dismiss the traditional concept of national liberation
and tried to redefine it in terms of liberation from economic backwardness:

I : So when you use this term, the struggle for social and national liberation, what do you mean by that?
R : ...There is what you might call a certain inertia of terminology. The
terminology that adequately reflected the situation in the past does not
[do so] in the present....I think this is fully applicable to the term
"national liberation." I think that with decolonization and independence, this term was permissible. [But] in the old sense, it's confined to
a few places. I think that generally, on the whole, the issue now is the
elimination of economic and cultural backwardness in that part of the

world. The problem of a new international economic order.... The
problem of liberation of those countries is still there in this sense.

I : Liberation from economic backwardness?

R : Yes, economic backwardness. But it can't be adequately described in
old notions.

He then explained that developing countries, to promote their development need to cooperate even with transnational corporations, though he
still tried to reinsert the concept of struggle in this relationship.

R : I am convinced that developing countries can't solve their problems on
the basis of only their domestic resources, on the basis of their national
resources. Recently I had a meeting with Latin American socialists and
I told them openly that they wouldn't be able to solve their problems
without somehow cooperating with transnationals. The transnationals
have their own selfish interests but everything coincides in the interests
of cooperation with international forces. The aspect of struggle is there
but at the same time there should be cooperation with transnational
corporations....

I : So what is the goal of the struggle?

R : National development. Primarily economic development.

I : Is that a struggle with the transnationals? What is the struggle?

R : It's a question of struggle. Why? Because the transnationals get profits
in those countries. They can take those profits or they can reinvest them
in the development of those countries. So that's why it's a struggle.

Consistent with this new definition of national liberation as being
primarily the liberation from economic backwardness, and given the poor
performance of socialist economies, there is a strong current in new thinking
that calls into question the very idea that socialism is a desirable path for
Third World countries. In regard to South Africa, Soviet policy has discouraged the African National Congress from seeking to bring about
socialism there.

This thinking has also led to a rejection of the idea that Third World
countries should necessarily follow the Soviet model. Shevardnadze has
said, "We are not now trying to act as mentors and do not consider ourselves
blessed with absolute truth...."[9] Alexei Kiva, in a lengthy article, described
how Soviets became gradually disillusioned with the belief that socialism
should and would become dominant in the Third World. He wrote with a
distinct tone of sadness and a touch of defensiveness:

Thus the hopes for rapidly ending the economic backwardness by following a noncapitalist road—hopes cherished by many new states—were dashed. So was our hope that new states of Asia and especially Africa would substantially reinforce world socialism by joining it. Who was destined to win the battle for the Third World, as we used to phrase it at the time, is clear now. We did not win it. But neither did the West. The winner was the logic of history, which put an end to many illusions. To give up illusions is not to be defeated.[10]

A Foreign Ministry official with whom we spoke in 1989 told us: "We are preparing some things showing that socialism does not work and that for developing countries was not a real success compared to capitalism."

In the interviews we even encountered a curious frustration, on the part of Soviets trying to get Third World leaders to let go of their orthodox Marxist positions. A Central Committee official explained:

> You see, there are powerful forces in those countries that are guided by socialist ideals....I've been to South Yemen, I met South Yemen leaders and they represent many people, a lot of the population, and they're for socialism. But from my point of view they are too left wing and less realistic. They understand their road to socialism as the road to no capitalism, nothing of capitalism. This leads to the already tested road to socialism: dictatorship, Stalinism. Right after the revolution, Lenin tried, he failed but he started looking for new ways—controlled capitalism, okay. But they don't want it, that means they do not allow any private enterprise. They don't want to deal with the transnationals....The idea of social equality, egalitarian approach, actually comes from the grassroots. And it negatively influenced the development.

A political analyst who specializes in Third World issues explained that such resistance stems partly from the fact that many Third World socialist leaders were originally educated in the Soviet Union:

> They saw what is going on here, and they also said this is the best way we've seen. But first of all it was not the best way to proceed here in the Soviet Union, and when artificially transplanted to a society where everything was completely different, completely different in terms of economy, social conditions, psychology, or such phenomena as tribalism, it becomes even more unrealistic, more artificial.

Several professors who train foreign cadres for the party described hot debates with young Third World cadres complaining that their mentors were giving up the faith. The communist parties of some countries, they explained, have even stopped sending their young people to Moscow, for fear they will be tainted by new thinking.

In a broader sense, as new thinking renounces the effort to promote socialism in the Third World, new thinking also stresses the importance of giving up the polarized world view that saw the world as an arena of competition between the Soviet Union and the United States. As one policy analyst explained:

> [In the past] we just examined [the Third World] from the point of view not only of the Soviet-American confrontation, but the confrontation of the two systems. Speaking about the Third World, we thought about it as an object of confrontation....We are trying to give up this method now.... We don't think about Soviet or American interests in the Third World.

Speaking with a group of Foreign Ministry officials one of them told us:

> In the Cold War years our policy in Africa, for example, was to do damage to each other. Americans to Russians and Russians to Americans. We forgot about Africans. And the only thing, it was like an obsession, was to do something wrong to the opposite side.

Another chimed in: "If we managed to do wrong to the United States, that would be better. But now not."

The past tendency to compete with the West to achieve dominance in various regions has been roundly criticized. Shevardnadze has said: "Divisions and redivisions of the world into spheres of influence are historically pointless. Today, we must all have only one sphere of influence— our planet."[11] Instead, there is an emphasis on allowing much greater independence on the part of smaller countries. Gorbachev has said that "new international relations can be built solely on the basis of an independent line."[12]

There is also a major trend away from seeing regional conflicts as being primarily a function of East-West conflict and seeing them, instead, as arising primarily from indigenous and nonideological factors. The scholar Y. Dolgopolov, in an article in *Krasnaya Zvezda*, wrote:

> Although regional conflicts vary in nature and in the nature of the conflicting forces, as a rule they arise on local grounds, as a result of contradictions engendered either by the colonial past, or by new social processes, or by throwbacks to the policy of aggression, or by a combination of all three. To make out that all these tangled contradictions are the result of East-West rivalry is not only wrong, it is also extremely dangerous.[13]

What flows from these changes in perspective is a thoroughgoing reorientation in the Soviet relationship to all countries. A. Vasilyev, deputy director of the Institute of Africa of the USSR Academy of Sciences, has written: "In the evolving nonconfrontational pattern of international relations we are ceasing to be the political, military, and (to the extent that we ever were) economic counterbalance to the West." He has warned: "Nowadays every revolutionary authoritarian dictator can hardly expect our unconditional political, moral, and material support simply because he utters a dozen 'Marxist-Leninist' slogans or pays lip service to anti-imperialism."[14]

Similarly, Andrei Kortunov has written:

> In mapping out future aid programmes, there is a need to discard as soon as possible the cold war stereotypes, when any anti-American regime in the Third World, declaring allegiance to Marxism-Leninism, could count on Soviet support.[15]

A policy analyst we interviewed complained that "some of our allies are a disgrace for us," Libya being a key example.

Perhaps most significantly, the shift in orientation also means a greater effort to build links with nonsocialist countries. Vasilyev has underscored that in "deideologizing interstate relations" the Soviet Union will not only be "preserving links with traditionally friendly states" but will also be "widening links with stable regimes which we consider conservative."[16] A policy analyst we interviewed said:

> I think the question is that we have to refurbish, to overhaul all our relationships....Maybe it's better to move towards a more balanced attitude towards all countries independently of their orientation....Of course, the United States looks askance at any Soviet attempt to deal with the Philippines or Taiwan. And now we are going to build new relations with those countries....The position is to create as many friends as possible.

The net effect of this shift is that, according to new thinking, the Soviet Union does not have to make dichotomous choices about with whom it will build good relations. As we will see below, Soviet diplomacy seems to be increasingly based on the assumption that the Soviet Union can have amicable and mutually advantageous relations with virtually all countries, whatever their ideological stripe. As Gorbachev has said, "our society is capable of being progressive and friendly toward all peoples."[17] Any interest in promoting socialism, to the extent it still exists, is being given a backseat to this pancongenial goal.

Building a New Order

New thinking does not call only for changes in Soviet behavior in the Third World. Rather there is a vision of a whole new order that flows from the efforts to eliminate ideological divisions and to maximize stability, integration, and the peaceful resolution of conflict. To this end, new thinking calls for a regime to mutually constrain the superpower competition, a policy of seeking national reconciliation in regional conflicts, limitations on the transfer of weaponry, and the withdrawal of the superpowers' global military presence.

A Regime of Mutual Constraint

The core concept in this new order is that the superpowers should agree to mutually constrain themselves from seeking unilateral advantages in regions of the Third World where there are conflicts. Karen Brutents, then deputy chief of the Central Committee International Section, said that this approach

> implies, first, a consistent policy to resolve these [regional] conflicts, not to exacerbate them. It also means not exploiting these conflicts to gain advantages in the struggle between the two blocs, to extend our sphere of influence, but proceeding instead from the real interests of the countries and peoples concerned, with a proper and balanced consideration of the interests of all sides involved...based primarily on fastidious respect for each people's right to choose their own path and to forge their own destiny without external intervention.[18]

To implement this principle new thinking calls for constraints on great-power intervention. Primakov has written that "only a code of conduct for great powers will lift the outside factors provoking regional conflicts."[19] The Soviet proposal to the United Nations for a Comprehensive System of International Peace and Security suggests that

> the permanent members could study the possibility of elaborating such measures, procedures and mutual obligations in the spirit of restraint and self-limitation, and respect for the freedom of choice of the peoples, which would rule out the involvement of major Powers in confrontations through regional conflicts.[20]

In the interviews we tried to find out if there are limits to this potential commitment to noninterference. For example, we asked numerous Soviets whether, if the United States stayed uninvolved, the Soviet Union would refrain from responding to requests for aid from progressive groups in Third World countries that are severely repressed or have their human rights grossly violated. On the whole the respondents seemed quite resolute. One policy analyst said, "If you keep your hands off, we will keep our hands off." A former Foreign Ministry official explained:

> Well, we are no longer that ambitious. We're not here to correct every situation, to defend every right in any country of the world. And, of course, we see the limits of what we can do. But again more importantly, there is a principle of noninterference. Sometimes [in the past] it was very close to what would be termed "lip service." Now we take it very seriously.

Naturally it is very difficult to come up with a real code of conduct that would cover all the situations that the superpowers may encounter in the Third World. On the whole, in the interviews, we got the impression that little effort has gone into really thinking through all of the potential predicaments and the appropriate response. However, there was one individual, Gleb Starushenko of the Institute of African Studies, who did present us with an unpublished paper in which he had worked out his "Policy of Preventing and Settling Regional Conflicts." He listed six standards for dealing with international conflict. Some are fairly uncontroversial, such as the principle of freedom of choice and prohibitions against efforts to "undermine or overthrow from outside another state's socio-political order or render assistance to anti-governmental forces." Others, though, are complex and potentially objectionable. He wrote:

> If anti-government activities in this state or that acquire a character of civil war, other states are obliged to stop rendering assistance to the lawful government as well. Otherwise this would be a violation of the people's right of self-determination....At the same time if it has been established for sure that the antigovernment forces are receiving outside help, it is already a question of repulsing aggression from the outside. That is why the government has the right of collective self-defence...[and] may appeal to any other state for aid and receive it.

He also added the exception that "[a]ll states have the right to render any assistance to liberation movements against racialism and colonialism because both colonialism and racialism are outlawed."

National Reconciliation

Beyond the constraints to be imposed on external intervention, new thinking also specifies the optimal approach to achieving the resolution of regional conflicts. Termed "national reconciliation," the goal is to incorporate all conflicting factions into a peaceful political process; the ultimate arbiter being the electoral process, not military force.

The details of this process of national reconciliation have been elaborated by Y.Dolgopolov in an article in *Krasnaya Zvezda*:

> The essence of this [national reconciliation] policy is that the conflicting sides are given the opportunity to promote the solution of general national problems without any outside interference through political dialogue rather than via armed struggle, which, as a rule, is futile.... Here it is possible to speak of a general pattern of settlement. First, dialogue is begun between the sides through mediators. Talks are also conducted with their help. In some cases the United Nations acts as the intermediary (the Geneva agreements on Afghanistan, and also the Iran-Iraq talks), while in others this role is played by groups of countries (the Contadora Group and the Support Group, and the ASEAN countries) or individual states. Second, the withdrawal of troops by the country involved in the conflict is balanced by political treaty obligations guaranteeing its interests. This approach can be seen in the Afghan, Cambodian and South African situations. Third, a guarantee system is used. The great powers and also the United Nations act as guarantors of compliance with agreements. The military aspects of the peaceful settlement of conflicts include the withdrawal of foreign troops from the relevant countries within a set deadline, the reduction or total removal of groups of foreign military advisers and specialists, the reduction or complete termination of foreign military aid, and so forth. [21]

Bovin has summarized such principles a bit more succinctly:

> 1. Direct talks between the sides involved in the conflict....
> 2. A cease-fire as a result of direct talks....
> 3. and 4. The formation of a provisional (transitional) government of national unity (national reconciliation) made up of representatives of all the groupings taking part in the talks and—after an agreed interval of time—general and free elections (possibly under international supervision). [22]

In the interviews we had the opportunity to press respondents about whether they were sincerely willing to accept the results of an electoral process that would be in their disfavor. On the whole they were unequivocal in their responses. The following is from an interview with a colonel from one of the military academies, who had expressed a number of traditional Leninist viewpoints:

Interviewer : If you pursue the policy of national reconciliation in certain countries...it's possible that this process could lead to a democratic election and in that election, the socialist forces may lose power.
Respondent : They can lose....That is why the policy of national reconciliation is new thinking and our policy. We are not afraid of that. Why are we not afraid of the changes that are taking place in Poland and in Hungary? We are not afraid. Let each country solve its own problems as it wishes, as it wants. That is the policy of new thinking.

With a Foreign Ministry official who deals with Third World issues we pressed further:

I : You are willing to have some kind of national reconciliation so that maybe your client is not the dominant force in the country. But you don't want a faction that is hostile to the Soviet Union in power, do you?
R : Why? You are talking on the basis of old thinking, you know, old traditional thinking. We don't care. We say that we respect the choice of the country. Look what's happening in Eastern Europe. Five years ago the situation could be completely different....We are trying our new ideas in the Third World and Africa in particular not because we want to impose our new influence. Sometimes we act contrary to our interests.

Controlling the Transfer of Conventional Weapons

Another key element in the concept of a new order in the Third World is the control of conventional arms transfers. The transfer of conventional weaponry is seen as playing a pernicious role in undermining regional stability. In June 1988 Shevardnadze said: "One of the obstacles impeding settlement of regional conflicts is the intensive transfusion of weapons into zones of increased confrontation."[23] Shevardnadze worried:

Access to conventional weapons in their most modern modifications is expanding. Their technological sophistication makes it easier to use them. There is now no need to spend much time and money on special training, and anyone can easily operate those infernal devices. In other words, conventional weapons are becoming part of everyday life, a common tool in the hands of too many people.[24]

Various Soviet writers have roundly criticized past Soviet behavior for engaging in arms transfers in the past. Andrei Kortunov has written:

> At a definite stage of history Soviet military aid assisted in strengthening newly-emergent states' independence. But in many cases it also added to the deformation of their political development, the excessive influence of the military, and the militarization of the whole social life. Sometimes this aid encouraged adventurism in foreign policy and bellicosity in relation to neighbors. Soviet military aid has been used by repressive regimes to suppress domestic opposition, national minorities and religious movements.... Sometimes Soviet deliveries are necessary to reestablish the regional balances of strength. But in this field, as on other spheres of military activity, Moscow has not always abided by the principle of reasonable sufficiency, thereby provoking a corresponding response from the west.[25]

In the interviews there was a doubt expressed even about the political advantages that accrue from military aid: "When it comes to influence it's usually a very diverse thing. Does that imply that if you supply arms to someone you have an influence? I don't think so frankly. Sometimes it's vice versa, the recipient which influences the supplier."

The consistent conclusion of this line of thinking is that there should be international efforts to control arms transfers. Shevardnadze has stated that "no nation should have the exclusive prerogative or absolute freedom to determine its own level of armament"[26] and that "the Soviet Union favors restrictions on the sales and supplies of conventional arms,"[27] and "a joint effort to constrain the international arms markets."[28] A high-level official we interviewed in the Foreign Ministry said that "the long-term goal" is to entirely eliminate arms transfers.

Some initial steps in this direction have been proposed. Yevgeni Primakov, an adviser to Gorbachev, has said that "the USSR and the United States could reach agreement on proportionate cuts in arms deliveries to the areas of conflicts."[29] Andrei Kortunov has written that the arms-exporting countries should "agree to ban the transfer of more sophisticated and dangerous military technologies to Third World countries."[30] There have been calls for "restricting sales of arms...on the basis of the principle of reasonable sufficiency."[31] Petrovsky has said:

> We can also accept another option, as proposed by Italy, namely, elaborating a code of conduct of suppliers and buyers of arms. Through joint efforts, states should resolutely combat illegal supplies of conventional weapons in the international black market, which is a dangerous phenomenon.[32]

A specific idea the Soviet Union formally proposed is to have, through the United Nations, an "arms supplies and sales register."[33] Addressing the UN General Assembly in September 1988 Shevardnadze said:

> The United Nations can become a real participant in resolving the issues of conventional arms limitation. The Soviet Union supports the idea of setting up within the United Nations a register of conventional arms sales and supplies and is ready to take part in developing the parameters of such a register.[34]

Soon after this proposal was made we asked a Foreign Ministry official involved with UN affairs:

Interviewer : What is the purpose of the register? Is it just simply a recording of activities?

Respondent : Yes, as a starting point it's a recording. In other words it helps to stop this black market in the arms sales field. But also it's a starting point to negotiate on the reduction of arms sales and regulation. And in the long run to finding some kind of political solution. This is the important first step. The starting point to dealing with these problems.

Later, in August 1990, in a letter to the UN Secretary General, Shevardnadze elaborated on his proposal, saying that importing as well as exporting countries should report on their arms transactions. Furthermore, countries should report on efforts to upgrade military facilities as well as training of military personnel (this would presumably require the Soviet Union to report on the activities of its military advisers). These measures he hoped would "open up the prospect of the elaboration under UN auspices of a draft convention on the restriction of international arms and supplies."[35] Shortly afterward Major General Vadim Makarevsky suggested that such a convention could be "similar to the Nuclear Non-Proliferation Treaty."[36] And the following month Shevardnadze argued that "we need to agree on principles governing the sale and supply of arms."[37]

Withdrawal of Global Military Presence

The world order proposed by new thinking also calls for the reduction and ultimate elimination of all forms of military presence outside of each nation's borders. This concept was first broached in July 1986 by Gorbachev in a speech he gave in Vladivostok. Speaking about security issues in the Asia-Pacific region, he said: "The Soviet Union is a convinced supporter of...the renunciation of foreign bases in Asia and the Pacific Ocean, and the withdrawal of troops from others' territory."[38]

In September of the same year, in a seminal article on collective security titled "The Reality and Guarantees of a Secure World," Gorbachev suggested: "The Security Council permanent members could...renounce demonstrative military presence...because such a practice is one of the factors of fanning up regional conflicts."[39]

Soon after, such ideas became regular themes in the speeches of Shevardnadze. Addressing the United Nations in June 1988, he called for a "mutual cessation of the presence of foreign troops and bases on foreign territories."[40] He elaborated:

> The question of military bases in other countries' territories and foreign military presence lies at the junction of the most urgent politico-military problems. It is the political pole where the meridians of international security and sovereignty, independence and national dignity of the peoples and countries converge.

He then made a bold proposal:

> The USSR proposes the goal of eliminating foreign military presence and military bases in foreign territories by the year 2000. This goal should be pursued gradually with regard for specific regional characteristics and for the real needs of security and defence. The United Nations would be invited to participate in verifying the withdrawal of troops from foreign territories. Where the presence of foreign troops is required to maintain peace they should be provided by the United Nations.[41]

The next year he made an unequivocal statement: "Our ultimate goal is not to have a single Soviet soldier outside the country."[42] And while in Nicaragua in October 1989, Shevardnadze not only called for "the elimination of foreign military bases" from the region but also "the withdrawal of foreign military advisers."[43]

Finally, in December 1989, Gorbachev offered a more specific time frame for these reductions saying: "We have proposed that all troops be recalled within their national boundaries by 1995-1996, and that all foreign bases be eliminated by the year 2000." [44]

Closely related to such proposals have been suggestions for limiting naval activities. Initially the major focus of such proposals was the Asia-Pacific region. In his July 1986 speech at Vladivostok, Gorbachev stated, "we propose starting talks on reducing the activity of naval fleets." He proposed that if the United States were to withdraw from its bases in the

Philippines the Soviet Union would respond appropriately, presumably meaning that the Soviet Union would withdraw from its positions in Vietnam.[45]

The next year, in an interview with the Indonesian newspaper *Merdeka*, Gorbachev spoke of "our readiness to lessen the activeness of the USSR and U.S. Navies in the Pacific Ocean" saying that "it is obvious that the border of confrontation here runs through the proximity of the fleets. Hence the danger of conflicts." He then proposed:

> Confidence-building would be promoted by limiting the scale of naval exercises and maneuvers in the Pacific and Indian Oceans and the adjacent seas: not more than one or two major naval (including naval aviation) exercises or maneuvers a year, notification of them in good time, and the mutual renunciation of naval exercises and maneuvers in international straits and the adjacent regions and of the use of combat weapons in the lines of traditional sea routes in the course of exercises. It would be possible to try out this "model" first in the northern Pacific, where there are not many "dramatis personae." And then to extend this practice to the southern part of the Pacific sea area and other countries in the region.[46]

Shevardnadze, in his June 8, 1988, speech at the United Nations, built on these ideas. Calling for "limitation of the number, scope, and area of (naval) exercises," he made a number of proposals:

> To enhance confidence it would be useful to compare data on naval potentials, to discuss the principles of the use of naval forces and to compare the goals of exercises and maneuvers at sea...establishing zones in the areas of major international ocean lanes of lower density of armaments and enhanced confidence and...withdrawing offensive forces and systems from such zones.

He expressed impatience with U.S. resistance to such naval arms control:

> From the standpoint of disarmament, naval forces still remain an 'off-limits area.' Some states which are ready to include even kitchen trailers in the military balance on the side of their opponents get nervous when they are invited just to talk about, for instance, aircraft carriers.

Ultimately, he envisioned, a United Nations naval force could replace the functions of national naval forces and suggested: "In the near future a joint trial activity could be conducted in which the fleets of the permanent members of the Security Council would practice maintaining freedom of navigation by United Nations forces."[47]

Consistent with this line of thought, as neutral ships were being attacked during the Iran-Iraq war, the Soviet Union proposed creating a UN naval force to protect shipping in the Persian Gulf. It also indicated a readiness to provide ships for this purpose, ships which would fly the UN flag.[48]

In July 1988 the Soviet Union tried to promote the ideas of naval arms control and reduced military presence at the UN conference on disarmament. Petrovsky reported a mixed response, saying: "All the delegations, except for the USA, supported us on [reducing] naval arms...[though] there wasn't the broad response on the question of military bases that we expected."[49]

The following September, at Krasnoyarsk, Gorbachev called for "consultations among the main naval powers of the region on the non-buildup of naval forces" in the Pacific region. He proposed a multilateral discussion of the question of reducing military confrontation in areas where the seaboards of the USSR, PRC [People's Republic of China], Japan, the DPRK [Democratic People's Republic of Korea], and South Korea are in proximity to one another, the aim being to freeze and commensurately reduce the levels of naval and air forces and restrict their activity.

This time he also made a more explicit offer:

> If the United States agrees to eliminate military bases in the Philippines, the USSR will be prepared, on agreement with the SRV [Socialist Republic of Vietnam] Government, to abandon its naval material and technical supply point in Cam Ranh Bay.[50]

Another means the Soviet Union has used to press for reducing the superpowers' military presence has been to consistently support the various proposals for "Zones of Peace, Friendship, and Neutrality." The most prominent of these proposals is the one to make the Indian Ocean such a zone. In Gorbachev's Vladivostok speech in 1986 he initiated an effort to revive the proposal from the dormant state in which it had been since passed by the UN General Assembly in 1971. The original declaration

> [C]alls upon the great Powers...to enter into immediate consultation with the littoral States of the Indian Ocean with a view to...eliminating from the Indian Ocean all bases, military installations and logistical supply facilities, the disposition of nuclear weapons and weapons of mass destruction and any manifestation of great Power military presence in the Indian Ocean conceived in the context of great Power rivalry.

Over the last years the Soviets have consistently reiterated support for this proposal, though to little avail given U.S. resistance.

Since 1970 in the United Nations and since 1975 in the Conference for Disarmament in Europe, there have also been efforts to make the Mediterranean a Zone of Peace that would exclude all foreign military presence from the region. Under Gorbachev the Soviet Union has become more emphatic in its support for such a proposal.

In 1971, the members of the Association of South East Asian Nations (ASEAN) declared Southeast Asia a Zone of Peace. Since then, however, the ASEAN nations have been ambivalent about whether they really want the United States to reduce its presence in the region. In any case, the Soviet Union has expressed its support for the idea.

In September 1988 the Soviet Union voted in favor of the UN General Assembly resolution declaring the South Atlantic a Zone of Peace. The resolution passed by an overwhelming majority, the United States being the sole dissenting voice. Riding on this sentiment, the next month Daniel Ortega, then president of Nicaragua, called for a Zone of Peace in Central America; a proposal also supported by the Soviet Union.[51]

Soviet Behavior in the Third World

Actual Soviet behavior in the Third World has a certain disjointed quality. In broad brush strokes, there have been dramatic and important changes consistent with the principles of new thinking. At the same time, though, when one looks closer into some of the details there are a number of ways that traditional behavior persists. The most significant change in Soviet behavior has been its general shift away from a competitive ideological orientation to one that emphasizes conciliation, cooperation, and negotiated solutions. There have also been some concrete steps in reducing Soviet military presence throughout the Third World and in reducing the flow of conventional weapons to the Third World. At the same time, though, the Soviet Union has in some ways continued to favor ideologically compatible nations, to send aid differentially to socialist countries, to maintain a major military presence throughout the Third World, and to maintain a high level of arms trade with Third World countries.

Deideologization and Conciliation

Perhaps the most dramatic change in Soviet behavior in the Third World has been its move away from trying to promote the victory of socialist factions over nonsocialist factions, promoting instead the policy of national reconciliation. In all of the regions that in the 1970s and up to the mid 1980s were the major points of contention with the United States, the Soviet Union has abandoned its support for a military solution and has instead promoted a negotiated solution leading to democratic elections with fair representation of all the feuding factions.

In Afghanistan, after nearly a decade of trying to prop up a Soviet-installed socialist government and to suppress an indigenous U.S.-supported Islamic insurgency, the Soviets have tried to promote national reconciliation, seeking ultimately to resolve the conflict through elections under UN supervision. In February 1989 they completed the withdrawal of their troops and have consistently supported UN efforts to achieve resolution through establishing a coalition government and ultimately holding elections. They have also expressed a desire to end military aid to all factions in the conflict (what has been called "negative symmetry"). When this position was criticized on the basis that the Soviets had already installed advanced weaponry in Afghanistan, they expressed a willingness to withdraw this weaponry as well. The United States, though, was resistant to the negative symmetry idea until after the coup failed: in September 1991 U.S. Secretary of State James Baker and the newly-appointed Soviet Foreign Minister Boris Pankin announced a mutual suspension of aid.

Similar policies were pursued in Angola. Starting in the middle 1970s the Soviet Union supported the socialist-oriented Angolan government led by the Movement for the Popular Liberation of Angola (MPLA), while the U.S. supported the insurgent Union for the Total Independence of Angola (UNITA). Beginning in the late 1980s, Soviet leaders began to hint at their interest in resolving the conflict through a national reconciliation process. For some time, though, they were careful not to put too much public pressure on the Angolan government, which at the time was reluctant to negotiate with UNITA. Presumably as the result of this pressure, in the later part of 1990 the Angolan leadership began to express willingness to engage in such a process. The Soviet Union and the United States, then, in a highly coordinated diplomatic effort succeeded in bringing their erstwhile clients to the bargaining table and on May 1, 1991, to agree to a cease-fire and free elections.

As with Angola, the Soviet Union at first refrained from openly urging the Ethiopian government to pursue a process of national reconciliation with its insurgent groups, though in interviews carried out in 1989, Soviets explained to us that this was the preferred approach. Finally, in early 1990 the Soviet government publicly stated that they saw negotiations as the only solution, began to withdraw their military advisers, and told the Ethiopian government that they would not renew their two-billion-dollar arms pact due to expire at the end of 1991. A Foreign Ministry representative even confirmed in May 1991 that the Soviet Union had established contacts with the rebels,[52] thus effectively positioning themselves for the imminent fall of the Ethiopian government to the rebels.

Yet another area of Africa where the Soviet Union has changed is Mozambique. For years the Soviet Union had supported the government of Joaquim Chissano in its struggle with the right-wing insurgency Renamo. Late in 1989, though, the Soviet Union withdrew its 800 military advisers, reduced its annual military aid from $150 million to $100 million, and encouraged the Chissano government to negotiate with the rebels. In June 1990 Herman Cohen, U.S. Assistant Secretary of State for African Affairs, exulted, "We're delighted...the Soviet Union is now fully supportive of negotiated settlement."[53]

The Soviet Union has also promoted national reconciliation in Cambodia. After the Vietnamese invaded Cambodia in December 1978 the Soviet Union supported the Vietnamese-installed government in its effort to suppress the three loosely allied insurgent factions, partly supported by the United States. Gorbachev, though, has consistently proposed a negotiated solution to the conflict and pressured the Vietnamese to withdraw their military forces, which they did in September 1989. The main thrust of the Soviet effort has been to work together with the United States and the other permanent members of the Security Council to establish, under UN auspices, an interim government and ultimately to hold elections.

In Central America Gorbachev has reversed years of Soviet efforts to further socialism through military means. In December 1987 at a summit in Washington, D.C., Gorbachev proposed that the United States and the Soviet Union make reciprocal pledges to refrain from delivering weapons to either the Contras or the Sandinistas in Nicaragua. This idea was rejected by the United States. Nevertheless, according to Soviet claims, the Soviet Union suspended military deliveries to Nicaragua at the beginning of 1989, saying that they would continue to exercise such restraint until the elections, to be held in February 1990. The U.S. government challenged whether the Soviet Union had actually eliminated all military deliveries but did affirm that military deliveries had at least been reduced.[54] In the period leading up to the Nicaraguan election Gorbachev repeatedly voiced support for the elections in Nicaragua. When the Sandinistas lost to the Uno party of Violetta Chamorro, the Soviets did not hesitate to recognize the new government.

The Soviets have also claimed to be holding back military support to the socialist-oriented insurgents in El Salvador fighting the U.S.-backed government and to favor negotiations. In late 1989 U.S. sources challenged this claim, saying that the weapons were simply being passed through Cuba and Nicaragua. In response the Soviets apparently made some serious efforts to get the Cubans and the Nicaraguans to stop. However, even U.S. officials conceded that the Soviet Union probably did not have the necessary leverage.[55] Later, though, in early 1991, Soviet pressure played a role in persuading the Sandinistas to get leftist rebels in El Salvador to return a number of surface-to-air missiles previously sold to them.[56] Then in August 1991, after a series of consultations, the Soviet Union and the United States formally joined forces in an effort to promote a diplomatic solution to the conflict. U.S. Secretary of State Baker and then Foreign Minister Alexander Bessmertnykh signed a letter to the UN Secretary General urging him to take an active personal role in negotiations—a step interpreted by U.S. State Department officials as a sign that the United States and the Soviet Union were no longer rivals in Central America.[57]

Finally, the Soviet Union has even changed its tune in relation to South Africa. Despite its many years of support for the African National Congress (ANC), which was committed to the violent overthrow of the South African government, Soviet officials have stressed the need for a peaceful resolution. In March 1989 Boris Asoyan, then a Foreign Ministry official, implied that the Soviet Union was ready to reduce its military shipments to the ANC and stated:

> In our opinion, we doubt that revolution in South Africa is possible, if you're talking of revolutionaries storming Pretoria....We support the ANC and we regard it as the main force in contemporary political life in South Africa. But we also believe that there is really no alternative to a peaceful solution.[58]

The Soviet government also began to reestablish diplomatic ties with the South African governnment, agreeing with the Pretoria government in February 1991 to establish "interest sections" in each other's capitals. In September 1991, Asoyan, then the Soviet ambassador to South Africa, stated that now that the dismantling of apartheid was irreversible he believed it was time to establish diplomatic relations.[59]

In addition to this conciliatory approach to conflicts within specific nations, the Soviet Union has also demonstrated a newly evenhanded approach to conflicts between states, even when one of those states is a client. In the tense relations between Israel and Syria the Soviet Union has taken a more amicable position toward Israel and discouraged Syria from its aspirations to achieve military parity with Israel. Moscow has also reduced its military aid to Syria. During the later stages of the Iran-Iraq war, though Iraq was a Soviet client, the Soviets encouraged both sides toward compromise and moderation, supported the UN ceasefire, and played a central role as mediator of the resolution. Though the Soviets supported

Iraq's position on ending the war, they also seemed to endorse Iran's position in regard to its border with Iraq.

As discussed above, Soviet new thinking stresses that the Soviet Union can have congenial diplomatic relations with virtually all nations. Differences in ideology, apparent conflicts of interest, or past tension need not be a barrier to amicable relations. There also seems to be an assumption that in situations in which there is a tension between two parties the Soviet Union can have cordial relations with both parties. Despite the apparently idealistic tone of this assumption, it has had a significant effect on Soviet diplomatic behavior.

In the Middle East, after years of siding with radical Arab states against conservative Arab states and Israel, the Soviet Union has begun to play both sides of the street. Diplomatic relations have been established with Saudi Arabia. More significantly, shortly after Gorbachev came into office, the Soviet Union began to expand its relations with Israel. In August 1986 the first official meeting in nearly twenty years occurred between Soviet and Israeli officials. Soon after, Shevardnadze met with Israeli Prime Minister Shimon Peres. In a strong gesture, Gorbachev said at a state dinner for Syrian President Hafiz al-Assad in April 1987 that the absence of diplomatic relations between the Soviet Union and Israel "cannot be considered normal."[60] In July 1987 a Soviet consular delegation arrived in Tel Aviv, and a year later an Israeli delegation arrived in Moscow. In September 1987 the Soviet Union proposed setting up diplomatic "interest sections" in Tel Aviv and Moscow. In October 1989 the Soviet Union newly refused to vote against Israel's membership in the United Nations. At a meeting at UN headquarters in September 1990 between Shevardnadze and Israeli Foreign Minister David Levi the two countries agreed to establish consular relations. And, finally, in October 1991, shortly before the Soviet-American-sponsored Middle East peace conference, full diplomatic relations were established. Also, in September 1991, the new Soviet Foreign Minister Boris Pankin denounced the "obnoxious [UN] resolution equating zionism to racism,"[61] which the Soviets have traditionally supported.

The Soviet Union has also been sidestepping the traditional divisions in Asia. After years of insisting that Korea should necessarily be one nation and clearly favoring the socialist north, the Soviet Union began building relations with South Korea, despite the displeasure of Pyongyang. In September 1990 the Soviet Union officially recognized South Korea. Addressing North Korean concerns, Shevardnadze commented, "good and fine relations between us do not contradict the interests of other countries."[62]

Perhaps the most significant development in Soviet diplomatic relations under Gorbachev has been the normalization of relations between the Soviet Union and China that occurred when Gorbachev visited Beijing in 1989. This was a hard-won achievement that Gorbachev had actively sought for some years. Nevertheless, Gorbachev has ignored Beijing's wrath in building economic ties with Taiwan.

The Soviet Union has also been strengthening relations with nations that, in the cold-war context, were considered to be on the 'other side.' Shevardnadze made the first visit by a Soviet foreign minister to Thailand and Indonesia in 1987. These visits were reciprocated by a visit to Moscow by the Thai Prime Minister Prem Tinsuanon in May 1988 and of Indonesian President Raden Suharto in September 1989. In December 1988 Shevardnadze made the first ever visit by a Soviet foreign minister to the Philippines as part of a larger effort to expand political and trade relations.

Similar diplomatic efforts have also been extended into the Western Hemisphere. Before Shevardnadze, no Soviet foreign minister had ever visited a Latin American country other than Cuba. But in October 1986 Shevardnadze visited Mexico and in the fall of 1987 Brazil, Argentina, and Uruguay. In October 1989 Shevardnadze also proposed establishing diplomatic relations with Honduras and El Salvador, something to which Honduras agreed in September 1990.

Global Military Presence

As was discussed above, a key tenet of new thinking is that it is undesirable for nations to project their military presence beyond their national borders. Soviet leaders have called for all nations to withdraw their military forces within their national boundaries by the year 2000.

In the realm of naval forces there have been some evident changes in Soviet behavior consistent with this principle. Soviet spokesmen claim that the Soviet Union has reduced its naval activities in the Pacific by half,[63] that 40 submarines, 41 surface ships, and 24 combatant craft were decommissioned.[64] They have said that by 1989 their Pacific Fleet was reduced by 57 ships,[65] and that by the end of 1991 another 16 warships would be decommissioned, including 9 large surface vessels and 7 submarines.[66] Admiral I. Kapitanets, deputy commander in chief of the Navy, also claimed in June 1991, that "after the completion of the last ships in the series, the building of large surface ships of the classes of the nuclear missile cruiser Kirov, the missile cruiser Slava, and the large antisubmarine ship Udalov will stop."[67]

Western sources have generally confirmed the trend toward reduced naval activity, though they do stress that many of the ships being decommissioned have reached the end of their serviceable life. U.S. Rear Admiral Thomas Brooks, director of naval intelligence, said in testimony to the House Armed Services Committee that the Soviets have removed significant numbers of ships from service, have reduced their Pacific fleet operations, are keeping their ships in port longer, and are spending less time at sea. He also reported that Soviet naval exercises tend to emphasize homeland defense and that there has been a "continued decline in out-of-area (OOA) deployments as the Soviets reduce their naval presence worldwide."[68] Westerners have observed that the Soviets also have reduced submarine deployments by half.[69]

Perhaps most dramatically, the Soviets have recently given up their naval supply station at Cam Ranh Bay. This is highly significant because this station has played a critical role in supporting their naval activities in the South Pacific, the Indian Ocean, and the South Atlantic. It was also politically costly in that the Vietnamese were reluctant to have the Soviets leave because they were seen as offsetting Chinese power.

However, despite these developments, there are still many features of external Soviet military presence that do not conform with the principle of new thinking. Despite the call for reducing global military presence the Soviets continue to maintain a substantial one. The activities of the Soviet navy go well beyond simply protecting the Soviet homeland; though there has been some reduction, Soviet ships still dock at far-flung ports in Yemen, Ethiopia, Angola, Guinea Bissau, Libya, Syria, and Cuba. In most of these countries Soviet aircraft also have access to airfields. Especially disturbing to the U.S. military, the Soviet navy, even as it has reduced its size and activities, has been pursuing a very active program of upgrading the quality of it naval capabilities such that the Soviet navy is perceived as having greater combat capabilities than it had in the past.[70] Finally, the Soviet Union still maintains military advisers in a long list of countries including Algeria, Angola, Cambodia, Congo, Cuba, Ethiopia, India, Laos, Libya, Mali, Mozambique, Peru, Syria, and Yemen as well as several thousand troops stationed in Vietnam, Mongolia, and Cuba (though the troops in Cuba are now slated for withdrawal).

Conventional Arms Transfers

Conventional arms transfers is yet another area in which Soviet behavior has a mixed quality. New thinking denounces such transfers as intrinsically problematic. And yet for the years 1987-1989 the Soviet Union was, by far, the largest exporter of weaponry to the Third World. During these years the Soviet Union represented respectively, 54.25 percent, 37.18 percent, and 38.48 percent of the world trade, with the United States in the second position during these years at 12.49 percent, 22.86 percent, and 23.6 percent.

At the same time there has been an important trend toward reducing such arms transfers. In constant 1990 U.S. dollars the value of Soviet arms transfer agreements with Third World countries decreased as follows:

1987 $25.280 billion
1988 $15.197 billion
1989 $13.041 billion
1990 $12.070 billion

In 1990 the Soviet Union even dropped behind the United States in the value of such transfer agreements (the U.S. was $18.496 billion) and as a share of the world market (the U.S. was 44.77%). Nevertheless, the Soviet Union still represents 29.22% of the world market and is, obviously, still a major exporter of conventional weaponry to the Third World.[71]

Even in the post-coup era it appears that there are no plans to significantly change this pattern of behavior. In September 1991, N.Vitchovsky, first deputy minister for the USSR Ministry of Weapons Industries, affirmed that though the Soviet Union was converting a major portion of its military industries to the civilian sector, it had no intention of withdrawing from the international arms market.[72] It appears that this behavior will persist under the Russian Federation. The Russian foreign minister Andrei Kozyrev affirmed in September 1991 that "international arms trade cannot be stopped," though he said it should take a "civilised character" and not be carried out for "ideological reasons."[73]

Roots of Persisting Traditional Behavior

Although the changes in Soviet behavior in the Third World are significant and impressive, there is, nonetheless, enough persistence of behavior contrary to the precepts of new thinking that one naturally wonders about its roots. According to statements made by members of the policymaking community it appears that there are numerous veins of thinking that would support traditional Soviet behavior or at least resist the directions of new thinking.

Legacy of the Old

Of course, the most obvious interpretation is that such behavior arises from the persistence of traditional Marxist-Leninist thinking in the foreign-policy elite. Since the failure of the coup, there has been little overt evidence of Leninist rationales for such policy behavior. In the period before the coup, expressions of such thinking were also quite unusual, but they would crop up upon occasion.

In a 1989 interview Nikolai Kosukhin of the Institute of Africa of the USSR Academy of Sciences supported an activist policy in Africa by sounding the traditional tocsin of social revolution: "We remain, as before, interested in the propagation of socialism, and we do not think the choice we made over 70 years ago was wrong....The USSR has no intention of abandoning its undertakings toward several African countries...."[74] Weakly attempting to reconcile such ideas with new thinking, Kosukhin also argued: "I would point to the Soviet leader's statement that the interests shared by the whole of mankind do not invalidate a class attitude. Thus the national liberation movements will remain within the sphere of our inter-ested attention."[75]

Mikhail Kapitsa, former deputy foreign minister and at the time direc-tor of the Institute of Oriental Studies and a member of the USSR Supreme Soviet Foreign Relations Committee, was reported as saying in September of 1989 that Moscow has been "a natural friend" of national liberation movements....The Soviet policy renounces war as a means for resolving disputes among various countries, but...any state facing an "imperialist offensive" has the right to self-defence and will subsequently be supported by Moscow by all means, including arms supply.[76]

Others defended the intervention in Afghanistan on the basis of such ideological principles. Alexander Prokhanov asserted that

> the entry of our troops into Afghanistan was not contradictory to the doctrine that we...were very interested in the birth of fraternal systems and structures around us. We have always helped the peoples of fraternal countries to preserve the revolution—not only because we are emotional internationalists, but also because this was our guarantee of survival.[77]

Some writers went so far as to resurrect the traditional Leninist argu-ment that violence is a legitimate means of furthering socioeconomic evolution. Speaking of "the historical foreordination of the triumph of socialism," Boris Kanivsky and Pyotr Sabardin of the Institute of Military History of the USSR Ministry of Defense wrote:

It goes without saying that violence and revolution are interrelated notions. From the standpoint of Marxism-Leninism, revolutionary violence can, in certain circumstances, play the role of a sort of accelerator of history, a midwife of an old society pregnant with a new one....In a given set of historical conditions, revolutionary violence is fully justified because it expresses the interests of the majority of people in a society and, therefore, has an objectively humane character while in other conditions, by virtue of the same reasons, it assumes the form of a struggle against reactionary violence....[78]

Despite the oft-repeated denunciation of the use of violence found in new thinking, as well as the above-mentioned insistence that the South African problem can only be resolved through peaceful means, Adamishin also asserted, in 1989, the legitimacy of violence in defending Soviet "assistance to liberation movements"[79] in South Africa. He declared: "As long as South African authorities continue to pursue a policy of violence, no one has a right to demand that people do not respond to it by violence."[80]

Despite Gorbachev's call for withdrawal of all military forces outside national boundaries, such forces were rationalized as necessary to maintain the cohesion of the socialist community and for the Soviet commitment to defend socialist governments around the world (concerns that would not necessarily be eliminated were Gorbachev's proposal to be accepted). For example, a prominent defense analyst we interviewed in 1989 explained why it was necessary to have forces in the Caribbean:

R : Cuba is a socialist country. We don't want them to feel alone so far away from us. We need some sort of lines of communication....
I : So the Soviet Union is still committed to the protection of the security of socialist allies outside of the main European area?
R : But of course. Just as the United States preserves and protects Japan and Korea.

In most cases the evidence of persisting traditional thinking appeared in an equivocal fashion, mixed with principles of new thinking. Individuals sometimes seemed to be conflicted, confused about what they think or groping for a way to reconcile old and new. For example, in an interview a senior policy analyst who has generally been noted for liberal foreign policy views showed an uncertain mix of views as he tried to explain the role of ideology in Soviet foreign policy:

The ideological rationale, I don't think it has completely evaporated. The ideological rationale exists and we will be siding and supporting some forces which we are thinking are working for the cause, like, for instance, our position in Chile. But first of all the means of support would be different. We would not get involved, you see. And then we will think about our own ideological motivations—whether it's necessary, to what extent and so on.

More commonly, though, individuals initially embraced principles of new thinking but on closer examination gradually reverted to more traditional postures. For example, a colonel from one of the military academies, in an interview in late 1989, initially espoused many of the principles of new thinking, even making the bold statement that the world is not ultimately moving toward socialism. He recognized that capitalism is more effective economically and asserted that socialism and capitalism are actually converging (his hands sweeping together and upward) into a form that will incorporate the best from both. This being the case, we asked why the Soviet Union continues to differentially support socialist factions over other factions. At this he abruptly changed his tune, saying:

R : That's the notion of ideology. We follow the principle of "Proletariats of all countries, unite!" We shouldn't leave our friends in trouble in this time. So the principles of ideology continue, we abide by these principles.
I : Of supporting socialist countries?
R : Yes....We would follow the principles which allow Marxist-Lenin ideology everywhere. This is a real principle, and one of our main principles....

But here, as was often the case, the colonel did not consistently adhere to traditional thinking. Moments later he shifted again and stressed that Soviet military aid to socialist countries was only "transitional" and they want "people to choose their own way of living." So we asked again why they render such aid. This time he stressed that "we are having a tendency to reduce this aid." We pressed:

I : Why do you do it? To say it's being reduced doesn't explain why you're doing it.
R : We have rendered help even to those governments who spoke in favor of socialism, we rendered help to them, gave aid to them.
I : Why?

His answer surprised us: he said "Because it was a mistake." But then he immediately reverted to a highly traditional ideological argument:

Now you should draw the line here. Here the principle of ideology comes in. Now we are not going to betray our friends. The principle of 'internationalism' and the principle of 'proletariat countries' unite. We understand the main principle of internationalism as proletariats of all the countries unite. All proceeds from this principle.

We then tried to find out what the colonel had meant when he had first said that such aid had been a "mistake." He then made a now-popular argument that it is a mistake to support underdeveloped countries that simply profess the principles of socialism but do not have the economic basis to really institute it. He mentioned Angola and Ethiopia as examples. However, on further questioning he seemed to reiterate the principle that, because of their ideological allegiance, these countries, despite their underdevelopment, should continue to receive support, though it should, he said, be reduced.

This same colonel showed similar inconsistencies on the issue of terrorism. Initially he espoused the new thinking that the United States and the Soviet Union should set aside their ideological biases and work together to solve such global problems as terrorism. However, when we probed into the specific case of the PLO, it turned out that his definition of terrorism was highly ideological:

I : Has the Soviet Union ever put pressure on the PLO to refrain from terrorism?

R : If they fight for their legitimate aims, is this terrorism?...

I : Are you saying, then, that if the interests are legitimate, if the goals are legitimate, then terrorism is a legitimate means to pursue those goals?...

R : But this is not terrorism. This is a national liberation war.

I : So what is terrorism? How do you define terrorism?

R : Small groups of armed people that capture objects, aircrafts, for example, and threaten some people and hold their lives.

I : But if people hijack aircraft in the service of the goal of national liberation, then it's not terrorism?

R : No....It's a very complicated question. We take one country and mix up things: terrorism and national liberation movement.

Another example of this tendency to initially embrace new thinking but then moments later to revert to a more traditional line is a public statement made in 1989 by Colonel General Nikolay Chervov, then spokesman for the General Staff. Initially, he concurred with the now-standard criticism of the intervention into Afghanistan:

Presumably not the best option for solving the Afghan problem was chosen....Apparently the military means were overestimated." But then moments later he seemed to equivocate. "On the other hand...the repeated appeals of the Afghan Government for help could not be ignored.[81]

Even individuals who are high-profile "new thinkers" have at times appeared to equivocate on key issues. Georgi Shakhnazarov, generally considered to be one of the architects of new thinking, has regularly called for the deideologization of Soviet foreign policy. However, in 1989, when asked whether Third World countries will have to "rely more on their own efforts and count less on Soviet aid," his reply seemed to hark back to an earlier time:

> [I]n regard to our own policy it certainly has not changed, because in that case we would have to give up our ideology. Our ideology is an internationalist one and quite simply we cannot do so, because we would be losing a part of our worth if we were to forget that we have to help the peoples which are embarking on the road of development, progress, and so on.[82]

In one of our interviews another prominent, though younger, proponent of new thinking also seemed to equivocate. After clearly denouncing Soviet overextension in the Third World he rather abruptly changed his tune, saying:

R : Maybe if everything else was okay with the Soviet Union it would go back to compete with United States in naval deployments in the Third World. But since everything else is not okay, even from the military point of view, you have much more urgent priorities. We should not waste a lot of our resources on very third-rate interests.

I : So if everything was okay economically then it might be a good idea for the Soviet Union to compete with the U.S. in Third World regions?

R : Yes, if everything was OK both economically, politically, ideologically, then why not? At least the military would say, "Well, maybe it would be dangerous, but why should we worry about it?"

A bit surprised and unclear about whether he was expressing his own views or the possible views of the military we asked, "Do you agree with this?" From his reply, though, it was still not clear whether he objected to foreign military presence as inherently problematic or as simply inadvisable because of current constraints on Soviet resources:

It's a very abstract, you know it's very abstract, very abstract logical construction, because it's never okay. And your resources are always limited....Overseas presence consumes a lot of resources, starving the much more important things.

Another recurring pattern was for Soviets to embrace the principles of new thinking but then back away from them in the event that they might threaten their ties to other socialist governments. This came up when respondents tried to explain why the Soviet Union continued to give aid to socialist governments (such as Angola or Ethiopia) facing longstanding insurrections rather than promoting the principle of national reconciliation.

This theme of needing to sustain socialist allies also appeared in an interview with a Central Committee official. Initially he made a number of very bold statements to the effect that capitalism is, in fact, a more advanced economic system than socialism. We then asked, if this is the case, whether it is best to encourage allies toward socialist or capitalist economic structures. He replied: "It would be wrong to persuade these countries to drop socialist ideas completely....You shouldn't deprive people of hope." Similarly, when we asked why the Soviet Union continues to support socialist countries facing insurrections, the official said the reason was primarily "ideological." He explained:

No one would understand if the Soviet Union, say, declines or rejects help to its friends, allies....There are still many who support the principles of old thinking. We can embark on a process of education, patience and enlightenment, right? Or we could say, 'To hell with them.' There is an internal element and you can see not everybody shares Gorbachev's ideas.

Finally, there were numerous interview respondents who themselves explained the persistence of traditional Soviet behavior in terms of a conflict within Soviets between old and new thinking. A young political analyst explained:

R : I think there is still in the ideological and political thinking of people, there is some idea of natural affiliation with nations that proclaim themselves sort of "socialist"....

I : Is there also support for the idea for pulling back from trying to spread Soviet influence in the Third World?

R : I don't know. It's hard to identify really because I think that there are both. I think one and the same person might say: "We are sick and tired of having to feed all these people." And, on the other hand, at the same time he will feel like that's something that we ought to do.

A senior political analyst stressed that the Soviet Union is going through a process of transition. He recognized that much of Soviet aid to Third World countries, such as sending fighters to Libya, does not really fit with new thinking. He explained:

> Momentum is a description of what's going on....One has to read this as something of a transition period. We are still going from where we had been for decades into something more rational, more cooperative, closer to normal in international relations....It's a mixed picture, because there are many elements which are of the legacy of the old confrontation period, and they're still there....We are somewhere in between....This is not something you can see as the model for the future, although we are, I think, already a long way from the total confrontation of the old time. This is not the kind of adversary relationship which used to be universal and almost absolute.

Another political analyst made the point a bit more colorfully. Stressing that "it's impossible to free yourself from the old prejudices at once," he referred to a French saying that "a man cannot become a European in one night even if he spends it with the most beautiful woman in Paris."

Great-Power Thinking

Besides these more traditional rationales, there is another distinct stream in Soviet explanations for the persistence of their behavior in the Third World that does not comply with new thinking. As discussed in Chapter 5, there is a strong trend among members of the Soviet foreign-policy elite to view the Soviet role in the world in classical great-power terms. Such thinking was evidenced when Soviets tried to account for Soviet behavior in the Third World.

In some cases this appeared in the form of highly pragmatic, narrowly self-interested rationales for behavior. For example, numerous Soviets explained that the extensive Soviet arms transfers were simply the result of an interest in hard currency. A Foreign Ministry official drew a picture of such decisions as being driven in a highly bureaucratic fashion:

> And one of the troubles we are having now in the economy has its roots in the power of the ministries, all-powerful ministries, bureaucracies. The Ministry of Finance is one of those ministries....I would imagine that the Minister of Finance is very eloquent whenever such questions such as [arms] sales comes up because the current [economic] situation is very difficult.

It was repeatedly stressed that such transfers were devoid of any ideological objectives. A senior political analyst explained:

> There is a difference between what existed before and now.... We send weapons, we transfer weapons, but now this has become an effort to get hard currency...as some sort of compensation for other kinds of transfers, but not to prepare for world revolution.

Such narrowly pragmatic rationales have also been used by military figures when explaining why it is necessary for the Soviet Union to have a global navy. For example, Admiral Konstantin Makarov, chief of the Navy Main Staff, stressed that in addition to territorial defense, one of the purposes of "our ships which now sail the world ocean" is "protection of Soviet fishing vessels in fishing areas or protection of our civilian shipping in international sea lanes such as, for instance, the Persian Gulf." [83] Ideological rationales such as "defending the gains of socialism," though one of the key rationales for originally building a global navy, have all but disappeared.

However, the strongest thrust in such great-power thinking was not that the Soviet Union should withdraw from the world scene and simply look out for its own narrow national interests. Rather, being a great power, it was regularly argued, the Soviet Union should play an active and dynamic role in shaping the world order.

Such thinking frequently came up when Soviets explained why the Soviet Union continues to have a global military presence in the form of a wide-ranging navy and military advisers in far-flung nations. In many cases, respondents admitted that the Soviet Union did not really want to entirely withdraw its military forces within its borders, even if the United States was willing to do so. Such ideas were dismissed as being largely ideal constructs meant for a time far in the future. Rather the immediate goal, it was explained, is to achieve stability within the existing status quo; not to simply allow the world to go its own way, but for the Soviet Union and the United States to work together, in part using their military presence, to stabilize the world order. Almost invariably there was some expressed interest in reducing the military component of the superpower's military presence, but not eliminating it. Clearly the goal was to maintain the Soviet Union as a great power, and some degree of military presence was seen as essential for that purpose.

Such thinking was expressed in an article by Sergei Blagovolin of IMEMO. He did call for some reduction of Soviet global military presence, but insisted that the Soviet Union should have some presence according to its national interests, interests he has articulated in great-power terms:

> Surely the Soviet Union is a great country and will continue to have economic and political interests in far-flung regions....Why does the Soviet Union need military power? In order to guarantee the comprehensive participation of the country in the processes of world development and for the support of the basic directions of foreign policy activity.[84]

Such thinking has also appeared in the military. Admiral Konstantin Makarov is reported as saying that the Soviet Union "needs a strong Navy...which would...correspond to the might of the country both quantitatively and qualitatively....This should be a fleet which acts to ensure strategic stability in the world."[85] Elsewhere he said: "Our fleet also plays an important role in implementing the Soviet state's foreign policy actions aimed at achieving measures of trust and easing international tension."[86]

In the interviews we were able to ask how Soviet military presence would play such a stabilizing role. To most this seemed self-evident and did not require any further explanation. However, they had some trouble reasoning how, given the relatively small Soviet presence in any particular region, the Soviet Union could hope to dissuade a determined adversary. A Foreign Ministry official, though, explained that the essence of the idea was that a military presence created a "linkage" such that any party initiating aggression would, by attacking Soviet forces, however limited, trigger the involvement of larger Soviet forces. In this way Soviet forces could help deter aggressors and maintain order in the world.

These efforts to give a military rationale for the Soviet global military presence were not, however, made with real conviction. Often it seemed the respondent was trying to remember a rationale that someone else had given them. More central, it seemed, was the attitude that the Soviet Union must necessarily maintain such a presence simply to maintain its status and image as a great power. This was often presented in terms of the need to match the United States.

I : If you were to unilaterally begin to reduce your naval presence, what would be the consequences? What interests are you defending through this presence?

R : We are a great power, as is the United States a great power. With your presence, there is our presence, too.

I : Is it that simple?

R : Well. it's the briefest that I can say. It's a reaction, it's not that you reacted to our presence but we reacted to your presence. Your globalism is official, our globalism is not so official. If there are some ships that can sail, why shouldn't they sail?...

I : But to what end? Just to imitate the United States?

R : What is the end of piling up arms? What is the end?

I : Well, there has been a stated principle that you want to move away from that, that you want to move toward defensive sufficiency, right? But in terms of projecting naval presence around the world—

R : (interrupting) There are American bases.

I : Is that a good reason?

R : It's just one of the reasons, but it's a good reason, of course.

I : If you don't imitate the United States, what then?...

R : Well, we both have scenarios of a global conflict, and act accordingly....

I : So you see it as tied to scenarios of global conflict. Do you also see it as tied to local conflicts, as tied to some scenarios that are more limited as well?...

R : Your staff and our staff have scenarios, yes, but...what you do, you do not ask why you do it: we do it because you do it.

Such great-power thinking was also used to explain why the Soviet Union continues to send conventional weapons to many countries in the world. Although some respondents disputed them, most accepted Western figures indicate that the Soviet Union (until 1990) was indeed the world's largest exporter of conventional weapons. In the interviews we pressed our respondents to explain why, if they saw conventional arms transfers as intrinsically problematic, they did not at least take the lead by unilaterally reducing their own. A frequent explanation was that the Soviet Union needed to maintain its position in the larger balance of power by continuing to support its clients.

In some cases this was presented as not only serving Soviet interests but as maintaining the equilibrium of the world order dominated by the superpowers. A policy analyst explained:

We have come to the present stage with some luggage of obligations and commitments, both the Soviet Union and the United States....If I were asked whether we should stick to those commitments or we should simply abandon them, I would strongly argue against abandoning those commitments since that would provide, in the present situation a kind of vacuum...and that could encourage even the United States to intervene, even for the sake of strengthening the order, the local order there, but to intervene.

Such thinking even appeared in respondents who seemed to be basically in favor of reducing arms transfers.

I : How do you understand the continued flow of arms to the Third World? It seems so inconsistent with the stated principles.

R : In a bureaucratic system you cannot deal with all problems. Gorbachev spends some political capital on the resolution of knotty problems. So it demands time to cut the inertia of old policy in other areas of the world. And definitely the intention of Gorbachev, Shevardnadze is to change the modus vivendi with our allies, our satellites if you like. In Africa and some other parts of the world. But it shouldn't be done in a way that would tip off in a drastic way. It shouldn't be done in a drastic way.

I : It would tip off what? Create an imbalance?

R : Yes. Not just in a geopolitical sense but it would arouse hostility on the part of our allies who are now just looking for some support and [if] we cut off this support they may be angry with us.

Others, though, spoke in a more self-interested fashion about the need for allies. As one policy analyst exclaimed, "We simply want more allies." A Foreign Ministry official elaborated how, for example, arms transfers were essential to maintaining India as an ally:

> There are very few items which can be attractive to our allies and partners. Take India, for example: Which other fields can we be complementary to each other? I mean, India may be useful to us in many fields: computers, textiles.... As for us, as for their interest in pursuing relations with us, it is, given our opportunities, it is military high technology. And it is submarines. So if we are going to keep our relations with India stable, and we are to stay high profile with these relations we should find some ways and means to do so and this is one of them...arms sales....It seems to me that the rationale for the military operation with India is...economic, military influence.

A policy analyst made a similar analysis of the Soviet decision to transfer submarines to India:

> My guess is that, first of all, it was kind of a symbolic gesture. We had a long process of developing foreign relations with India. Economic relations, cultural relations and political relations and I think that it was just another step in the direction just to prove to the Indians that they are really very special to us and so on and so forth....India was very important for the Soviet Union from a geopolitical point of view, when we had very bad relations with China.

In another interview we pushed to find the roots of this concern for having allies. The initial question was about Soviet support for the Angolan government.

R : So I can't very well imagine our government even if it is convinced that the war in Angola can't be won by the Dos Santos government to take such a step as cutting aid to the Angolan government. Because first: it would be considered all over the Third World as a sign of weakness. A kind of betrayal of the Angolan government. Because nobody can prove right now that they can't win the war. So as long as any hope remains that they can win the war and crush UNITA, in this kind of situation, to cut aid to Angola would be such an inadmissible pressure from the point of view of our principle.

I : OK, the other Third World countries perceive the Soviet Union as weak in this case. Why is that so important? What are the larger objectives of the Soviet Union that would be undermined by this kind of perception?

R : Well, now we have a different kind of relationship with the United States than we used to have. And, of course, we are interested in making accommodations everywhere that is possible. But this rejection of the confrontation approach from our part doesn't mean that the competition has come to an end. All over the world we are going to have competition by peaceful means, but still it is competition. It is a rivalry for many years to come. But not in the realm of confrontation. We must have allies all over the Third World. And the importance of such allies is, in my view, greater than it used to be.

I : For what reason?

R : I'll tell you. We used to look at the world as divided in black and white. United States on one side, and we on the other side. And the Third World was kind of a reserve, or kind of our ally. Now we have come to a very interesting situation in which we have to deal not only with the U.S. and the West in general, but also with a lot of more countries....And nobody can say that the U.S. government is a very reliable partner in this sphere. So we must have allies, we must have support from nations which are...whose views coincide more or less with our views. That have our—not military bases—but bases of support somewhere in Africa and in Asia.

I : Because then if you don't what will happen?

R : If we don't? Well you know that the United States is stronger than we are—not in the military but in the economic field, I mean. And the U.S. has a lot of allies and a lot of countries which will support them in the

United Nations and elsewhere. I believe that we are entering in all fields a period of very tough negotiations with the U.S. Not only in the disarmament issue, but also in the issue of resolving internal conflicts and new economic order, and many other things. And so we must have a network of allies all over the world....Angola is just a small part of the whole pattern. The pattern is that we must not let our international prestige among our allies sink very low.

Later in the interview, we asked a series of questions to see if this concern for allies was masking some traditional ideological aspirations. However, he was quite emphatic in stressing that the Soviet Union should in no way try to further socialist revolution in the world. Rather the pursuit of allies was seen as intrinsic to Soviet national interests.

Interestingly, in some cases even Soviets who emphatically embraced traditional Leninist foreign-policy objectives would also reveal underlying great-power concerns. For example, the academic Mikhail Muntyan initially rebuffed, on ideological grounds, criticism of Soviet involvement in the Third World:

Our involvement in regional conflicts is interpreted as excessive in many cases and unwarranted in some others. I think to renounce our internationalist duty, which is to assist and support the forces of social progress all over the world, would be tantamount to repudiating the very essence of Marxism-Leninism. We must show political skill precisely by fulfilling this internationalist duty in forms strengthening socialism's positions in the world and not weakening them.

But then in the next sentence he also showed a more politically pragmatic concern for enhancing the Soviet geopolitical position, implying that in some cases this must take some precedence over more ideological objectives:

At the same time, the art of international politics consists in winning as many allies and friends as possible or, at any rate, in neutralizing obvious adversaries. Moves and actions which prevent or fail to serve the achievement of this aim must not be exalted to the rank of policy.[87]

In some cases the idea of supporting socialist allies initially seemed to be derived from an ideological orientation, but on closer analysis it became clear that the concern was primarily a great-power concern for maintaining allies. For example, a prominent expert on the Third World was trying to explain why, at the time, the Soviet government was refraining from putting pressure on the Angolans to pursue a policy of national reconciliation with UNITA:

R : So we recognize, we admit...there is no problem of instigating a kind of world revolution all over the world. But still at the same time we are a socialist country, the first socialist country. We have a lot of friends and allies, movements committed to the socialist cause. So I believe that if the Angolan government were not socialist-oriented, things would have been slightly different. But since it is, and we don't have so many of them right now you know, Ethiopia, Angola, Mozambique, maybe Congo, South Yemen. That's all.

Then in an oddly convoluted line of logic he explained that, though the Soviet Union was not really interested in promoting socialism in the world, it was necessary for the Soviet Union to still behave as if it was, and not put pressure on socialist forces to seek accommodation, so as to maintain its position with its allies.

R : So my point is, if we apply pressure, to any of this kind of government, be it Angolan government or Ethiopian government, one of the few governments which support our cause, which are committed to the idea of socialism, if we apply against their will a kind of pressure to make them accommodate with their enemy...then we lose a lot of prestige among leftist movements all over the world. Then all the insinuations that are evident even now, that the Soviet Union is not interested in national liberation movements, is only interested in accommodation with America with Western help and technology, all these kinds of accusations and insinuations will increase to a very significant degree. And it will be very difficult for us to defend our position. So if the Angolan government itself comes to the conclusion that it can't win the war and must come to a kind of condition, then we would have been only too glad to mediate, and try to arrange things as smoothly as possible to set up a kind of coalition government and so on. But once they are stubborn and adamant and want to continue the war, it is very difficult to find arguments to tell them no you mustn't wage war anymore, you must come to an agreement, you must try to set up a coalition government, you must recognize UNITA as a legitimate partner, not as an enemy, as a rebel. But as a legitimate opposition which must find its place within the future structure of your state.

I : This is a description of a sort of passive or hands-off policy of national reconciliation, that is, if the circumstances exist to support that, to go

with it, but not to push it.
R : Yes. It is just this. It's a practical, pragmatic consideration....We can't very well turn our back on our allies, after all they've been brought up here in Moscow. What is the ruling party in Angola? Its core consists mainly of people who were educated here or followed our advice and so on. So if now we come to them and say it was wrong, so you've come to power but you mustn't think you're a legitimate government.
I : You must not disinherit your children?
R : Sure. That's the point.

In some cases the sense of loyalty to socialist allies has even been given a kind of moral coloring. For example, Shevardnadze, in the same October 23, 1989, speech in which he denounced the intervention in Afghanistan as immoral, he also said, "We are not morally entitled to deny support to the Afghan people." He argued that the Soviet Union cannot abandon commitments to its friends and allies and furthermore that to do so "would devalue all the sacrifices made by our people."[88] On another occasion Shevardnadze commented, "We must remember that we are a great power and to tell any nation that we needed you yesterday but not today is simply not done."[89]

Even Soviets who from a new-thinking perspective actively criticized the scope of Soviet activism in the Third World would at other moments also reveal such great-power concerns, perhaps reflecting some inner conflict. For example, a political analyst initially denounced Soviet external presence as "counterproductive," complaining:

Whenever you have your military presence, you become a hostage to that presence. You cannot take out the troops if, for example, you don't have any need in keeping them since you have your obligations, you have prestige. This will be regarded as a sign of weakness.

However, later, when we pushed him to say whether he thought the Soviet Union should, together with the United States, withdraw from the Third World, he balked:

It's not a problem of withdrawal. The Soviet Union and the United States have become the global, so to say, powers, present everywhere. So the problem now is not to withdraw from some areas and say, let's forget about that, just they do what they like: It's impossible.

He then tried to reconcile this position with new thinking by saying that such responsibility is, in fact, consistent with new thinking as long as there are some efforts to reduce its military dimension:

> Global responsibility is still there in the new political thinking. The global responsibility of the Soviet Union and the United States for the situation, well, everywhere in the world....The military component of that responsibility should be diminished, which doesn't mean just simply abandoning it.

Similarly, a Foreign Ministry official initially proposed that the Soviet Union should greatly reduce its naval presence around the world, roundly criticizing the traditional notion that the Soviet Union should invariably try to match the United States. However, when we asked specifically whether this meant that the Soviet Union should ultimately withdraw from the Caribbean, he stiffened and said:

> Well, there is one more problem to this story. That is, like you, we also have global interests and we have allies and friends in all parts of the world and we have to be aware of this reality and you have to be aware of this reality also. If you remember, the Cuban missile crisis was because of our perception of an imminent threat to Cuba and this may be the case with certain regions of the world today, including Cuba, including North Yemen or South Yemen, Vietnam, and so on.

We asked: "So you see that you're playing some protective function to those countries? Even a stabilizing function in that a crisis can occur if there are not forces in the area that compensate for any vulnerability of your allies?" He answered: "Yes, yes. You will agree that it is an inevitable function for a superpower. [chuckles] Well, it is an open question whether we are still a superpower, but still we see ourselves as such."

Finally, there were Soviets who explained persistent Soviet activism in the Third World in terms of great-power competition, but at the same time recognized that this was inconsistent with new thinking. For example, a senior political analyst explained Soviet behavior as being driven by a desire for "political and military returns," recognizing that this "does not exactly fit into the overall political atmosphere of new political thinking." A high-level Foreign Ministry official described the dynamic of the super-powers each trying to move into any geopolitical void, like playing a game of chess. With frankness he said, "Now, I don't think that we have as yet come to an understanding that this game has ended. And it hasn't ended perhaps as yet." But, he said:

We are pushing to this understanding...that we shouldn't consider the foreign policy as a zero-sum game, that we have to occupy every single square that is possible to occupy, we have to transfer every nation or state into clients, as if we have to push it everywhere we can. So this is one of the first steps of new political thinking.

In both cases, these comments were made with a certain sadness, as if it was somewhat painful for these Soviets to recognize the difficulty the Soviet Union has in restraining its competitive national impulses even when largely relieved of the ideological rationale for such competition. Nonetheless, there was still a dominant tone of hopefulness: encouragement from the extent of the change seen and anticipation that, perhaps, as the United States moderates its own competitive behavior in light of Soviet changes, this could ultimately prompt even greater Soviet restraint.

7

Europe

In this chapter we will explore how the changes in Soviet ideology have influenced Soviet policy and behavior in Europe. The most dramatic change was the gradual relinquishment of Soviet domination over Eastern Europe. This led to the collapse of Soviet-dominated governments throughout the region, the removal of the Berlin Wall, the reunification of Germany and its inclusion in NATO, and, finally, the disbandment of the Warsaw Pact.

Although these changes have been more persistent and vivid than the changes in Soviet behavior in the Third World, they have, nonetheless, been neither smooth nor easy. At every point along the way Soviets made diplomatic and conceptual efforts to impose some limits on the unraveling of the old order.

However, in a remarkable example of the power of ideology, the logic of new thinking consistently prevailed. Clearly the Soviet Union had the military means to prevent such unraveling, just as was true in the past. But once it was established that the principle of national sovereignty superseded any ideological principle that might prompt intervention, the legitimizing foundation of Soviet hegemony as well as the implicit threat to use force were undermined. It was only a matter of time before the Warsaw Pact would come unglued.

Concurrent with the process of unraveling the old order in Eastern Europe there have also been efforts, within new thinking, to define a new order for Europe as a whole. This began with Gorbachev's vague proposal for establishing a Common European Home and evolved into the notion of a pan-European security system to replace the alliance structure.

The Gradual Decline of Soviet Hegemony

Before new thinking there was little ambiguity about the Soviet position in relation to Eastern Europe. According to Soviet ideology, the emergence of socialist governments in Eastern Europe was an expression of the inevitable process of evolution toward socialism. Efforts toward undoing this development were seen as arising from malignant counterrevolutionary forces and therefore required intervention by fraternal socialist governments. Of course, because the Soviet Union was the dominant power in Eastern Europe, this principle of fraternal assistance to maintain socialist, and therefore necessarily friendly, governments could not be easily differentiated from raw Soviet hegemony over Eastern Europe.

The principle of fraternal assistance was not simply an empty idea. On repeated occasions—in East Germany in 1953, in Hungary in 1956, in Czechoslovakia in 1968, and in indirect ways in Poland in 1980—the Soviet Union did intervene to abort departures in Eastern Europe from the Soviet-sanctioned line. On the occasion of the 1968 intervention in Czechoslovakia, the ideological rationale for such intervention was clearly formulated in what became known in the West as "the Brezhnev Doctrine." An article in *Pravda* on September 26, 1968, titled "Sovereignty and the International Obligations of Socialist Countries," outlined the principle of limited sovereignty for socialist countries, saying that any decision of socialist countries

> must damage neither socialism in their own country nor the fundamental interest of the other socialist countries nor the worldwide workers' movement, which is waging a struggle for socialism. This means that every Communist Party is responsible not only to its own people but also to all the socialist countries and the entire communist movement. Whoever forgets this by placing sole emphasis on the autonomy and independence of communist parties lapses into one-sidedness, shirking his internationalist obligations.[1]

Early in Gorbachev's tenure he stressed, to the contrary, that all governments have the right to choose their own form of government and that intervention into the affairs of another country is inadmissible. Initially, though, such pronouncements made little impact in the West. For decades Soviet leaders had, in their typical double-think style, also voiced such principles at the same time they also embraced the notions of the Brezhnev Doctrine. With Gorbachev there was still no observable change in Soviet behavior.

Furthermore, Gorbachev also made other statements that suggested some remnants of old-school hegemonistic thinking may have still been alive. In a major article published in September 1987 Gorbachev did speak of the right of each country to choose its own path, but he also stressed that each country has the right to maintain the status quo. This had a familiar ring similar to the traditional Soviet argument that the Eastern European countries were already expressing their freedom of choice in their choice of the path of socialism. Furthermore, at another point in the article, in reference to East European countries, he used the term "one of our own,"[2] suggesting a definite hegemonic relationship.

However, by the year 1988, there were some indications that genuine changes were occurring. In March 1988, while in Yugoslavia, Gorbachev signed a Soviet-Yugoslavian joint statement saying that the two countries "have no pretensions of imposing their concepts of social development on anyone" and that they "prohibit any threat and use of force and interference in the internal affairs of other states under any pretext whatsoever."[3]

Although these words were not in themselves strikingly new, Soviets with whom we spoke shortly afterward read this speech as signalling a genuine departure from the Brezhnev doctrine. They portrayed the change as not yet complete, but affirmed that Soviet policy was in the process of rapidly evolving toward a position that East European socialist countries, could "go their own way" in regard to their domestic governmental system.

Soviet academics also began to make unusually bold statements that directly challenged earlier Soviet behavior. For example, in June 1988 Oleg Bogomolov commented that in the past the Soviet Union was "eager for our experience to be copied," but that

> [W]e now assert that no one has a monopoly on the truth, each country seeks the best solutions, and we must not impose our experience on each other but learn from each other's experience. It seems to me that henceforth the kind of actions or the kind of policy which used to be interpreted by the Western press as the "doctrine of limited sovereignty" will become impossible.[4]

Dashichev was even bolder, saying:

> We are trying to free our relations with the socialist countries from the deformation of the periods under Stalin and Brezhnev, on the basis of total independence, equality, and noninterference....If we free ourselves from the shadows of the past, this will also have a favorable effect on East-West relations.

When asked whether this means "no more interventions like the one in Prague in 1968," Dashichev answered, "I think that under today's conditions something like that is impossible..." and that though the Soviet Union may try to influence East Bloc countries through political means "in no case, however, is military force permitted. This must finally belong to the past....We can build the common home of Europe only if hegemonism is finally liquidated." He even stated that, provided relations between Berlin and Bonn continued to improve, "the Wall will disappear in the course of time."[5]

Some Soviets described the process of going through this shift in attitudes. The All-Union radio commentator Viktor Levin, discussing the principle of equality and noninterference in relations between socialist countries, said:

> Let us be frank: Not so very long ago many of these concepts I have referred to appeared to some to be seditious, and supposedly to run counter to the principles of socialist internationalism....Now a process is under way not an easy process, and one should be frank about that—a process of purging ourselves of these dogmas.[6]

However, it was not until Gorbachev's speeches in Poland in July 1988 that the larger world began to take serious note of the change in Soviet thinking. Addressing the Polish Sejm (or parliament) Gorbachev implicitly recognized that support of the principle of equality and independence by previous Soviet administrations was largely empty:

> The foundation of principles upon which cooperation in the socialist world is based has recently been substantially renovated, although there were plenty of good principles before as well. What suffered was the readiness to be guided by them in earnest. Now equality, independence, and joint tackling of problems in common are becoming the immutable norms of our relations. They are rid of the elements of paternalism and coming to rest totally and completely on the foundation of voluntary, committed partnership and comradeship.[7]

Later he quipped, "I think the notion of socialist pluralism is also applicable to relationships between the parties and countries of the socialist world."[8] He also signed a Soviet-Polish Joint Statement embracing the principles of equality, independence, and the "right to independently solve questions of the country's development."[9]

In the ensuing months Soviets began to repeatedly break taboos governing the interpretation of past Soviet policy in relation to Eastern Europe. The historian L.S. Yagodovsky of the Institute of Economics of the World Socialist System made a then-heretical statement that the goals of perestroika and the Prague Spring of 1968 were "largely identical."[10] He implied that there was indeed a kind of "Brezhnev Doctrine" though he still felt a need to do so in a convoluted way.

I think the idea of such a doctrine was a fabrication from the first, but it must be said that grounds for this fabrication were apparently provided to some extent by some not entirely clear statements made by L.I. Brezhnev, among others, in the late sixties....Today, however,...suffice it to recall M.S. Gorbachev's statements to the effect that the CPSU proceeds from the premise that the ruling party in each socialist country is fully autonomous....No one has the right to lay claim to a special position in the socialist world.[11]

High Party officials were no less active in making bold departures from past positions. When Nikolay Shishlin, then head of the Central Committee Propaganda Department, was asked about the potential for trade union pluralism in Poland, he said that this was a decision for the Polish and implicitly criticized past Soviet behavior by ruling out a "repetition of the 1980 events," and said that "we would not be afraid if Solidarity re-emerged."[12]

Georgi Korniyenko, then deputy head of the Party's Foreign Affairs Department was the first to bluntly recognize and denounce the Brezhnev Doctrine. In September 1988 he said to the Italian Communist Party, "We have given up the Brezhnev principle of limited sovereignty....No state or party has the right to impose its own path of development, even if it is the best."[13]

Soviet officials were also not shy about sending such messages to Eastern European countries. In an interview on Hungarian television Bessmertnykh clearly stated the principle of nonintervention, implicitly denounced the Brezhnev principle of limited sovereignty, said that the events of 1968 could not be repeated, and predicted that Soviet troops would be withdrawn from Hungary in the near future.[14]

In a series of interviews we carried out in October 1988 we heard even starker statements. For example, an analyst at IMEMO said: "The Brezhnev Doctrine or the violation of sovereignty is completely dead. It completely contradicts new thinking. The principle of peaceful coexistence has to be spread even in the countries of socialism."

Another senior and influential analyst at IMEMO even insisted that the Soviet Union would allow the reunification of Germany and the withdrawal of Eastern European countries from NATO. He explained:

I am convinced that we would not try to obstruct (withdrawal from the Warsaw Pact) by any military means. We would maybe call the Political Consultative Committee of the Warsaw Pact....We would say that you would all the same leave the COMECON. We would tell them that you would then be violating and breaking all the economic principles in the socialist countries. We would say that you are going to violate the balance

of forces between east and west. We would remind them of socialist
solidarity. By these methods we would act, but I don't think by any other
methods.

Overall, it seemed that Soviets we interviewed were even a bit surprised
that we took seriously the prospect that they might intervene. To them it
seemed self-evident that the political costs of intervention would be so high
that it would be unthinkable.

At the same time many of these same Soviets had a surprising confidence
that the East European countries, given this freedom, would not want to
withdraw from the Warsaw Pact or even depart very far from socialism.
They assumed that populations in these countries had grown accustomed
to the social guarantees of socialism, that they would want to stay closely
aligned with the Soviet Union because of their dependency on it for gas and
oil, and, in the case of Poland, they would look to the Soviet Union for
security guarantees against Germany. For example, one analyst from the
USA Institute explained:

> I think that what Gorbachev is trying to achieve is some mature political
> alliance in Eastern Europe. It means that this alliance will be based on
> diversity in social and economic spheres, on different models, different
> ways of development. Then it will be based on diversity in some, at least
> marginal foreign policy interests...and most difficult to achieve, the alliance
> should be based on the organic interest of the countries and not just on the
> perceived threat from the West. And if he achieves it I think there will be
> less incentive for East European countries, even if some change happens
> there, to withdraw from the Warsaw Treaty.

At the same time, however, there were also, during this period some
clear indications of more traditional positions on the relation of the Soviet
Union to the Eastern European countries. For example, there were persisting
positive evaluations of the 1968 intervention in Czechoslovakia. In August
1988 *Pravda* and *Izvestiya* reported sympathetically on Czech articles that
defended the need for the 1968 intervention. Alexander Kondrashov, in
Izvestiya, reiterated the traditional argument that the Prague Spring was
largely due to Western subversive efforts to "wrest the CSSR [Czechoslo-
vakia] from the socialist community and change the correlation of forces in
Europe in its favor," playing upon the "political irresponsibility and opportunism of a section of the then CPCZ [Czech Communist Party] leadership." Kondrashov asked rhetorically, "Could that really leave all the
friends and allies of socialist Czechoslovakia indifferent?" He stressed how
the Prague Spring efforts were not really in the Czech interest because

Czechoslovakia was so dependent on the Soviet Union for oil, gas, and ore. Then with satisfaction he exclaimed, "How the country has risen up and straightened itself since surmounting the crisis of 1968-69!"[15]

The interpretation of the invasion of 1956 was also controversial. In July 1989 the Hungarians held a ritual reburial of Imre Nagy, leader of the 1956 Hungarian effort to liberalize Hungary and pull it out of the Warsaw Pact. In a sympathetic gesture the Soviet ambassador attended the event. There were also supportive articles in the press. One of them by Yevgeniy Ambartsumov, referred to the "treacherous capture" of Nagy and condemned the Soviet Union as the "guilty party" for his execution.[16] However, other voices in the Soviet media stressed that the events of 1956 were counterrevolutionary in that communists were killed[17] and the Soviet government continued to refrain from any revision of the official interpretation of the events.

Perhaps most central, there was also apparent controversy about whether the Eastern European countries were now free to depart from socialism. The controversy was even surprisingly public. In February 1989 Bogomolov said that it would represent no danger if Hungary were to become a Western-style bourgeois democracy.[18] However, days later, Politburo candidate member Nikolai Talyzin said he disagreed with Bogomolov.[19]

Overall, the dominant position stressed the right of Eastern European countries to decide their fates. In May 1989 Valentin Falin took this position when he was asked whether he could envisage a social democratic Hungary and a Christian democratic Poland.[20] Alexander Yakovlev affirmed: "If a certain people selects a certain road, it thus implements its interests, and we must take this into consideration no matter what choice was made, provided the choice has really been made by the people."[21] In a politically significant gesture *New Times* magazine published an interview of Lech Walesa in February 1989.[22] The following July, Vadim Zagladin affirmed that the Soviet Union "will maintain ties with any elected Polish government....Any solution adopted by our Polish friends will be accepted by us."[23]

Others, though, held that the Eastern European countries must adhere to socialism. Karen Brutents, then deputy chief of the Party's International Department, insisted that new forces in Eastern Europe must "respect the socialist option already adopted."[24] Articles also appeared in the Soviet media criticizing the new liberalizing developments in Eastern European countries and comparing them unfavorably to 1956 and 1968.[25]

Ultimately, this apparent conflict was embodied in the equivocal positions taken by Gorbachev. Gorbachev repeatedly affirmed the right of countries to determine their own fates and, while in Hungary in March 1989, he publicly expressed his approval of a multiparty system in Hungary.[26]

However, in a series of speeches in France in July of 1989 he was remarkably equivocal. Perhaps most convoluted was a comment he made in a news conference with French President Francois Mitterrand:

> If you and I agree that the construction of a common European home does not mean and will not mean the ousting of ...this or that system...but on the contrary...each remaining the same as he is, but at the same time changing too...it would mean that each people would retain its freedom of choice. [27]

The next day, though, he seemed to be more explicitly open to the possibility that countries could indeed depart from socialism. Addressing the Council of Europe he made one of his most definitive repudiations of the Brezhnev Doctrine:

> Social and political orders changed in the past and may change in the future as well. However, that is exclusively the affair of the people themselves. It is their choice. Any interference in internal affairs of whatever kind, any attempts to limit the sovereignty of states, both of friends and allies, no matter whose it is, is impermissible.

He also excluded the possibility of using force not only between alliances, but "within an alliance" as well. [28]

However, several days later, at the Sorbonne he once again injected an ambiguous, even faintly threatening tone.

> There are those who would like to see...the removal of the division of Europe via the ousting of socialism. That is unrealistic; furthermore, it is dangerous. I think that in scientific research and in politics everything must begin from the realities. In this case, it is necessary to retain one's ideological attachments. Let everyone remain as he is with his own choice. [29]

Such controversies also constellated around the reevaluation of the past interventions in Czechoslovakia in 1968. In an interview with Hungarian television in July 1989 then Politburo member Igor Ligachev was asked whether the Soviet Union might once again intervene as in 1968. He brushed off the question, pointing to Gorbachev's principle of nonintervention and adding that "I support this principle in its entirety." However, when he was asked whether the 1968 intervention was being reassessed, he insisted that in 1968 the Dubcek government was not serving the interests of the people and "therefore, when the Prague request for assistance was voiced we were forced to extend help." Nevertheless, he also reiterated that "the only correct principle" is that "we must not interfere in internal affairs, and the party of the given country is sovereign and independent."[30]

Equivocations such as these also appeared in the press. On the twentieth anniversary of the 1968 invasion Soviet newspapers ran stories that recalled the events in exclusively positive terms.[31] The next year, in August 1989, the discussion reflected much greater ambivalence. Reported were interviews with several Soviet participants in the 1968 events. Ivan Pavlovsky, then deputy defense minister and commander of forces sent to Czechoslovakia, was a bit defensive: "Everything is being criticized today. All was different. But, this issue should be regarded in the context of the military-political situation which existed at that time. I am a man of convictions and my views do not change."[32]

Kiril Mazurov, a Politburo member at the time who was directly involved in the invasion, made a more convoluted statement suggesting some inner conflict: "I would never have agreed to conduct such an operation today. But in the concrete situation of August 1968, I acted in accordance with my convictions, and if a similar situation had arisen today I would have behaved the same way." Later he also said: "If today a situation arose such as the one in 1968 in Czechoslovakia, in my view there would be no intervention. No one among our present leadership would even think of such a thing. At the time, however, it seemed quite normal."[33]

Despite the renunciation of the rationale for the 1968 invasion Soviet government officials were, for a period, also reluctant to criticize it. Foreign Ministry spokesman Yuri Gremitskikh in August of 1989 argued that the events in 1968 need to be viewed in the context of their time.[34] Even Shevardnadze on October 27, 1989, refused to criticize the 1968 invasion and repeated the old defense that Soviet troops were invited in.[35] In our interviews, though, government officials made it clear that the reason for this reluctance was a desire not to antagonize the Czech government. Mazurov also commented publicly: "There is evidently some kind of tacit agreement which prohibits us from speaking about this unpleasant topic. Because as the saying goes, in the house of a hanged man it is not seemly to talk about the rope."[36] By the next December 4th, though, after the Czech government fell, the Soviet Union joined the Warsaw Pact in denouncing the 1968 invasion as "illegal."[37]

During fall 1989 there were also a number of important steps in the direction of renouncing the Brezhnev doctrine, even by name. With characteristic elan, then Foreign Ministry spokesman Gennadi Gerasimov announced that the Brezhnev Doctrine had been replaced by the "Sinatra doctrine": "In the Soviet Union of today we replace the Brezhnev Doctrine...with the Frank Sinatra doctrine from the title of one of his famous songs, "I Did it My Way"....I think, in fact, that each Eastern country is doing it its own way."[38]

With a heavier hand IMEMO analyst Viktor Sheynis, in an article in *Izvestiya*, damned the Brezhnev Doctrine as a violation of international law:

> [T]he Molotov-Ribbentrop pact, the invasion of Czechoslovakia, and the "international assistance" to Afghanistan are links in one and the same chain which cannot be separated. Our society's moral health lies in overcoming the imperial syndrome....The time has come to publicly and clearly admit our responsibility for the "Brezhnev Doctrine." It is dead to all intents and purposes. The only thing left to do is admit this.[39]

Yevgeni Primakov, referring to the presumptuousness of the Brezhnev doctrine, stated: "Unlike what used to be the case in the past, we no longer think that we are all but holding God by the beard and that we are closer to the truth than anybody else."[40]

In fall 1989 there were also rapid changes in the attitude about the Berlin Wall. As late as August 1989, on the anniversary of the erection of the Berlin wall, the wall was described by the Soviet press in positive terms saying that it "lead to the re-creation of more positive conditions for building socialism in the GDR," that "the republic acquired prestige in the international arena,"[41] and that it "placed a solid barrier" in the way of Western forces that sought "the elimination of the GDR and the reversal of postwar realities in Europe" and by so doing "saved peace."[42] However, by the following October the Soviet Union was actively promoting the idea of tearing down the wall.

Needless to say all of these changes did not occur without substantial emotional difficulty. In some cases individuals found it painful to recall past Soviet behavior in light of the newly emerging norms of behavior dictated by new thinking. V. Shutkevich, a correspondent for *Komsomolskaya Pravda*, wrote in September 1989:

> Tragic dates and pages cannot be erased from the people's memory. The further they recede into the past, the more painfully and the more often they resurface, just like fragments embedded in the flesh, appearing years later. I am convinced that we still have not emptied our bitter cup of repentance, and the feeling of shame for some deeds by our forebears will still, time and again, make us blush.[43]

More common, though, were expressions of pain about the obvious breakdown of the socialist commonwealth. When the exodus of East Germans began, Zagladin spoke of "the pain" the sight elicited in him[44] and Portugalov spoke of "bitter feelings."[45]

Not all Soviets, however, responded with such a quiet, philosophical attitude. Clearly there were those who also responded with anger and irritation. Reportedly in a November 27, 1989 press conference Defense Minister Dimitri Yazov, when asked about events in Eastern Europe, was so testy that he seemed out of control. And, as a number of Soviets recently explained to me, during this period there were high-level military and party officials pressing for the Soviet Union to intervene militarily to prevent the breakdown of the Warsaw Pact.

Overall, though, what is most striking is the extent to which Soviets even seemed enthusiastic about seeing Communist governments fall in the Eastern European countries. This was quite apparent in the interviews and was clearly reflected in the Soviet behavior through this period. In August 1989, when the new Polish government was being formed, Gorbachev reportedly telephoned leaders of the Polish Communist Party and successfully pressed them to be more accommodating to Solidarity.[46] Shortly after Gorbachev's visit to East Germany in October 1989, East German President Erich Honnecker stepped down and the government began to undertake a rapid series of reforms. In November there were rumors that Gorbachev telephoned then Czech leader Milos Jakes and urged him to loosen his grip over Czech society.[47] And in December 1989 the Soviets not only openly supported the forces overthrowing the Communist Party regime of Nicolae Ceausescu, but even sent them medical and relief aid.

There was, however a point past which it was difficult for even some of the most ardent new thinkers to go: This was the idea of a reunified Germany in NATO. In the public debate not only conservatives warned against the perils of a reunified Germany, but even Shevardnadze painted ominous images saying: "The ghost of revanchism is roaming Europe, hand in hand with the ideas of unity and unification....The new status of the German question has raised dangerous hopes for redrawing of borders."[48]

Overall there was a good deal of inconsistency in positions taken by leading Soviet figures as to whether they would accept the idea of a reunified Germany in NATO. When Dashichev was asked, "Are you afraid of a reunified Germany?" he answered, "No, not at all. The German people themselves must be able to decide on the national question" though he added confidently, "If reunification will be attained at all it will certainly not come very soon."[49] Primakov said that the Soviet Union will not use force to prevent the GDR from leaving the Warsaw Pact,[50] and Alexander Yakovlev said that the Soviet Union would not interfere with the reunification of Germany, that it was a matter to be decided by the Germans.[51]

However, when Gerasimov was asked whether the Soviet Union would interfere if a democratic GDR chose to withdraw from the Warsaw Pact he replied that "governments change, governments come and go, but international commitments remain....We have our commitments to this [Warsaw] Pact."[52] Gorbachev also showed a peculiar contradictory position. In an interview with *Pravda* in February 1990 he both referred to "the German's right to unity" and said that "history has decided that there be two German states."[53]

In our interviews Soviets were distinctly uncomfortable with the German question. Although a few Soviets as early as fall 1989 predicted that reunification was inevitable, most held to the idea that it was simply not feasible. Some argued that the Helsinki accords established the borders of Europe and that it would now be a violation of international law to change them. Others emphasized that neither the Soviet Union nor most of the European powers wanted reunification to occur, as if this entirely settled the question. They seemed to rely on the hope that the Four Powers would put on the brakes.

At times Soviets explicitly tried to draw on Western fears that Germany might become too strong. In a comment by Gerasimov in November 1989 he seemed to be appealing to U.S. fears that it might lose its hegemonic domination over Germany. "To be honest, the prospect of a united Germany, transformed from being strong to being mighty and disobedient, will hardly please our Western allies whatever they might say about it in public at present."[54]

There are even indications that during fall 1989 and winter 1990 the possibility of intervening militarily to prevent unification was considered. In the interviews at that time, when we asked whether such intervention was possible, we received an uncertain response. More recently, Soviets with whom we have spoken have indicated that in fall 1989 and winter 1990 such options were being suggested at high levels. At the time there were few public indications of such considerations though the Canadian Press News Agency did report in February 1990 on a nonattributed interview with a spokesman for the Central Committee who said that the Soviet Union would consider using military force to prevent reunification on unacceptable terms.[55]

Eventually, though, as the Western powers came to support the idea of German reunification the Soviets seemed to accept reunification conditional on the United Germany not being part of NATO. The rationale for this resistance was based on very traditional concerns about the balance of power on the continent. Even Shevardnadze said in May 1990 that German membership in NATO "would very concretely affect our security interests, it would mean an acute violation of the balance of power in Europe, it would create for us a dangerous military-strategic situation."[56]*

However, the logic of new thinking still made it difficult for the Soviets to hold to this position. They still could not come up with a rationale for denying the Germans the right to choose what alliance they wanted to join. In a conversation with Bush in Washington on June 1, 1990, Gorbachev let slip the question of whether it "shouldn't be the German people who decide whether they are not in NATO." Bush pressed Gorbachev to say how the Germans could demonstrate their wishes but failed to pin him down.[57]

Meanwhile, in the Soviet Union an intense debate ensued. The notion of a unified Germany in NATO was too much for the conservative forces to bear. The criticism of Shevardnadze and his entire East European policy reached an even more feverish pitch, with public denunciations from even high-level military officials, asking why Soviet troops were not putting things in order the way they had in 1956 and 1968.[58] Shevardnadze, though, was unrepentant. He attended the ceremony officially closing Checkpoint Charlie in late June. And he responded directly to criticism, comparing his detractors to the McCarthyites in the U.S. who asked "who lost China?" and saying:

> What can I say to those who ask why the changes in East Europe were allowed to happen and why we agreed to withdraw our troops? The subtext to this is clearly: Why did we not use tanks to "restore order?" Can we seriously think that is possible, that the problem can be solved that way? Have we really learned nothing; can we not remember the lessons of Afghanistan if we have already forgotten those of 1956 and 1968? Haven't we had our fill of funerals and internationalist invalids?...It is time to realize that neither socialism, nor friendship, nor good-neighborliness, nor respect can be produced by bayonets, tanks or blood.[59]

Ultimately, though, he stressed the principles of new thinking as the basis of his position, principles that should take precedence over the concept of national interest:

---

*Interestingly, in his memoirs written in 1991, Shevardnadze at one point explained that "we did not consent to Germany's membership in NATO" because of "Soviet public opinion." But at another point he maintained that to accept a unified Germany in NATO in mid 1990 would have "tip[ped] the balance of forces in Europe." He also did not explain clearly how this concern for balance was finally obviated. Eduard Shevardnadze, *The Future Belongs to Freedom* (New York: Free Press, 1991) 132, 138.

[Intervention] would have contradicted the logic of our own actions and the principles of the new political thinking. Furthermore, even if what is happening in Eastern Europe were at variance with our interests, even then we would exclude any interference in these states' affairs. It is impossible, for today we acknowledge in deeds and not just in words, the equality of nations, the sovereignty of peoples, noninterference in their affairs, and their right to freedom of choice.[60]

In the end Shevardnadze's position prevailed. On July 16, 1990, Gorbachev finally accepted a unified Germany in NATO, saying that "we made realpolitik."[61] Despite the tremendous storm of resistance that Shevardnadze had to weather in promoting this policy, and despite the sting of disapproval he apparently continued to feel, in his memoirs, written in 1991, he viewed this outcome as an inevitable result once the principles of new thinking were established: "[I]t was clear from the outset that we would not resist the unification of Germany. Such opposition would run counter to our political principles."[62]

The final remnant of Soviet hegemony was the institution of the Warsaw Treaty Organization (WTO). Since its inception in 1955, the alliance had been a means for the Soviet Union to effectively dominate Eastern Europe. Here again, the principles of new thinking implied that any such association should be purely voluntary. Although Hungary and Czechoslovakia did make some calls for disbanding the alliance, on the whole the Eastern European countries did not loudly proclaim their wish to leave the alliance. Nevertheless, it gradually became clear that this was the emerging sentiment. In the end Gorbachev beat them to the punch and on February 12, 1991, proposed disbanding the military structures of the Pact.

This decision, though, was hard in coming. For the year and a half leading up to the decision there were a series of efforts to try to stanch the flow toward dissolution. In the fall of 1989, as the Eastern European communist governments were falling, a widely expressed idea was that the Warsaw Pact needed to be demilitarized, deideologized, and, instead, politicized. There seemed to be a hope that common interests, especially economic ones, would continue to hold the alliance together. Even conservative elements accepted the idea that the WTO would be deidologized. Akhromeyev said that the WTO will become "an alliance of interest" and will "free itself from its ideological superstructures."[63] But the underlying message was that the WTO would nonetheless persist. Akhromeyev also stressed: "The West must realize this: The Warsaw Pact existed in the past, exists now, and will exist in the future too."[64] Stripped of its ideological rationale, Akhromeyev seemed to be trying to tell the West that the Soviet

Union still saw the WTO as an important instrument for its great-power aspirations.

Nevertheless there was still a need to give a rationale for maintaining the WTO, to specify the basis of this "alliance of interests." There were some efforts to uphold the idea that the WTO nations faced a military threat from the West. But this argument ultimately collapsed when in the summer of 1990 the WTO and NATO officially declared that they are no longer adversaries.

In interviews in Moscow in May 1990 Soviet academics and Foreign Ministry officials spoke about the Warsaw Pact as collapsing or being effectively finished. By the end of June 1990 even General Alexei Lizichev, chief of the Soviet Army and Navy Main Political Directorate, said, "The Warsaw Pact as a military organization is on the decline. Our officers have understood and accepted that."[65]

Although there were efforts to try to tie the disbandment of the WTO to the disbandment of NATO this was eventually dropped. In July 1990 General Geli Batenin, an adviser to the CPSU Central Committee, said that "the USSR would regard NATO as a partner"[66] and in the same month the Soviet Union established formal diplomatic relations with NATO.

During this period there continued to be intense criticism from conservatives about the loss of Soviet control over Eastern Europe and unhappiness about the potential for the dissolution of the Warsaw Pact. Much of this criticism was aimed at Shevardnadze. As it became more intense and as Gorbachev, evidently cowed by conservatives at the time, failed to defend Shevardnadze, it eventually led to his resignation in December 1990.

In addition, there were conservative efforts to slow the process by obstructing the treaty reducing conventional forces in Europe, the cornerstone of the new European order. Using a technical loophole, military leaders tried to reassign a number of troops and weapons to the navy so as to remove them from the purview of the treaty.

However, ultimately all these efforts failed. In February 1991 it was announced that on April 1 the military structures of the WTO would be dissolved and on July 1, 1991, at a quiet ceremony in Prague, the Warsaw Pact officially disbanded. After the ceremony Czech President Vaclav Havel noted the irony of its occurring in Prague, the scene of the 1968 intervention, saying, "Prague, once the victim of the Warsaw Pact, is the city where the Warsaw Pact is meeting its end as an instrument of the cold war."[67]

However, even as the Warsaw Pact was folding, some members of the Soviet elite still hoped to exert some control over East European countries. In June 1991 a document drawn up in the Information Department of the

CPSU Central Committee was leaked to the German press. It described the goal of imposing certain limits on Eastern European countries. It was quoted in the German newspaper *Frankfurter Allgemaine* as follows:

> It is very important that these [East European] states pursue a policy of friendship towards us, that they not be a source of anti-Sovietism....Under no circumstances can there be a real or potential threat to the military security of the USSR emanating from the East European region. No matter how events of the region unfold, they must remain free of foreign military bases and armed forces....It is necessary to act against the accession of our former allies to other military blocs and groups, especially NATO.

Differentiating this position from traditional Soviet hegemonism the document continues:

> This type of policy requires firmness in defending Soviet interests with a renunciation of attempts to dominate and with an understanding of the essential difference between interference, which we reject, and the use of legitimate levers of influence.

These "legitimate levers" are then explicitly described as being the Soviets control over the flow of oil and gas to the Eastern European countries.

It is difficult to assess the influence of this kind of thinking. The document was written in a plaintive tone, as if the authors clearly felt that the Soviet government, heretofore, had not been acting on such ideas. Reportedly, during this period the Soviet government apparently did try to get the Eastern European countries to agree not to join alliances in which the Soviet Union is not represented.[68] Since the failed coup though, there have been no fresh indications of such Soviet efforts, the Soviet Union has not tried to employ its "levers" and, most significantly, the several Eastern European countries have felt free to apply to join NATO and have suffered no untoward consequences.

The Common European Home

In new thinking, even more fundamental than the concept of the illegitimacy of Soviet hegemony over Eastern Europe has been the concept of the "common European home." This concept has challenged the entire bipolar ideological structure of the European continent. Consistent with the new-thinking emphasis on the unity underlying the appearance of fragmentation, the concept of a common European home stresses that amicability and cooperation, devoid of ideological considerations, are the most natural and appropriate state for European relations.

In his book *Perestroika* Gorbachev described in some detail how he arrived at the concept of the common European home:

> Having conditioned myself for a new political outlook, I could no longer accept in the old way the multicolored, patchwork-quilt-like political map of Europe....I felt with growing acuteness the artificiality and temporariness of the bloc-to-bloc confrontation and the archaic nature of the "iron curtain." That was probably how the idea of a common European home came to my mind, and at the right moment this expression sprang from my tongue by itself. Then it came to have a life of its own, so to speak and appeared in the press.

This insight, he explained, was derived from "pondering on the common roots of such a multi-form but essentially common European civilization." Elaborating this theme, he wrote.

> Europe "from the Atlantic to the Urals" is a cultural-historical entity united by the common heritage of the Renaissance and the Enlightenment, of the great philosophical and social teachings of the nineteenth and twentieth centuries. These are powerful magnets which help policy-makers in their search for ways to mutual understanding and cooperation at the level of interstate relations. A tremendous potential for a policy of peace and neighborliness is inherent in the European cultural heritage. [69]

A political analyst we interviewed explained that with the idea of the common European home Gorbachev's aim was to elicit in people the feeling of an "all-European identity."

Gorbachev has also tried to elicit a feeling of the unity of Europe and to emphasize that it can be achieved through peaceful means. Speaking in the German Democratic Republic in 1989 he read from the poet Fedor Tyutchev the following verse:

> The oracle of our times has proclaimed unity,
> Which can be forged only with iron and blood,
> But we will try to forge it with love,
> Then we will see which is more lasting.

and then explained: "The lyrical poet Tyutchev expresses by the word love everything that we, at the close of the 20th Century, put into the notions of concord, cooperation, interaction, and human relations as applied to Europe." [70]

Counterbalancing this idealism Gorbachev also brought in a more sobering note implying that a failure to cooperate raised the specter of nuclear war. He wrote that only through such cooperation can Europeans "save their home, [and] protect it against conflagration and other calamities,...The concept of a 'common European home'...combines *necessity with opportunity.* "[71]

Gorbachev did not go very far in defining the form for such cooperation but he did emphasize that he was not simply talking about vague diplomatic niceties but rather a concrete normative structure. At times Gorbachev described such a structure in more informal terms as "sensible norms of coexistence."[72] At other times he stressed the need for a clear legal structure: "We are convinced that a reliable, law-based foundation must underlie the common European process. We think of the common European home as a law-based community...."[73]

As with the notion of nonintervention, the idea of a common European home pointed logically to a series of steps that Gorbachev and others might not have originally fully comprehended. For example, if there was indeed the potential for such security cooperation within Europe and the underlying conditions for such amicable relations truly obtained, it was not clear why the Warsaw Pact needed to array such enormous and preponderant forces against NATO. This implication was not lost on some Soviets. In 1988 some Soviets began to call for the Soviet Union to make some unilateral reductions in Soviet forces in Europe. Vitali Zhurkin commented at the time:

> I think that one should think more daringly about more decisive initiatives in this sphere. For example, Europe is particularly concerned with our side's vast superiority in tanks. This is but one of the imbalances which exist in Europe. Why can't we give some thought and then take some decisive measures and unilaterally begin eliminating some of these imbalances? Can we not take some courageous steps in the sphere of certain reductions, say in the number of armed forces we have abroad? What I am leading to is this: Within the style of the new thinking, it appears there is a need to think in terms of new, radical initiatives which would capture the imagination of the people and the world public, as well as the political circles of other countries.[74]

Conservative figures, especially in the military, though, insisted that all such reductions should be made on a bilateral and equal basis.

We were able to raise this subject in interviews we carried out in Moscow in October 1988. It was clearly a very emotional subject. Some Soviets we spoke with clearly favored such a unilateral cut, emphasizing how Soviet forces in Europe were oversized. Others, though, would respond to the idea with a stony face or show some offense at the implication that the Soviet Union might need to show its good faith by taking the first step. A widely recurring response was a faint sneer and the comment "you know, it takes two to tango."

For many, the question elicited conflict. For example, a prominent political analyst agreed that the Soviet Union, because of the disproportionate size of its conventional forces in Europe, could easily make unilateral reductions without jeopardizing its security. He also felt that this would make a serious impact on the Europeans, who would then put pressure on the Americans to be generally more forthcoming with the Soviets. Nevertheless, he rather abruptly expressed opposition to the idea of making unilateral reductions. When we pressed him to explain why, he became quite uncomfortable. Using the analogy of clothing, he said it was very hard for him to imagine taking off his coat when the other side refuses take off their coat. When we asked him why this mattered if he didn't really need his coat, he squirmed and said that he was afraid that this would lead the other side to ask for more and more until he would finally be naked. As he said this his voice became increasingly agitated and he began to protectively clutch his clothing.

Nevertheless, the thinking in favor of unilateral steps did make some real impact on Soviet behavior. Particularly dramatic were the unilateral cuts in Soviet forces announced by Gorbachev in his speech at the United Nations on December 7, 1988. These cuts included 500,000 troops overall, a reduction of 50,000 troops from Eastern Europe, and a total of 10,000 tanks, 8500 artillery systems, and 800 combat aircraft from the region including Eastern Europe and the European part of the USSR. Remaining forces were also to be configured in a more defensive fashion.

Even more significant, the Soviets began to show a remarkable flexibility in the negotiations on reducing conventional forces in Europe. For years they had insisted that the cuts should be equivalent on both sides. This would have left their superior position in place. Now the Soviets not only accepted reductions to equal levels, but they also accepted limits on the numbers of forces that could be held by a single country. Because the Soviet Union contributed such an overwhelming majority of the Warsaw Pact forces, limiting the contribution of a single nation had the net effect of actually reducing Warsaw Pact forces below the level of NATO forces.

Not surprisingly, many Soviets were not enthusiastic about this evolution of the Soviet position. Within the Supreme Soviet conservative delegates openly criticized these developments, in particular pinning the blame on Shevardnadze's policies. (This criticism become so vitriolic, it contributed significantly to his decision to resign.) The military also resisted the final resolution of the treaty negotiations by harping on minor sticking points, so that it was not finally signed until 1991.

Another point of contention that occurred early on was about attempts of Western countries to build relations with members of the Warsaw Pact—something that should be unobjectionable from the point of view of building a common European home. This controversy arose in May 1989 when George Bush made a trip to Poland and Hungary. In response to a question anticipating some Soviet nervousness, Gennadi Gerasimov stated calmly:

> The Soviet Union considers trips by statesmen to be a very positive phenomenon....Contacts favor the construction of the "general European home." Consequently the Soviet side has and can have no objections to President Bush's plans to visit the two East European countries.[75]

Other Soviets, however, were not so sanguine. Manki Ponamarev wrote in *Red Star*:

> There is no doubt that Washington is attempting to drive a wedge between the socialist countries of Eastern Europe and change the correlation of forces on the continent. Bulgaria's *Rabotnichesko Delo* was right when it wrote that G. Bush is 'very likely the first U.S. president to try to question the historical realities in Europe since World War II. [76]

Even some government officials expressed some wariness. Vadim Perfileyev, first deputy chief of the Foreign Ministry's Information Administration has commented:

> Attempts to use the process of forming a government in Poland in order to destabilize the situation in the country and inflict any sort of damage on its alliance obligations, including those regarding the Warsaw Pact and on Soviet-Polish cooperation are not in accordance with the interests of stability in Europe.[77]

A Pan-European Security System

Certainly the most significant idea to evolve from the concept of the common European home has been that of replacing the bipolar alliance system with a pan-European security system. As with all such ideas, there were contributing factors besides the basic orientation of new thinking. Soviet leaders could, most likely, see that once East European countries really believed they were free to make their own political choices, there was a good chance that the Warsaw Pact would begin to come apart. A Pan-European Security System was seen as a means to soften the political blow of such an event by effectively absorbing both alliances into a single system.

In May 1989 the Warsaw Pact officially sent a message to NATO calling for the dissolution of both blocs. On the surface this was not an entirely new idea. It had been a standard Soviet proposal for decades. Soviet commentators even recognized that in the past such proposals were not entirely sincere. Vitali Zhurkin, director of the Institute for European Affairs of the USSR Academy of Sciences has commented: "In the past we frequently proposed eliminating NATO and the WTO...but no one in the West took these appeals seriously, and I believe that there was a certain amount of diplomatic guile on our side."[78] But now, Zhurkin and others emphasized, the Soviet Union was speaking seriously. Deputy Foreign Minister Ivan Aboimov stated:

> We don't regard the existence of the Warsaw Treaty and NATO as permanent factors of the future....Favoring their simultaneous disbandment in the long run, we think this can take place as we proceed on disarmament, confidence-building and the development of cooperation in Europe.[79]

In late 1989, though, as the move to reunify Germany began to pick up steam, the Soviet Union began to back away from talk about disbanding the alliances. Apparently there was some hope that the alliance structure would prevent the reunification of Germany. In December 1989 Vladimir Petrovskiy commented that "before the two blocs can be dismantled, it is possible to imagine that, for an interim period, these two alliances might serve as stabilizing elements in Europe."[80] Gherman Gvintsadze of the Foreign Ministry even said:

> We do not deny the role of NATO as a significant element of the established balance of forces....But we expect that officials in the capitals of NATO countries also come to realize the importance of the Warsaw Treaty Organization for the maintenance of stability and security in Europe.[81]

The dominant theme was that, as a first step, the alliances should be transformed from being primarily military to being primarily political, with the gradual elimination of military structures.

But as it became clear that the Soviets could do little to stop the reunification of Germany and that the Warsaw Pact's days were numbered, there was a renewal of interest in the idea of a Pan-European system that would absorb the alliances. Some Soviets, even Gorbachev, half-joked that the Soviet Union should apply for membership in the North Atlantic Treaty Organization (NATO).

A whole spectrum of concrete ideas was proposed to help make more concrete the notion of a Pan-European security system. Some were relatively tame. A frequently repeated suggestion was to strengthen the Conference on Security and Cooperation in Europe (CSCE), by having regular meetings of foreign ministers or heads of state. Armed Forces Chief of Staff General Mikhail Moiseyev proposed

> establishing a telephone hotline between the command points of NATO's supreme allied commander in Europe and the USSR Armed Forces General Staff and, when necessary, exchange operations groups with those organs for the prompt receipt of information and monitoring each other's military activity.[82]

Shevardnadze suggested that the Soviet Union and other East European countries join the Council of Europe.[83]

A somewhat more ambitious idea was to develop a conflict reduction or prevention center within the CSCE. Here, too, there was a range of ideas. Andrey Kozyrev, then head of the Foreign Ministry Department for International Organizations, commented:

> I see a conflict reduction center as a body in which we can exchange data on a daily basis, for example, on military maneuvers, troop movements, and other things affecting European security. If any party is worried by what is happening, misunderstandings can quickly be sorted out.[84]

Others described the center as one to mediate in conflicts between nations or even between ethnic groups within nations.

But in many cases the aspirations for such a center were considerably more grand. Some saw the center as the foundation for building a real collective security system. In November of 1990, addressing the CSCE summit in Paris, Gorbachev commented:

> I would like to single out the center for conflict prevention—a kind of regulator of the military-political situation. We anticipate a great future for it—its gradual transformation into a kind of pan-European Security Council possessing effective measures to extinguish the sparks of any conflict.[85]

This comment was consistent with earlier comments by Vadim Zagladin, one of Gorbachev's closest advisers on European affairs. Zagladin stated that the Soviet objective in creating a Pan-European Security System was nothing less than a collective security system:

> We aspire to the formation of an all-European system—that is, a system which is not aimed against anyone but serves as an instrument of the joint assurance of security for all its participants. For this reason, it seems to me, either the term 'joint security' or 'all-European collective security' would be more appropriate.[86]

As part of this system, Zagladin explained, it is necessary to have a transnational body with the power to arbitrate as well as mediate conflicts.

> There is a need to have some kind of a pan-European body. That is, a body which would be a permanent connecting link between the countries participating in the pan-European process...which could serve—if the need arose with the United Nations or some other body along with it—as a judge in the event of disputes uprising—of conflicts between nationalities or of a new type—in order to prevent Europe in the future...from returning to the situation of 1913, or 1938 or 1937 when Europe was a powderkeg.[87]

In the interviews we were able to press Soviets to define more fully what they had in mind for such a collective security system in Europe. A Foreign Ministry official specializing in European affairs envisioned an all-European pact that would fix and guarantee borders. He also saw that a governing body would be established with the power to prescribe the levels of reasonable sufficiency for the armed forces of the member states. The governing body would also have executive powers to resolve conflicts that may arise. However, he had not really worked out the problem of how this body would enforce its decisions. When we raised the question of whether this body might have transnational peacekeeping forces at its disposal he became somewhat uneasy and failed to clearly embrace or reject the idea.

A political analyst at one of the think tanks of the Academy of Sciences was considerably bolder. He envisioned a Pan-European Security Council modeled after the UN Security Council. There would be five permanent members (the Soviet Union, the U.S., France, Britain, and Germany) as well as rotating members, and it would be based in Berlin. This Security Council would have extensive powers to regulate troop levels in member states and dictate the terms of disarmament. Most significantly, it would command an all-European armed force that could intervene in internal as well as interstate conflicts. The Council would even have control of all tactical nuclear weapons in Europe. Interestingly, he made these proposals in a low-key, matter-of-fact style, as if he did not regard them as particularly remarkable.

Naturally all these ideas about a Pan-European security system were not universally embraced. Conservative voices have clung to the traditional notion of security as being derived from a bipolar structure. A recurring theme has been that the changes being proposed through arms control negotiations or by the unification of Germany would upset the "balance of forces" in Europe and thereby threaten Soviet security. For example, Prokhanov wrote in January 1990:

> The entire geopolitical structure of Eastern Europe, the building of which cost our country dearly, tumbled down overnight. The balance of European forces has been destroyed, and the consequences are unpredictable. The sentimental theory of "our common European home" has brought about the collapse of Eastern Europe's communist parties, a change in the state structures, and imminent reunification of the two Germanies. By the end of this century, the German industrial giant will tower over Europe— full of energy, inspired by Pan-Germanic ideas, and attracting traditionally German lands into its gravitational field. As the colours and contours of Europe's political map are changing, the bones of Russian infantrymen stir in unknown graves. [88]

This concern for the balance of forces was not, however, limited to conservative voices. As mentioned above, even Shevardnadze expressed such concerns, saying in May 1990 that German membership in NATO "would very concretely affect our security interests, it would mean an acute violation of the balance of power in Europe, it would create for us a dangerous military-strategic situation."[89]

At times there was a failure to recognize the logical tension between the bipolar notion of the balance of power between the alliances and the idea of a Pan-European security system based on the principles of collective security. For example, an official statement of the Foreign Ministry blithely spoke in one sentence about trying to achieve both "the preservation of stability and the balance of forces which has developed on the continent," and "further development of the general European process, including the creation of new structures of collective security."[90]

Nevertheless, in the interviews there seemed to be some awareness of this conflict. A Foreign Ministry official spontaneously addressed this persisting concern for the balance of forces saying:

> In many respects old thinking is preventing a new analysis of the situation. For example, the concept of the balance of forces, I think is a thing coming

back to us from the past. I don't actually believe that a concept of the balance of forces is something on which we can build a safe future in Europe. It is something belonging to confrontation; to alliances. If we want to do away with alliances, then we have to do away with the balance of forces. It would be a different system. But it is an uncertain system. Until now we have a certainty. Not a productive certainty but a certainty although a dangerous certainty....We are living the old ways but we haven't yet assumed the new ones. It is a most difficult and uncertain period....We have to apply some measuring sticks by which to measure this process of transition....and up to a certain degree in a certain period, the concept of the balance of forces has to be applied....Because it is a period of transition. You are doing away with armaments. On what basis are you doing away with armaments? Various states belong to various alliances still. Various states have different levels of armaments. You have to compare them. By comparing them you apply this notion of the balance of forces. But perhaps [in the future] we can switch over from the notion of the balance of forces to something new in which—I imagine—we can think in terms of why do we have armed forces at all?

Gradually, though, as the Warsaw Pact has disintegrated, even conservative voices have begun to downplay the bipolar model. For example, Defense Minister Dimitri Yazov, who in July 1990 had strongly objected to the idea of disbanding the Warsaw Pact because NATO was still standing and even growing stronger,[91] in November of 1990 stated sanguinely, "The Warsaw Pact will no longer exist. We are not opposed to NATO," though he did express hope that the alliance structure would be integrated into "a new European security structure."[92]

Finally, the notion of the common European home has been extended beyond security concerns to address an array of normative issues. A recurring theme in Soviet statements is that Europe as a whole should be integrated into a singular normative system. Speaking at the second CSCE conference on the Human Dimension in June 1990, Shevardnadze said: "The optimum design for the human community in today's integral and interdependent world demands the unity of rights and responsibility."[93]

The Soviets have also enthusiastically embraced the idea of a "European legal space." Yuri Deryabin, chief of the USSR Foreign Ministry Security and Cooperation in Europe Department, explained that in the pursuit of such a legal space the European nations should try to "bring about compatibility of legal standards where this is possible. And, finally, the ultimate goal is to achieve single all-European legal norms and standards, that is, the formation of a European legal space...." More than a simple coordination of laws, Deryabin added that in the future these agreed-on norms should "acquire international legal force."[94]

The most prominent function for these proposed shared norms is in the realm of human rights. Soviets have supported the idea of not only establishing universal norms of human rights but also in some way trying to enforce them. Also at the CSCE Human Dimension conference Shevardnadze said:

> I will recall that, speaking to the United Nations, M. S. Gorbachev voiced the Soviet Union's intention to extend its participation in international monitoring mechanisms on human rights. We are prepared to reach a point whereby such bodies not only record violations of rights and freedom of the individual, but also prevent them from occurring.[95]

Closely related to the concern for human rights, the Soviet Union has supported a Swiss proposal for having foreign observers at court trials.[96]

Deryabin has underscored that applying the principles of human rights within the CSCE structure implies some erosion of national sovereignty. In September 1991 he stated, "the CSCE has always proceeded from the fact that the principle of noninterference in internal affairs does not extend to the sphere of human rights." He then proposed that the CSCE develop more intrusive mechanisms for inspecting for human rights abuses, adding that "participants in the all-European process will be deprived of the right to refuse to cooperate with the inspectors in accomplishing their tasks under the pretext that this would amount to interference in internal affairs."[97]

Perhaps most dramatically the Soviets have also embraced the principle of democracy as a universal norm. They signed the Paris Charter of the CSCE, which established democracy as such a norm for the members of the CSCE. Deryabin, commenting on the Charter, said confidently, "Democratic principles have been formulated and all of Europe will have them in common."[98] The Soviets also supported a CSCE initiative by the United States and Britain proposing a declaration establishing the principles of a democratic political system, based on free elections, a multiparty system, and political pluralism.[99]

Finally, Soviets have supported the notion of addressing problems of the environment in a collective fashion. Gorbachev has outlined an ambitious proposal:

> The common European home will need to be an ecologically pure one. Life has taught us bitter lessons. Large-scale ecological problems have long since outstripped national borders. The shaping of a regional system of ecological security is an urgent task. It is perfectly possible that the common European process will move quickest of all in precisely this truly priority sphere. A first step could be the working out of a long-term ecological program. Our proposal to create a center for urgent ecological

aid within the United Nations is well known. Such a center or agency with an early warning and control system is one which Europe desperately needs. One might also think about establishing a common European institute for ecological research and expertise, and, in time, establishing a body with powers to make binding decisions.[100]

Soviet officials have also suggested means of strengthening the CSCE. Deryabin said that the CSCE should no longer be limited by the principle of consensus as it is now. He also said the idea of a CSCE peacekeeping force is "an idea whose time has come," explaining that, "if we reach the common conclusion that the CSCE should be an instrument of stability and security, then it must have such a force at its disposal,"—though he did add that it is still too early to fully implement this idea.

It also appears that the thrust initiated with the concept of the common European home will persevere under the Commonwealth of Independent States. In October 1991 the Soviet Union was invited to join the North Atlantic Cooperation Council—a new body consisting of the members of NATO and the nations of Eastern Europe. The first meeting of the Council was held shortly after the dissolution of the Soviet Union and the institution of the Commonwealth of Independent States in December 1991. Yeltsin sent to the conference a representative for the Commonwealth and had him read a statement.

The most striking element in Yeltsin's statement was a proposal for Russia to join NATO. In a press conference held shortly after the statement Independent States, Yeltsin elaborated on this proposal. He said that, "the general command of our community must in the longterm probably merge with NATO and form the unified forces of Europe." But he was also quick to add that "this is a long-term prospect," more than five to seven years in the future when there are no nuclear weapons.[101]

Overall, Yeltsin's statement to the North Atlantic Cooperation Council echoed many of the themes of the idea of a common European home. He spoke of "a new system of security from Vancouver to Vladivostok" and of "forming a reliable collective security system in Europe with the participation of the members of the Commonwealth of Independent States, as well as the United States and Canada." He said that "relations can be based on joint recognition of common values and single vision of ways of ensuring international security." [102]

8

Universalism, New Thinking, and the New World Order

Although many Soviets portray new thinking as having sprung *sui generis* from the brows of the Soviet elite, new thinking is actually the most recent development in a line of thought, often described as "universalism," that goes back at least as far as the aftermath of World War I. This line of thought, originally associated with Woodrow Wilson, asserts that modern weapons technology has grown so destructive that it is no longer viable for nations to resolve their disputes through war. Thus it is necessary for nations to enter into a normative system that regulates their behavior and to establish an international institutional system for peacefully resolving conflicts.

Although this line of thought now has a great deal of currency, it was not universally accepted at the time of its proposal. Even in the United States in the pre-World War I period there had been a strong tradition that glorified military conquest and happily embraced the notion of, and even the term, imperialism. Support for the notion of a collective security system was so lukewarm that, even after the formation of the League of Nations had been spearheaded by President Wilson, the United States Senate refused to ratify U.S. membership. More dramatically, during the decades between the wars, Germany, Japan, and Italy embraced highly militaristic ideologies that extolled the value of war and derided the concept of trying to resolve disputes through international institutions.

The Soviet ideology that was established by Lenin in 1917 also embraced military violence as a legitimate instrument of policy and an essential feature of socioeconomic evolution. Efforts to suppress military violence were rejected as intrinsically biased in favor of the status quo and therefore inconsistent with the revolutionary Soviet ideology.

Accordingly, the Soviet Union was initially very suspicious of international institutions. It avoided involvement with the League of Nations for many years after the League's founding in 1920. Typical of the Soviet attitude to the League is the following communique, issued by the Soviet Narkomindel, the Commissariat for Foreign Relations: "The Soviet Government is still convinced that this allegedly international body really serves as a mere mask, designed to deceive the broad masses, for the aggressive aims of the imperialist policy of certain Great Powers or their vassals.[1]

However, already in the 1930s the Soviet Union began to feel some pressure to at least superficially adapt to the prevailing world system. Stalin apparently came to view the League of Nations as a potential brake on the aggressive actions of other states.[2] In 1934, the Soviet Union became a member of the League. Later when Italy invaded Ethiopia the Soviet Union joined with the League, using the prevailing normative language, in denouncing Italy. Apparently, though, this did not reflect a deep-seated change of heart on the part of the Soviets, as in 1939 they invaded Finland on the flimsy pretext of self-defense, thus leading to their expulsion from the League.

Though the League turned out to be ineffective in preventing the outbreak of World War II, the horrors of that war and the specter of the potential for atomic war in the postwar era revitalized the interest of Western countries in establishing a normative international order, thus leading to the institution of the United Nations.

This wave of universalist thinking was particularly prominent in the United States. The destructive potential of a general war was seen as so great that the very concept of war was delegitimated except for defensive purposes (thus the Department of War was renamed the Department of Defense). Ambitious ideas were considered for reordering the world so as to eliminate the potential for war. The notion of world government was viewed seriously and numerous U.S. senators identified themselves as world federalists. Even President Harry Truman said that he carried in his pocket a copy of the portion of Tennyson's poem "Locksley Hall" that predicted a "Parliament of Man, the Federation of the world," Truman explaining "that's what I have been working for."[3] There was a remarkable willingness to consider subordinating national sovereignty to international institutions, most notably in the unsuccessful effort to establish an international body that would control atomic weapons—a notion that would not be seriously considered today.

Though no single spokesman articulated the postwar U.S. universalist position, it was, nonetheless, undergirded by a coherent line of logic that flowed from U.S. values. This logic was founded on the notion that legitimate power was not derived from the ability of a government to forcefully assert its will, but from the will of the governed expressed through democratic process. This principle flowed naturally into the notion of consensually derived international law as the basis for peacefully regulating the international order.

Of course, there was a fly in the soothing ointment of this thinking in that many governments were themselves not democratic or representative of the will of the people. This logically undermined the legitimacy of the international legal process. It also raised the question of whether an order based on international law and the peaceful resolution of disputes might be intrinsically conservative and serve to maintain regimes that were not reflective of the will of the governed.

Such questions were not simply of an academic nature. The Soviet Union, particularly given its behavior in Eastern Europe, was becoming a major case in point. Although Western nations had come out of the war convinced that military force was no longer a viable instrument of policy between states, it appeared that the Soviet Union had learned the opposite lesson. Traumatized by Hitler's invasion, the Soviet Union was determined to establish a buffer zone in Eastern Europe, and thus it kept its occupying armies in place and used the threat of force to install puppet governments in Eastern European capitals.

On the surface the Soviet government joined in the formation of the United Nations and ostensibly embraced Western universalist notions of international cooperation. As many Americans perceived it then, and as we know now from Soviets who were then part of the government, these moves were simply cynical efforts to soften the West. Underneath the Soviets were still deeply steeped in a highly competitive ideology that ultimately sought to overcome the capitalist West largely through superior military capability. Legitimacy for them was derived not from democratic process or international law but from the rightness of their ideological aspirations.

Americans, correctly assessing Soviet attitudes (though perhaps overestimating their willingness to take military risks in the pursuit of their goals), largely pulled back from the heady universalism of the early postwar period. Having rapidly disarmed after the war, they began an intensive period of military expansion, increased the size of their defense budget several fold, and maintained it at high levels for the ensuing decades. Interest in using the United Nations as a means for resolving international conflict dropped off precipitously. Instead, the dominant paradigm for the international order became the military and political containment of the Soviet Union.

The U.S. military buildup based on the model of containment, of course, fit neatly into the Soviet concept of an inevitable conflict between socialism and capitalism. As the Soviets accelerated their own military building, developing atomic and then nuclear weapons much sooner than the United States anticipated, the cold war and its attendant arms race was soon in full bloom.

Not long after Stalin's death in 1953, though, there were already some signs of uncertainty in the Soviet elite about the viability of the confrontation with the West and the Soviet emphasis on military force. These signs arose from an awareness of the destructive potential of nuclear weapons. Georgi Malenkov, then chairman of the Council of Ministers, asserted that a general nuclear war would mean "the destruction of world civilization."[4] This idea was not well received and this apparently played a role in Malenkov's fall from power. Nevertheless, in 1956 Party General Secretary Nikita Khrushchev recognized that nuclear weapons made war so destructive that it required a revision of Marxist-Leninist dogma: A general war with the West, previously viewed as a necessary outcome of the tension between capitalism and socialism, was no longer seen as "fatalistically inevitable."

Khrushchev also began to articulate some of the key features of the condition of mutual vulnerability. In 1960 he explained that in a war between nuclear-armed states even "the state which suffers [an all-out surprise attack]...will always have the possibility to give the proper rebuff to the aggressor." And with more emphasis, he asserted, "Nuclear war is stupid, stupid, stupid! If you reach for the button you reach for suicide." As Khrushchev moved to act on the logical implications of this thinking he tried to reduce the size of the Soviet military, provoking a strong reaction, which, played an important role in his ultimate deposition.

Under Brezhnev the problem of mutual vulnerability was dealt with in a contradictory, almost schizophrenic fashion. On one hand Brezhnev recognized that the consequences of a nuclear war would be so great that it required the Soviet Union to follow a policy of "detente" with the West, to pursue treaties that would limit and even reduce the superpowers' nuclear weapons arsenals, and to strike a generally more cooperative posture in areas of potential confrontation. This new approach reached its zenith in 1972 with the signing of the first Strategic Arms Limitation Treaty (SALT I), which included an Interim Agreement limiting strategic offensive weapons and an open-ended agreement banning antiballistic missiles. This latter agreement was significant because it, in effect, made explicit the condition of mutual vulnerability and committed both sides to refraining from attempts to upset it through defensive systems. Concurrently the superpowers also signed a joint statement on the Basic Principles of Relations between the Soviet Union and the United States. This agreement, a key precursor of the new thinking that would come later, said that the two countries will proceed from the common determination that in the nuclear age there is no alternative to conducting their mutual relations on the basis of peaceful coexistence. Differences in ideology and in the social systems of the USA and the USSR are not obstacles to the bilateral development of normal relations based on the principles of sovereignty, equality, non-interference in internal affairs and mutual advantage.

...The USA and the USSR attach major importance to preventing the development of situations capable of causing a dangerous exacerbation of their relations. Therefore, they will do their utmost to avoid military confrontations and to prevent the outbreak of nuclear war. They will always exercise restraint in their mutual relations, and will be prepared to negotiate and settle differences by peaceful means. Discussions and negotiations on outstanding issues will be conducted in a spirit of reciprocity, mutual accommodation and mutual benefit.

Both sides recognize that efforts to obtain unilateral advantage at the expense of the other, directly or indirectly, are inconsistent with these objectives. The prerequisites for maintaining and strengthening peaceful relations between the USA and the USSR are the recognition of the security interests of the Parties based on the principle of equality and the renunciation of the use of threat of force....

The USA and the USSR regard as the ultimate objective of their efforts the achievement of general and complete disarmament and the establishment of an effective system of international security in accordance with the purposes and principles of the United Nations.

But on the other hand, under Brezhnev, many traditional Leninist positions apparently at odds with the principles of detente were, at the same time, sustained. Although Brezhnev had ostensibly accepted the need for a new approach to international relations in light of the condition of mutual vulnerability, this attitude was simply grafted onto the body of traditional Leninist thought in a piecemeal fashion; it did not really alter the underlying foundation. In response to questions about whether detente signified a departure from the Leninist path, Brezhnev reassured the faithful that he was simply pursuing Lenin's method of peaceful coexistence, which would mollify the West while giving socialist forces a chance to build their strength. He explained that detente "creates favorable conditions for the struggle between the two systems and for altering the correlation of forces in favor of Socialism."[5] Equally disturbing to Americans, under Brezhnev, military writers continued to write about the possibility of winning a nuclear war with the West. But most disturbing of all, the Soviet Union continued to pursue a competitive foreign policy, supporting socialist factions in the Third World, expanding the conventional capabilities of its army, dramatically increasing the size of its nuclear arsenal, and ultimately invading Afghanistan.

These developments dashed U.S. hopes about the potential for detente and left many Americans with the impression that the entire effort had been little more than a charade to put the West off its proper guard, while underneath the Soviets had not really changed. This impression, though, was mistaken. The insights that led Soviets to seek out detente were very real. The problem was that many of these insights contradicted key principles of Leninism. Because Soviets were not ready to directly challenge Lenin, these new perspectives existed side-by-side with traditional Leninist thought.

A prime example of this contradictory thinking could be found in military writings about the potential for victory in a nuclear war. Military writers would frequently recognize that a nuclear war would be devastating to all parties, irrespective of who attacked first. But at other moments they would assert that in the event of a nuclear war the Soviet Union would indeed be victorious. On closer analysis it appears that the belief in victory was sustained, at least in part, because it was seen as essential to the Leninist framework. According to this framework, socialism, by its nature as a superior form of social organization, must necessarily prevail over capitalism. Then Chief of Staff Marshall Nikolai Ogarkov asserted in the Soviet Military Encyclopedia that "the advanced character of its social and state structure...creates for [the Socialists] the objective possibilities for victory."[6] The notion that victory was impossible in such a war was rejected by other military writers, not on the basis of a military argument but because such a belief would weaken "class and defensive vigilance"[7] and because the proper Marxist-Leninist view is not "one of futility and pessimism."[8]

With time, though, it became more and more difficult to maintain this contradictory position; it was politically problematic because Westerners were alarmed by the claim that victory was possible and it was psychologically problematic because it is stressful to maintain such inconsistencies. In a key speech in Tula in 1977 Brezhnev, as part of his denunciation of nuclear superiority, declared the impossibility of winning a nuclear war. There was still some slight ambiguity, though, in that he specifically said that the imperialists could not hope to achieve victory, leaving open the possibility that the socialists might achieve it. However, at the Twenty-sixth Party Congress in February 1981, he dispelled any uncertainty, declaring categorically that "to expect victory in nuclear war is dangerous insanity."[9] For a few more years the notion of such a victory still persisted in the military press, but by the mid-1980s it finally had disappeared from the Soviet discourse.

The recognition of the inability to win a nuclear war was not the only anomaly to contradict the prevailing Leninist paradigm. As was discussed earlier, the failure of the insular Soviet economy to compete with the West, the unsatisfactory results of Soviet support to socialist factions in the Third World, and the debacle in Afghanistan all contributed to a growing sense that the radiant future promised for decades was not obtaining.

But it was primarily the reality of mutual vulnerability and the consequent nonutility of military force for resolving disputes between the world systems that ultimately led Gorbachev to incorporate many of the key principles of universalist thinking into his new thinking. Initially this did not seem so radically new because past Soviet leaders had also ostensibly embraced these principles. What was different was that Gorbachev embraced such principles not merely politically but intellectually as well. He was ready to genuinely accept the new premises and then follow them through to their logical consequences.

It is now clear that Gorbachev did not originally expect that the consequences of embracing these principles would be as dramatic as they turned out to be. He seemed to think that there was a way to sustain Soviet hegemony over Eastern Europe and especially to keep East and West Germany divided. He also did not anticipate the ultimate fragmentation of the Soviet Union.

But universalist thought says that political orders that are held in place by military force are both morally illegitimate and politically unstable. Ultimately the popular will seeks to assert itself, thus leading to violent confrontations. Such violence has the potential to escalate to dangerous proportions. Thus, the only viable political form rests on the will of the governed. Once Gorbachev genuinely accepted these principles it was only a matter of time before the will of the governed did assert itself in Eastern Europe and in the Soviet republics.

What was particularly remarkable was that once this new framework of legitimacy was established it was largely irreversible. From the beginning Gorbachev had the military capability to prevent any of these changes, just as previous Soviet leaders had. But once this kind of intervention was delegitimated in Soviet society it would have been very difficult for Gorbachev to use such force, or the threat of it, even if he had wanted to.

This was vividly demonstrated by the failure of the August 1991 coup leaders, who stepped in with the apparent intention of using the threat of force to prevent the fragmentation of the Union. The coup leaders were not able to muster an alternative framework to legitimate their efforts. Interestingly, they did not even try to draw on the Leninist framework. Rather they portrayed themselves as following the same line established by Gorbachev—apparently the only viable basis of legitimacy available. But obviously this did not make sense; Gorbachev's framework explicitly denounced just the kind of extralegal and forceful intervention the coup leaders had made. Without a coherent framework of meaning for their efforts, they failed to galvanize the military and the internal security forces to respond to their command, and thus the coup fizzled.

In addition to the changed attitude about military force, universalist thinking also prompted a great interest among Soviets in the United Nations, international law, and the notion of collective security. In a 1987 article Gorbachev in effect announced that the Soviet Union would hitherto look to the United Nations and international law as a critical instrument for creating a comprehensive security system in the world. At a September 27, 1988, speech before the United Nations General Assembly, Shevardnadze proclaimed: "[W]hat we are speaking of now is voluntarily delegating a portion of national rights in the interests of all and, paradoxically enough, in order to strengthen national security while at the same time strengthening universal security.[10]

Then, in his historic speech at the United Nations on December 7, 1988, Gorbachev said that the new thinking

> concept of all-embracing international security is based on the principles of the UN charter, and proceeds from the obligatory nature of international law for all states....Our ideal is a world community of states based on the rule of law, which also make their foreign policy activity subordinate to the law. The attainment of this would be facilitated by an accord within the UN framework on a uniform understanding of the principles and norms of international law, and their codification, taking account the new conditions, and also the formulation of legal norms for new spheres of cooperation.[11]

At the time of this speech, in a meeting with Secretary General Javier Perez de Cuellar, Gorbachev also made the curious but revealing comment that "God is on your side at the United Nations."[12]

Beyond these more general statements there were also proposals for making these principles more concrete. Soviet leaders made a number of efforts to put greater military power at the disposal of the United Nations. In September 1988, the Soviet Union issued UN document A/43/629, which contained a myriad of proposals for expanding the role of UN peacekeeping forces. Closely related was an oft-repeated call for renewing the Military Staff Committee, the moribund military arm of the United Nations staffed by the chiefs of staff of the permanent members of the Security Council. Though it was not entirely clear at the time what Soviet leaders had in mind for the Military Staff Committee, Shevardnadze recently explained in his memoirs that by putting military forces at the disposal of the Security Council it "could act as a full-fledged guarantor of peace in any region."[13] Also the Soviets supported the notion of having a UN naval force police the Persian Gulf during the Iran-Iraq war and later, perhaps most significantly, proposed that a permanent UN naval force police sea lanes around the world.

The Soviets also backed up these proposals with some concrete steps. They began to make substantial payments on their past debts for peacekeeping operations and offered to commit a Soviet armed forces contingent to the UN and to give material support and training to UN forces. They also participated in airlifting UN forces to monitor the Iran-Iraq conflict and the spring 1990 elections in Namibia.

There were also efforts to strengthen the power of the International Court of Justice (ICJ). On several occasions Soviet spokesmen called for nations to agree to the compulsory jurisdiction of the ICJ on a wider number of issues. In March 1989 the Soviet Union said that it would accept such jurisdiction over six human-rights agreements to which it is a signatory. And in October 1989 Shevardnadze and Baker agreed to submit to ICJ jurisdiction seven treaties dealing with terrorism and drug trafficking.[14]

In October 1990 the Soviet Union proposed a UN control authority to monitor the implementation of international agreements. Such an authority, it was proposed, would have the right to carry out on-site inspections, and their findings would be used by the ICJ in the adjudication of disputes regarding the enforcement of such agreements.

Members of the Soviet elite have also made some remarkable comments about the potential for international institutions to intervene into the domestic affairs of states—something of which the Soviet Union has been historically extremely wary in the past. In May 1991 Shevardnadze (after his resignation as foreign minister and before his reappointment), commented: "If I had remained a member of the Soviet government, I would not object to UN involvement in resolving internal conflicts." He then specifically explained that this included the possibility of the UN intervening in the interethnic conflicts in the Soviet Union, adding that what is needed is a new definition of national sovereignty.[15]

Naturally, one might question whether Shevardnadze's attitude reflected that prevailing among the Soviet elite. But a comment made by Deputy Foreign Minister Vladimir Petrovsky the following August follows in the same vein. Petrovsky said, "The principle of noninterference doesn't apply to the cause of protecting human rights and democracy" and that "democracy and observance of human rights in the USSR should have not only national, but also international guarantees."[16]

Given that this was said immediately after the coup failed, it appears that Petrovsky was trying to say that he would have regarded it as appropriate for the UN to intervene in some way to contravene the coup. Deryabin seemed to be making a similar allusion when, in September 1991, he spoke of "providing guarantees for democracy" and then related this concept to "the August events in the USSR."[17] In the same vein in September 1991, shortly before the CSCE human rights conference in Moscow the new Foreign Minister Boris Pankin said:

> The principle of noninterference in internal affairs of other states, which we have always observed and which has sometimes been used here to stall matters so as not to permit democratic changes in our own country, must not be a purpose in itself.... We support the establishment of a system of observers and rapporteurs who can be sent to any country at the proposal of other states.[18]

This does not mean that there are no limits to the Soviet willingness to subordinate its sovereignty to international institutions. As we have observed, there is a strong stream of thinking in the Soviet elite that is very concerned with maintaining Soviet status as a great power. For many interview respondents, this goal seemed to require that the Soviet Union be very protective of its national sovereignty. In the interviews we asked whether the Soviet government would be willing to submit arms control treaty disputes to the ICJ or some other third party. Nearly all respondents asserted that the Soviet government would not (though one high-level Kremlin official affirmed with some emphasis that it would). Also, as we have discussed, nearly all respondents felt that, despite the new-thinking emphasis on the equality of all nations and the democratization of international relations, the Soviet government would not be willing to give up the power of the veto in the Security Council even if other members of the Council were willing to do so. Soviets also expressed no interest in shifting power from the elitist Security Council to the more egalitarian General Assembly.

It is also important to note that these attitudes are likely to persist even if the Soviet Union comes unglued and the Russian republic effectively displaces the Soviet Union in the international sphere. Discussions with officials in the Russian government suggest that it will be equally concerned about its great-power status and symbols of its national sovereignty.

Nevertheless, there are still good reasons to believe that the Soviet Union or Russia will most likely take a leading role in efforts to realize the universalist agenda in the world. First, new thinking is so actively aligned with the universalist agenda that new thinkers tend to think of it as their own. And in the Soviet government, and even more so in the Russian government, universalist new thinking is the dominant orientation.

Second, though the great-power orientation may lead Soviets or Russians to be protective of their national sovereignty and their great-power status, there are also important great-power considerations that would now favor the development of stronger general constraints in the international arena. In the Cold War era the Soviet Union had ambitions that could have been thwarted by such constraints. But now, with domestic political and fiscal limitations being as strong as they are, the Soviet Union has little to lose by accepting a more regulated international environment. More important, without such constraints there is the potential that the United States as the sole superpower will attempt to dominate the world at the Soviet Union's expense. Therefore, in the interest of preventing the United States from totally eclipsing the Soviet Union on the world stage it makes sense for the Soviet Union to champion the cause of a more elaborate and effective web of international constraints.*

The fact that Soviets see some strategic advantage in promoting a strong regime of international law should not be interpreted as meaning that they think they can manipulate it to their ends. There is no reason to believe that they will have any unique advantage in an international legal system based on third party adjudication—rulings are no more likely to be in their favor than for any other country—and by all indications it seems that they recognize this. Their attitude is that they are simply taking a realistic position, that the only alternative to a law-based international system is one based on the distribution of military power, and they regard that as too dangerous and too costly.

---

*Shevardnadze seemed to be addressing this kind of thinking in his memoirs when, explaining the need for military forces to be at the disposal of the UN Security Council, he said: "Today many claim that after the Persian Gulf crisis a Pax Americana or 'American Century' will begin, and from now on the United States exclusively will keep order in the world. If this is undesirable (and it is), then all the more imperative to create the appropriate U.N. mechanisms as rapidly as possible to elevate the role of the U.N. and make it a real center for collective actions." Eduard Shevardnadze, *The Future Belongs to Freedom* (New York: Free Press, 1991) 107.

Raising the West One

As we know, Soviets have historically shown a penchant for comprehensive solutions to big problems and, as we have observed, having accepted a certain set of principles they tend to follow them through to their logical conclusion. Therefore, it is not surprising that now that the Soviets have come back into the Western fold and accepted the notion of a universalist international order, they have not only shown a willingness to match the Western model, but, with characteristic zeal, have also raised the stakes. Soviet new thinkers have proposed certain principles that take the universalist model into realms that the West has not seriously contemplated.

For example, they would like to see an expansion of the compulsory jurisdiction of the ICJ into a wider array of issue areas. Turning the tables on the United States in the realm of human rights, Soviet leaders have, in a number of instances, shown less squeamishness than the United States about the prospect of compromising national sovereignty. To an extent that has befuddled other countries, they express much more readiness than most to put military power at the disposal of the United Nations. They also seem to sincerely support the notion of giving the UN genuine policing powers, for example, supporting the establishment of a UN naval force to protect sea lanes.

On a normative level the Soviet new thinkers have also posed some principles that go further than anything the West has considered. Not only have they embraced the notion that, on a domestic level, legitimacy flows from the will of the largest social whole, they have tried to apply this principle to the international domain as well. They insist that the United Nations is not only a forum for negotiating conflicts, but that solutions derived from the democratic process of international bodies are imbued with a special legitimacy that all nations should honor. This legitimacy does not only flow from such normative principles as fairness but also from a concern for the survival of humanity. According to new thinking, in an interdependent nuclear-armed world it is essential to build consensus. Unless nations agree to a democratically based international process for dealing with disputes, it will only be a matter of time before a conflict will erupt that will escalate to a devastating nuclear exchange.

Consistent with this thinking the Soviet new thinkers support a militarily strong United Nations and have challenged the very notion of the legitimacy of individual nations actively seeking to amass power through the actual or threatened use of military power. From their point of view they, for moral reasons, intentionally relinquished some of their militarily derived power in the world. They now appeal to others to do the same.

Concretely, the Soviet government has called for a general reduction of military power through disarmament and for all nations to withdraw their military forces within their borders by the year 2000.

As we have seen, the sentiments in these high-toned appeals are not shared by all Soviets nor does Soviet behavior entirely conform with the principles prescribed. There are many Soviets who are still highly protective of national sovereignty and are still quite interested in the prospect of expanding the national power of the Soviet Union. And it is easy to identify a number of unilateral steps that the Soviet Union has not taken that would be consistent with the new-thinking principles prescribed, such as further reducing the size of their army, withdrawing their troops and military advisers stationed abroad, reducing their far-flung naval activities, and accepting the compulsory jurisdiction of the ICJ on a wider range of issues.

This does not mean that the Soviets are disingenuous in promoting principles along these lines. If other countries were more willing to take such steps it is hard to say how far the Soviets would be willing to go. As far as I can tell, the Soviets are not entirely sure themselves. As long as they perceive themselves as willing to go further than other countries, they tend not to trouble themselves with the question of their own limits. Nonetheless, it is important for Westerners to have some idea of how far the Soviets are willing to go.

There is the possibility that the great-power orientation will set in and that the Soviet Union will simply behave the same as other countries and be highly protective of their sovereignty. It is also possible that as more power devolves to the republics they will feel an especially strong need, for symbolic reasons alone, to assert their sovereign rights.

On the other hand, the Soviet people have historically demonstrated an imperative need to feel that they are on the cutting edge of the most promising solution to global problems. The changes that have occurred in Soviet foreign policy only became possible when Gorbachev was able to propose changes in the context of a grand ideological vision.*

The ousting of Leninist ideology does not signal an end to the role of ideology in the Soviet Union but rather a renewed demonstration of its power. Though some members of the Soviet elite are influenced by the great-power line of thinking, it is likely that the idealistic streak in Soviet

---

* The difficulty Soviets have in making comparable changes in their economy may well be derived from the fact that their leaders have not been able to present the need for economic changes in an equally coherent and well-elaborated ideological framework.

political culture will persist. Even if the union further fragments, such that the role of the Soviet Union is largely displaced by the Russian republic, it is likely that this trait will persevere and may well even be enhanced. Also, there is no ideology on the horizon that is seriously competing with new thinking, therefore it appears that it will persevere as the dominant value system.

In short, I see no reason to believe that the Soviets (or the Russians) have reached the limit of their willingness to submit to an international regime based on strong international institutions and international law. I would also point out that since Gorbachev came into office, Westerners have consistently underestimated how far the Soviets are willing to go in directions previously foreshadowed by their statements of principle.

Responding to the New Soviet Challenge

The fact that the Soviets have embraced universalism poses a new challenge to the United States. In the years immediately following World War II the United States was the primary champion of the universalist approach to international order. Much of the U.S.A.'s status in the world and self-image at home has rested on the idea that it was ready and willing to enter into a universalist order if only the Soviet Union would give up its messianic ideology and join the world community. The competitive posture of the United States in the world was explained as necessary for the long range goal of ultimately pressing the Soviet Union to behave cooperatively. But now, as the Soviet Union has finally come around, thus putting the ball back into the U.S. court, the United States has responded ambivalently.

This ambivalence has its roots in the period shortly after World War II. Although immediately after the war the dominant stream of thought in U.S. policymaking circles was of a universalist persuasion, there was also a strong stream of thinking, eventually dubbed "realism," that was dubious about the potential for international cooperation based on international law. Similar to the Soviet great-power thinking described above, it viewed the struggle for power as an inevitable feature of international relations. The struggle for influence between the Soviet Union and the United States was seen as a natural state of affairs.

When it became clear to the U.S. policymaking community that the Soviet Union was not genuinely interested in a cooperative world order, this stream of thought gained ascendancy, originally in the formulation of the policy of containment. Since then, realist thinking has continued to have a powerful effect on U.S. policymakers, even while the universalist stream of thought has continued to be prominent in U.S. declaratory policy. But as long as the Soviet Union was perceived as unwilling to enter into a cooperative world order, the tension between these two streams of thought was not an issue.

By the beginning of the Bush administration in 1989, this situation began to change. There was a growing consensus, joined even by former President Ronald Reagan, that the Soviets had indeed moved far enough from their traditionally competitive posture that a new response was required on the part of the United States. But the Bush administration, heavily influenced by realist thinking, was slow to respond. In its first year in office the administration did conduct a review of U.S. policy in light of the changes in the Soviet Union. But the conclusion of the study was that the United States should follow a policy characterized by the oxymoronic term "status quo plus," which essentially implied no significant changes in policy. Administration figures at times even seemed to express nostalgia for the stability and predictability of the cold war period.

It was not until late 1990, when the United States faced the problem of the Iraqi invasion of Kuwait, that the administration rather suddenly began to embrace the newfound possibilities for a universalist order. With Soviet support in the UN Security Council, the United States was able to success-fully lead a coalition of countries against Iraq and to have it almost universally viewed as legitimate. Delighted with this new state of affairs, Bush waxed effusive about how there was now a "new world order."

In the ensuing months Bush elaborated the idea of a new world order, making it clear that what he had in mind was essentially the classical universalist idea. He spoke of "a vision of a new partnership of nations...a partnership based on consultation, cooperation, and collective action."[19] He emphasized that this partnership will not only be a vague commitment but will be governed by "the rule of [international] law, not the law of the jungle,"[20] and that it will be based primarily in the United Nations, which is now "poised to fulfill the historic vision of its founders"[21] and "its promise as the world's parliament of peace."[22]

He implied that this new order will also impose constraints on the powerful. Quoting Winston Churchill, he defined the new world order as one in which "the principles of justice and fair play protect the weak against the strong."[23] Perhaps most dramatically he implied that nations are constrained from using military force without international authority, saying that "a just war must also be declared by legitimate authority," which he specified as the United Nations.

At other moments, though, Bush seemed to backpedal from this univer-salist vision. On April 13, 1991, he virtually contradicted his earlier definition of the new world order as constituting "rules of conduct" saying that it is not "a blueprint that will govern the conduct of nations, or some supranational structure or institution." Rather he injected a much more unilateral character saying, instead, that the new world order "really describes a responsibility imposed by our successes."

He tried to wiggle out of the constraints on the United States implied by the need to look for international consensus by arguing that there is already an emerging consensus based on a set of "shared ideals" that "have received their boldest and clearest expression in our great country, the United States."[24] In other words, the difference between the new world order and the original U.S. efforts to promote its preferred ideals, is simply that a growing portion of the world likes those ideals. The unilateralist element in U.S. thinking was also foreshadowed on February 1, 1991, when, speaking to a military audience, Bush growled that when the war ends Saddam Hussein and the rest of the world will know "that what we say goes."[25]

Equally significant are the many issues that the United States has not addressed. There has been no reevaluation of intervention in Panama, though this was not sanctioned by the UN, as Bush now says is necessary. Despite the newfound enthusiasm for multilateral action, there has been no reconsideration of the U.S. effort to maintain and increase its unilateral power in the world through its global military presence. There has been little thought of expanding the range of issues subject to the compulsory jurisdiction of the ICJ.

Nevertheless, universalist thinking continues to exert a growing influence on U.S. policy. After having gone to the United Nations to sanction the use of force against Iraq (thus setting an important precedent for the future), the United States continues to use the UN to monitor and enforce the terms of the ceasefire. U.S. planes being put at the disposal of UN inspectors have even been repainted with UN flags. The U.S. has agreed to a UN-sponsored mutual cessation of aid to the Afghan factions and is working together with the Soviet Union, in some cases under UN auspices, to resolve conflicts in Cambodia, El Salvador, and the Middle East. Most dramatically, Bush announced that the United States will make substantial unilateral cuts in its nuclear arsenal.

Equally significant, President Bush continues to use universalist language in his speeches. Addressing the United Nations General Assembly on September 23, 1991, he reiterated the notion of a new world order based on "the rule of law," and "the cooperative settlement of disputes," and based largely in the United Nations. To counter charges that the United States is "striving for a Pax Americana" he insisted that "we seek a Pax Universalis, built upon shared responsibilities and aspirations." But even in this speech, realist tones persisted as he insisted that within the new world order "no nation must surrender one iota of its sovereignty"—an idea somewhat at odds with the idea of nations submitting to a system of international law.

In closing I would suggest that the changes in thinking in the Soviet Union and the United States have generated significant prospects for the two countries to more fully realize the universalist ideals that both countries embrace. Naturally, there are many difficulties inherent in the problem of international cooperation and, of course, many prospects rest on the willing participation of other countries as well. But it is hard to overestimate the significance of the convergence of the superpowers around a shared value system. As the image of the contentious Vladimir Lenin fades from the Soviet aura, it is now possible for the Soviet Union and the United States to begin to weave a singular political culture.

Interestingly, this shared political culture includes, on both sides, a strong presence of realist or great-power thinking. This is not inherently problematic. Realism can steer policymakers to consider carefully the national interests of their country, and universalism can guide policymakers to align those interests with a long-term cooperative vision.

Problems can arise, though, when realism becomes not only a concern for national interests but a belief that national interests are so intrinsically polarized that cooperation is all but impossible. Just as Leninism, in a similar way, had narrowed the scope of Soviet policymakers' thinking, it was largely the exaggerated influence of realism that caused Western observers to fail to even consider the possibility of the remarkable events of the last few years. The voluntary Soviet withdrawal from Eastern Europe, the dissolution of the Communist Party by its own general secretary, the Soviet-American solidarity against an erstwhile Soviet ally, and even the substantial unilateral reductions of the U.S., and then Soviet, nuclear arsenals all seemed, within the realist framework, well beyond the range of what is possible.

It is hard to say to what extent this narrowing effect of realism grew from something intrinsic to the U.S. policymaking community and to what extent it was a response to the ideological rigidity of the Soviet Union. Faced with a foe that insisted that conflict and confrontation were inevitable, there was probably a strong pull toward a world view concurring with this pessimistic position. Such a world view likely gave meaning to the conflict and relieved the frustration of daily diplomacy by raising the phenomenon to the philosophical plane of the eternal verities.

But now as Lenin, that seemingly intractable antagonist, appears headed for his earthly burial, and as Soviets slough off the restrictive influence of his thought and change their behavior accordingly, this somber vision may seem less certain. Surely it will continue to be inherently difficult to achieve international cooperation even though there are new forces—the potential for nuclear war, the growing integration of the world economy, the emergence of a global culture—generating greater pressures for its realization. Surely the new world we now encounter carries within it the seeds of problems not yet realized. And even as the Soviets continue their conciliatory posture, there are other nations showing no such signs of reform. But the very fact that such a massive and seemingly stubborn nation as the Soviet Union could go through such a radical and unanticipated change suggests that the universe of possibilities that we now face is greater than we have hitherto assumed.

Appendix

Design of the Study

To study, as a function of Soviet political culture, the changes in Soviet ideology and foreign policy that were initiated with the ascension of Mikhail Gorbachev to the leadership of the Soviet Union, two key sources of materials were analyzed: (1) statements made by members of the foreign-policymaking community as part of the Soviet public discourse and (2) interviews carried out with members of the foreign-policymaking community.

Public Discourse

Materials analyzed include:

- Official statements and speeches made by government officials, especially President and former CPSU General Secretary Mikhail Gorbachev and former Foreign Minister Eduard Shevardnadze;
- Articles, books, and yearbooks written by members of the foreign-policymaking elite including government officials, policy analysts from the various institutes of the Academy of Sciences, and journalists. Articles originally appeared in *Izvestiya, Pravda, Mezhdunarodnya Zhizn* (International Affairs), *Novoye Vremya* (New Times), *Moscow News, Krasnaya Zvezda* (Red Star), *Literaturnaya Gazeta* (Literary Gazette), *Sovetskaya Rossiya, Argumenty I Fakty, Komsomolskaya Pravda*, and others. In most cases articles appeared in translated form in the Foreign Broadcast Information Service: Daily Report, Soviet Union.
- Published transcripts of radio and television transmissions including press conferences of government spokespersons, and discussion programs, interviews, and call-in talk shows with government officials, academics, and journalists. Radio transmissions included programs designed for foreign as well as domestic consumption. These appeared in translated form in the Foreign Broadcast Information Service: Daily Report, Soviet Union.

In examining such material, attention was paid to the formulation of general ideological principles as well as to rationales given for specific foreign policy positions.

Interviews

Respondents

The individuals selected for interviews were part of the Soviet foreign-policymaking community. As is indicated by the listing of their institutional affiliations, these included individuals who are part of the larger intellectual community involved in analyzing foreign policy (academics and journalists) as well as officials in the various branches of the Foreign Ministry, the Defense Ministry, and the Communist Party.

The interviews were carried out over a period from October 1988 through May 1991. In a few cases Soviets were interviewed in the United States, but mostly the interviews occurred in Moscow. In some cases a group of respondents were interviewed together, but in most cases there was a single respondent. Several respondents were interviewed more than once.

This study was carried out as part of a larger research project that included Gloria Duffy and Jennifer Lee as co-researchers. Dr. Duffy and Ms. Lee were participants in approximately half of the interviews.

My institutional host in Moscow on four of the trips was the Institute for World Economy and Foreign Relations (IMEMO) and on one trip the Institute of Social Sciences of the Central Committee of the Communist Party. In each case my hosts arranged interviews, but I also initiated contacts for interviews on my own. Most difficult to access were members of the military, but I did ultimately gain some interviews with them as well.

Procedure

At the beginning of the interview we (or I) explained who we were and the purpose of the study: to better understand new thinking in Soviet foreign policy. We asked for permission to tape record the interview, assuring the respondent that the material would not be for attribution. In every case we were given permission. (My experience shows that this willingness is in marked contrast to previous years when most Soviets would not allow tape recording. It is also different from my experience interviewing American policymakers, 10-15 percent of whom refuse to be tape recorded.)

We would usually begin the interview asking some general questions about the nature of new thinking, why they thought it had emerged, and their attitude about it. In virtually every case respondents ostensibly embraced new thinking even if, in some cases, they criticized some of the policies that seem to flow from it. Whenever we could, we would try to elicit criticism of new thinking.

To the extent respondents embraced specific principles of new thinking, which was nearly always the case, we then began to focus on areas of Soviet foreign policy behavior relevant to these principles. In particular we zeroed in on Soviet behavior that seemed inconsistent with such principles. Our point in doing this was not simply to make them uncomfortable but to see what principles they used to rationalize such behavior. At some moments we had to be a bit aggressive to prevent them from simply evading difficult questions. Once they explicitly or implicitly presented such principles we would try to get respondents to elaborate.

At some point in the interview, if it did not occur spontaneously, we would bring up the subject of Lenin and Marxist-Leninist ideology. We tried get a sense of how they viewed Lenin and how they felt about the discrepancies between Marxism-Leninism and new thinking. Often this produced some resistance, with efforts to try to obscure these discrepancies. Here again, in some cases we had to be a bit pushy, reminding them of things that Lenin said that are quite different from new thinking or simply steering the conversation back to the original question when we got an evasive reply. Overall, we used whatever methods we could to try to flush out any residual Leninist thinking.

In some cases, individuals fully embraced new thinking and accounted for the discrepancies in Soviet behavior in terms of the attitudes of others in Soviet society who were said to be influencing policy. In this case we would ask them to elaborate how they understood these attitudes, who held them, how strong they were, how influential they were, and what were their underlying roots. Often such explanations were quite illuminating.

Naturally, the question arises of whether respondents were genuinely sharing their real thoughts and feelings or if they felt some compulsion to mouth the party line. There were some cases in interviews with officials in the government or in the Central Committee in which it appeared that this may have been occurring. This is not to say that it seemed that they were simply making statements contrary to their beliefs, but that they would avoid talking about subjects that might force them to be too explicit about a criticism they might have had. Such behavior, though, can easily be regarded as endemic to government officials—I have found it to an equal magnitude interviewing U.S. officials.

In the case of respondents who were not officially representing the government it is very hard to conclude that they were mouthing a party line, because there was such a wide range of view expressed. Some respondents almost seemed to take pleasure in saying, with the slightly exaggerated emphasis of a newfound freedom, that they disagreed with Soviet policy. On the whole, I would say that there was even a greater pluralism of views expressed in Moscow than is generally found in Washington, D.C. Respondents were also not shy about disagreeing with their colleagues and superiors. In some cases, when we were interviewing groups of respondents (with their superiors present) the range of opinions expressed was about as great as one could possibly imagine.

The following is a list of interview respondents grouped by institutional affiliation.

Government Officials
Foreign Ministry 17 (3 former)
Defense Ministry 1
Presidential Adviser 1

Washington, D.C., embassy 2
United Nations Mission 2
Supreme Soviet Delegates
    (dealing with defense issues) 4
Arms control treaty negotiators 3 (2 former)
Defense Ministry of the Russian Republic 1
Foreign Ministry of the Russian Republic 2

Military
Flag rank 2
Other officers 8 (2 former)
Editors, Red Star 2
Professors at military academies 4

Central Committee, CPSU
Information Department 3
Institute of Social Sciences 6

Academy of Sciences
Institute of the World Economy and International
                Relations (IMEMO) 27
Institute for the Study of USA and Canada 10
Institute for Europe 2
Institute for Africa 1

Other
Institute for International Relations 3
Journalists 5

Total: 82 (Note: The totals from the above listed categories is greater because some individuals fell into more than one category.)

Notes

Chapter 2

1 . Quoted in Louis Fischer, *The Life of Lenin* (New York: Harper Colophon, 1964), 422.

2 . Ibid., 424.

3 . V.I. Lenin, *Collected Works*, Vol. 33 (London: Foreign Languages Publishing House, 1960), 499-500.

4 . The Communist Party of the Soviet Union, "The Programme of the Communist Party of the Soviet Union," (Moscow: Novosti Press Agency, 1986), 23-24.

5 . Ibid., 7.

6 . TASS report, "19th All-Union CPSU Conference: Foreign Policy and Diplomacy," *Pravda*, July 26, 1988, 4; cited in *FBIS: Soviet Union*, July 26, 1988, 30.

7 . Eduard Shevardnadze, interview by Massimo D'Alema and Sergio Sergi, *L'Unita*, November 28, 1989, 11-13; cited in *FBIS: Soviet Union*, December 4, 1989, 6.

8 . "Striving for Comprehensive Security. Speech by E.A. Shevardnadze, Head of the Soviet Delegation, at 43d UN General Assembly," *Pravda*, September 28, 1988, 4; cited in *FBIS: Soviet Union*, September 28, 1988, 9.

9 . "In a Friendly Atmosphere" *Pravda*, October 19, 1988, 2; cited in *FBIS: Soviet Union*, October 19, 1988, 41.

10 . Mikhail Gorbachev, *Perestroika: New Thinking for Our Country and the World*, (New York: Harper & Row, 1987), 148.

11 . "M.S. Gorbachev's Speech at the UN Organization," *Pravda*, December 8, 1988, 1-2; cited in *FBIS: Soviet Union*, December 8, 1988, 13.

12 . Lenin, *Collected Works* , Vol. 29, 153.

13 . Quoted in Albert L. Weeks and William C. Bodie, *War and Peace: Soviet Russia Speaks* (New York: National Strategy Information Center, 1983), 6.

14 . Gorbachev, *Perestroika*, 147.

15 . Quoted in Prof. Shalva Sanakoyev, "Peaceful Coexistence in the Context of Military-Strategic Parity" *International Affairs*, February 1988, 75.

16 . Gorbachev, *Perestroika* ,146.

17 . Quoted in A. Mikhalyov "USSR-Poland: Toward New Frontiers," *Za Rubezhom*, November 8-24, 1988; cited in *FBIS: Soviet Union* , November 30, 1988, 23.

18 . "An Interview with Gorbachev," *Time*, September 9, 1985.

19 . Mikhail Gorbachev, Speech to the French Parliament, *Moscow News*, 1985,5.

20 . Gorbachev, *Perestroika*, 147.

21 . Mikhail Gorbachev, *"Political Report of the CPSU Central Committee to the 27th Congress of the Communist Party of the Soviet Union,"* (Moscow: Novosti, 1986), 81.

22 . Lenin, *Collected Works* , Vol. 23, 95.

23 . Gorbachev, *Perestroika*, 147-148.

24 . Eduard Shevardnadze, "Foreign Policy and Perestroyka," Oct. 23 speech to plenary session of the USSR Supreme Soviet, *Pravda*, October 24, 1989, 2-4; cited in *FBIS: Soviet Union*, October 24, 1989, 48.

25 . "Gorbachev Addresses Plenum," *Pravda*, July 26, 1991, 1; cited in *FBIS: Soviet Union*, July 26, 1991, 27.

26 . "Gorbachev, Yeltsin: Communism failed," *San Jose Mercury News*, September 6, 1991, A1.

27 . Thomas Kuhn, *The Structure of Scientific Revolutions* (Chicago: University of Chicago Press, 1970).

28 . See Chapter 11 in Steven Kull, *Minds At War: Nuclear Reality and the Inner Conflicts of Defense Policymakers* (New York: Basic Books, 1988).

29 . Anatoli Adamishin, "Humanity's Common Destiny," *International Affairs*, February 1989, 4.

30 . "Bogomolov Argues for Undogmatic Socialism," *Komsomolskaya Pravda*, October 3, 1989, 2; cited in *FBIS: Soviet Union*, November 25, 1989, 95.

31 . "The USSR and the Third World," *International Affairs*, December 1988, 136,144.

32 . Ibid., 145-146.

33 . "'Studio 9' Discusses Perestroyka's World Image," Moscow Television Service, October 28, 1989; cited in *FBIS: Soviet Union*, November 2, 1989, 11.

34 . Valentin Falin, interview by Fritjof Meyer, Rudolf Augstein, and Joerg R. Mettke, *Der Spiegel*, February 19, 1990, 168-172; cited in *FBIS: Soviet Union*, February 22, 1990, 35.

35 . Alexei Kiva, "Developing Countries, Socialism, Capitalism," *International Affairs* , March 1989, 60-61.

36 . Igor Yanin, "Returning to Simple Truths" *International Affairs*, March 1989, 110.

37 . David Remnick, "Lenin's Birthday Less Than Happy," *Washington Post*, April 22, 1991, A11.

38 . Marina Pavlova-Silvanskaya, "Can We Avoid Coming Full Circle?" *Sovetskaya Kultura*, October 1, 1988, 5; cited in *FBIS: Soviet Union*, October 6, 1988, 55.

39 . V.K. Chernyak, "Viewpoint": "We Are in the Same Boat," *Komsomolskaya Pravda*, October 15, 1988, 3; cited in *FBIS: Soviet Union*, October 26, 1988, 5-6.

Chapter 3

1. "M.S. Gorbachev's Speech at the UN Organization," *Pravda*, December 8, 1988, 1,2; cited in *FBIS: Soviet Union*, December 8, 1988, 12.

2. TASS Report: "For the Peaceful, Free and Prosperous Future of Europe and All Other Continents: Meeting With French Parliament," *Pravda*, October 4, 1985, First Edition, 1-2; cited in *FBIS: Soviet Union*, October 4, 1985, G4-G5.

3. Ibid., G5.

4. "Striving for Comprehensive Security. Speech by E.A. Shevardnadze,

Head of the Soviet Delegation, at 43d UN General Assembly Session," *Pravda*, September 28, 1988, 4; cited in *FBIS: Soviet Union*, September 28, 1988, 7.

5. Gorbachev, *Perestroika*, 12.

6. Ibid.

7. Ibid., 146.

8. Vladimir Petrovskiy, "At the USSR Mission's Headquarters in the United Nations," interview by Hisham Milhim, *Al-Qabas*, October 14, 1988, 18; cited in *FBIS: Soviet Union*, October 18, 1988, 19.

9. "Interview with M.S. Gorbachev by DER SPIEGEL Magazine (FRG)," *Pravda*, October 24, 1988, 1-2; cited in *FBIS: Soviet Union*, October 25, 1988, 30.

10. Gorbachev, *Perestroika*, 140

11. "Priority to Political Means," *International Affairs*, August 1989, 61.

12. A.N. Yakovlev, Press Conference at the National Press Club, TASS, November 16, 1989; cited in *FBIS: Soviet Union*, November 17, 1989, 13.

13. Mikhail Kaloshin, "The Global Dimensions of Ecology," *International Affairs*, April 1990, 94.

14. "Shevardnadze Addresses United Nations," *Pravda*, September 27, 1989, 4; cited in *FBIS: Soviet Union*, September 27, 1989, 13.

15. "Text'of speech by President Mikhail Gorbachev at dinner hosted by King Carlos I in Madrid on 26 October," *Pravda*, October 28, 1990, 2; cited in *FBIS: Soviet Union*, October 29, 1990, 19.

16. "Gorbachev Meets 'Survival' Committee," *Pravda*, January 17, 1991, 1; cited in *FBIS: Soviet Union*, January 1, 1991, 27.

17. "Presentation of Indira Ghandi Prize; Speech by M.S. Gorbachev," *Pravda*, November 20, 1988, 2; cited in *FBIS: Soviet Union*, November 21, 1988, 20.

18. "M.S. Gorbachev's Speech at the UN Organization" *Pravda*, December 8, 1988, 1,2; cited in *FBIS: Soviet Union*, December 8, 1988, 13,14.

19. Mikhail Gorbachev, message to Pugwash Conference, TASS, August 29, 1988; cited in *FBIS: Soviet Union*, August 29, 1988, 10.

20. Anatoli Adamishin, "Humanity's Common Destiny," *International Affairs*, February, 1989, 5.

21. TASS report, "Gorbachev Speaks at Dinner," June 1, 1990; cited in *FBIS: Soviet Union*, June 4, 1990, 18.

22. TASS report, "M.S. Gorbachev's Answers to Questions From Representatives of the French Intelligentsia," *Pravda*, July 6, 1989, 2; cited in *FBIS: Soviet Union*, July 10, 1989, 39.

23. "Striving for Comprehensive Security. Speech by Head of the Soviet Delegation, at 43d UN General Assembly Session," *Pravda*, September 28, 1988, 4; cited in *FBIS: Soviet Union*, September 28, 1988, 2.

24. "Priority to Political Means," *International Affairs*, August 1989, 60.

25. Professor Vadim Valentinovich Zagladin, interview by Viktor

Nikolayevich Levin, Moscow Domestic Service Broadcast, June 7, 1990; cited in *FBIS: Soviet Union*, June 8, 1990, 20.

26. TASS report, "Visit Ends," *Pravda*, September 22, 1988, 4; cited in *FBIS: Soviet Union*, September 23, 1988, 36.

27. Eduard Shevardnadze, "Second Renaissance," *Izvestiya*, November 24, 1989, 7; cited in *FBIS: Soviet Union*, November 29, 1989, 47.

28. A.N. Yakovlev, press conference, November 16, 1989, at the National Press Club, TASS, November 16, 1989; cited in *FBIS: Soviet Union*, November 17, 1989, 13.

29. TASS, May 18, 1989; cited in *FBIS: Soviet Union*, May 18, 1989, 17.

30. "International Security and Law," *International Affairs*, April 1989, 93.

31. TASS report, "E.A. Shevardnadze's Speech," *Pravda*, June 9, 1988, 4-5; cited in *FBIS: Soviet Union*, June 9, 1988, 9.

32. "In order to win the struggle against global-scale dangers, it is necessary that [the] universal approach prevail over...egoism." Mikhail Gorbachev, message to Pugwash Conference, TASS, August 29, 1988; cited in *FBIS: Soviet Union*, August 29, 1988, 10.

33. Eduard Shevardnadze, "Foreign Policy and Perestroyka," Speech to Plenary Session of the USSR Supreme Soviet, *Pravda*, October 24, 1989, 2; cited in *FBIS: Soviet Union*, October 24, 1989, 45.

34. *TASS*, September 4, 1990; cited in *FBIS Soviet Union*, September 5, 1990, 4.

35. "The New Thinking Is Not a Doctrine But a Method" *Izvestiya*, July 2, 1989, 4; cited in *FBIS: Soviet Union*, July 28, 1989, 86.

36. E.A. Shevardnadze, press conference March 26, 1990, *TASS*, March 26, 1990; cited in *FBIS: Soviet Union*, March 27, 1990, 28.

37. "International Security and Law," *International Affairs*, April 1989, 93.

38. Aleksandr Yakovlev, "New Political Thinking Is Dictated by Centuries-Old Moral Aspirations," interview by Boyko Vutov, *Rabotnichesko Delo*, September 30, 1989, 1,6; cited in *FBIS: Soviet Union*, October 5, 1989, 77.

39. TASS report, "Text of the Spanish-Soviet Joint Political Declaration," *Pravda*, October 28, 1991, 1; cited in *FBIS: Soviet Union*, October 29, 1990, 24.

40. Anatoliy Karpychev, "'Third Party' in Dialogue Between Presidents," *Pravda*, August 10, 1991, 6; cited in *FBIS: Soviet Union*, August 15, 1991, 6.

41. Eduard Shevardnadze, speech at the "International Open Skies Conference" in Ottawa, February 12, 1990, TASS, February 12, 1990; cited in *FBIS: Soviet Union*, February 13, 1990, 1.

42. Mikhail Gorbachev, "The Socialist Idea and Revolutionary Perestroyka," *Pravda*, November 26, 1989, 1-3; cited in *FBIS: Soviet Union*, November 27, 1989, 75.

43. Mikhail Gorbachev, "The Socialist Idea and Revolutionary Perestroyka,"

Pravda, November 26, 1989, 1-3; cited in *FBIS: Soviet Union,* November 27, 1989, 75.

44. Gorbachev, *Perestroika,* 148

45. Eduard Shevardnadze, interview by Massimo D'Alema and Sergio Sergi, *L'Unita,* November 28, 1989, 11-13; cited in *FBIS: Soviet Union,* December 4, 1989, 4.

46. "Top Priority" radio broadcast, July 15, 1988; cited in *FBIS: Soviet Union,* July 19, 1988, 4.

47. A. Maslennikov, "Another Stage Completed. Thoughts Following the Visit," *Pravda,* June 3, 1988, 5; cited in *FBIS: Soviet Union,* June 6, 1988, 19.

48. Eduard Shevardnadze, speech at the "International Open Skies Conference" in Ottawa, February 12, 1990, TASS, February 12, 1990; cited in *FBIS: Soviet Union,* February 13, 1990, 3.

49. Victor Kremenyuk, "International Negotiations Need a Scientific Approach" *International Affairs,* June 1989, 101-102.

50. Gorbachev, *Perestroika,* 142.

51. TASS report, "Poland: On Principles of Equality," *Sovetskaya Rossiya,* August 20, 1989, 5; cited in *FBIS: Soviet Union,* August 21, 1989, 34.

52. "Studio 9," Moscow Television Service, October 15, 1988; cited in *FBIS: Soviet Union,* October 18, 1988, 89.

53. Mikhail Gorbachev, interview by Pravda editorial board, TASS, January 16, 1989; cited in *FBIS: Soviet Union,* January 17, 1989, 2.

54. "Time for Action, Time for Practical Work. M.S. Gorbachev's Speech in Krasnoyarsk," *Pravda,* September 18, 1988, 1-3; cited in *FBIS: Soviet Union,* September 20, 1988, 37.

55. Mikhail Gorbachev, "The Reality and Guarantees of a Secure World," *Pravda,* September 17, 1987, 1-2; cited in *FBIS: Soviet Union,* September 17, 1987, 25.

56. Mikhail Gorbachev, *"Political Report of the CPSU Central Committee to the 27th Congress of the Communist Party of the Soviet Union"* (Moscow: Novosti, 1986), 81.

57. S. Akhromeyev, "Our Military Doctrine," *Za Rubezhom,* November 10-16, 1989, 1-3; cited in *FBIS: Soviet Union,* December 5, 1989, 115.

58. "M.S. Gorbachev's Speech at the UN Organization," *Pravda,* December 8, 1988, 1,2; cited in *FBIS: Soviet Union,* December 8, 1988, 12.

59. "M.S. Gorbachev's Speech at the UN Organization," *Pravda,* December 8, 1988, 1,2; cited in *FBIS: Soviet Union,* December 8, 1988, 13.

60. "Speech by A.N. Yakovlev," *Pravda,* January 7, 1989, 4; cited in *FBIS: Soviet Union,* January 9, 1989, 47.

61. "Petrovskiy Discusses 'New Internationalism,' UN," *Za Rubezhom,* September 21, 1990, 9; cited in *FBIS: Soviet Union,* October 3, 1990, 12.

62. Quoted in Stanley Kober, "Idealpolitik," *Foreign Policy*, Summer 1990, no. 79, 17.

63. Quoted in Zbigniew Brzezinski, " Selective Global Commitment ," *Foreign Affairs*, Fall 1991, 5.

64. AFP, December 1, 1989; cited in *FBIS: Soviet Union*, December 1, 1989, 13-14.

65. TASS, March 28, 1989; cited in *FBIS: Soviet Union*, March 29, 1989, 3.

66. Georgi Shakhnazarov, "Governability of the World," *International Affairs*, March 1988, 16-24.

67. Eduard Shevardnadze, "Foreign Policy and Perestroyka," speech to Plenary Session of the USSR Supreme Soviet, *Pravda*, October 24, 1989, 2; cited in *FBIS: Soviet Union*, October 24, 1989, 45.

68. TASS correspondent Mikhail Kochetkov, TASS, October 7, 1989; cited in *FBIS: Soviet Union*, October 11, 1989, 6.

69. TASS correspondent Mikhail Kochetkov, TASS, October 7, 1989; cited in *FBIS: Soviet Union*, October 11, 1989, 5, 6.

70. E. Shevardnadze speech before the 45th U.N. General Assembly session, TASS, September 25, 1990; cited in *FBIS: Soviet Union*, September 26, 1990, 7.

71. Vyacheslav Dashichev, interview by Elfie Siegl, *Frankfurter Rundschau*, February 8, 1990, 6; cited in *FBIS: Soviet Union*, March 8, 1990, 6.

72. Andrei Kolosovsky, "Risk Zones in the Third World," *International Affairs*, August 1989, 42, 41.

73. "Conversation between F.M. Burlatsky, chairman of the Public Commission for Humanitarian Cooperation and Human Rights of the Soviet Committee for European Security and Cooperation, and Deputy Foreign Minister A.A. Adamishin," *Literaturnaya Gazeta*, January 25, 1989, 2, 14; cited in *FBIS: Soviet Union*, January 27, 1989, 11.

74. "Speaking Out Before the 28th CPSU Congress," *Pravda*, June 29, 1990, Second Edition, 2; cited in *FBIS: Soviet Union*, June 29, 1990, 40.

75. Vyacheslav Dashichev, "Socialist Concept of Power Through the People Has Been Neglected in the GDR," interview by Peter Henker, *Frankfurter Rundschau*, October 16, 1989, 2; cited in *FBIS: Soviet Union*, October 18, 1989, 90.

76. A.N. Yakovlev, "Speaking Before the 28th CPSU Congress: Finding the Strength and Courage for Real Renewal," interview by *Pravda*, June 23, 1990, 5; cited in *FBIS: Soviet Union*, June 25, 1990, 41.

77. "Speech by USSR President Gorbachev at a Meeting with Representatives of U.S. Intelligentsia in Washington on May 31," Moscow Television Service, June 1, 1990; cited in *FBIS: Soviet Union*, June 4, 1990, 17; "Speech by USSR President Gorbachev at a dinner given in his honor by U.S. President George Bush in Washington on May 31," TASS, June 1, 1990; cited in *FBIS: Soviet Union*, June 4, 1990, 19.

78. Alexander Tsipko, "Sources of Stalinism: Separating the Myth from the Reality," *Moscow News Weekly*, No. 16, April 23-30, 1989, 8-9.

79. "Openness in Politics," *International Affairs*, August 1989, 119.

80. G.I. Yanayev, "To Take A Broad, Unblinkered View of the World," interview by G. Vasilyev, *Pravda*, August 13, 1990, 1,5; cited in *FBIS: Soviet Union*, August 15, 1990, 6.

81. Igor Malashenko, "Non-Military Aspects of Security," *International Affairs*, January 1989, 40.

82. "PERESTROIKA, the 19th Party Conference and Foreign Policy," *International Affairs*, July 1988, 6.

83. Anatoli Adamishin, "Doomed to Discord," *New Times*, March 28-April 3, 1989, 8-10.

84. Eduard Shevardnadze, "Foreign Policy Begins at Home," interview by Galina Sidorova, *Novoye Vremya*, No. 28, July 7, 1989, 8-10; cited in *FBIS: Soviet Union*, August 3, 1989, 46.

85. "From Balance of Forces to Balance of Interests," account of Literaturnaya Gazeta Press Club session, *Literaturnaya Gazeta*, June 29, 1988, 14; cited in *FBIS: Soviet Union*, June 30, 1988, 4.

86. Alexei Izyumov and Andrei Kortunov, "The Soviet Union in the Changing World," *International Affairs*, August 1988, 51, 54-55.

87. TASS report, "The Intellectual Charge of Restructuring. M. S. Gorbachev's Meeting with Cultural Figures and Scientists from the Polish People's Republic and the USSR," *Pravda*, July 15, 1988, 2, 3; cited in *FBIS: Soviet Union*, July 15, 1988, 38.

88. Mikhail Gorbachev, "The Socialist Idea and Revolutionary Perestroyka," *Pravda*, November 26, 1989, 1-3; cited in *FBIS: Soviet Union*, November 27, 1989, 74.

89. Andrei Kozyrev, "A New Lease on Life," *New Times*, September 19-26, 1989, 8.

90. "Interview with Colonel General N. Shlyaga, chief of the Soviet Army and Navy Main Political Directorate, by A. Gorokhov and V. Izgarshev: 'Does a Present-Day Chapeyev Need a Present-Day Furmanov?'" *Pravda*, September 30, 1990, Second Edition, 3; cited in *FBIS: Soviet Union*, October 3, 1990, 58.

91. Leonid Radzikhovsky, "An Economy of Sacred Cows," *Moscow News*, No. 23, June 11-18, 1989, 12.

92. TASS report, "The Intellectual Charge of Restructuring. M.S. Gorbachev's Meeting With Cultural Figures and Scientists From the Polish People's Republic and the USSR," *Pravda*, July 15, 1988, 2, 3; cited in *FBIS: Soviet*

Union, July 15, 1988, 39.

93. Len Karpinsky, "His Beard Must Be Cut Off," *Moscow News*, No. 41, October 15-22, 1989, 3.

Chapter 4

1. Gorbachev, *Perestroika*, 50.

2. "Vremya" newscast, Moscow Television Service, March 1989; cited in *FBIS: Soviet Union*, March 21, 1989, 29-30.

3. "The Cause of Perestroyka Needs the Energy of the Young: M.S. Gorbachev's Speech at the All-Union Student Forum 15, November 1989," *Pravda*, November 16, 1-3; cited in *FBIS: Soviet Union*, November 16, 1989, 65.

4. Gorbachev, *Perestroika*, 25-26.

5. Ibid., 145.

6. TASS report, "The Intellectual Charge of Restructuring. M.S. Gorbachev's Meeting with Cultural Figures and Scientists from the Polish People's Republic and the USSR," *Pravda*, July 15, 1988, 2-3; cited in *FBIS: Soviet Union*, July 15, 1988, 38-39.

7. Eduard Shevardnadze, "Wars Are Losing Ground—Restructuring and Diplomacy—Shevardnadze on Troop Withdrawal," interview by Ferenc Varnai, *Magyarorszag*, November 4, 1988, 4-5; cited in *FBIS: Soviet Union*, November 28, 1988, 7.

8. Gorbachev, *Perestroika*, 25.

9. Quoted in A. Mikhaylov, "USSR-Poland: Toward New Frontiers," *Za Rubezhom*, November 8-24, 1988; cited in *FBIS: Soviet Union*, November 30, 1988, 23.

10. David Remnick, "'I Cannot Go Against My Father,'" *Washington Post*, National Weekly Edition, December 17-23, 25.

11. Mikhail Gorbachev, *The August Coup* (New York: Harper, Collins, 1991), 47-48.

12. Serge Schmemann, "A Russian is Swept Aside By Forces He Unleashed," *New York Times*, December 15, 1991, A23.

13. Akhmed Iskenderov, "Leninism and the National Liberation Movement," *International Affairs*, November 1987, 75.

14. TASS report, "International Seminar," *Pravda*, September 30, 1989, 5; cited in *FBIS: Soviet Union*, October 6, 1989, 4.

15. "International Observer's Roundtable," Moscow Radio broadcast, November 12, 1989; cited in *FBIS: Soviet Union*, November 14, 1989, 3.

16. *Pravda*, April 22, 1989, 1-3; cited in *FBIS: Soviet Union*, April 24, 1989, 48-49.

17. Yuri Krasin, "International Security and the Social Renewal of the World," in *International Security and World Politics* (Moscow: Nauka Publishers, 1988), 50-57.

18. Interviewed in N. Zhelnerova, "Socialism Has a Colossal Resource and It Cannot Be Improved by Capitalism," *Argumenty I Fakty*, October 21-27, 1989, 1-3; cited in *FBIS: Soviet Union*, October 25, 1989, 65.

19. Ye. K. Ligachev, speech, *Pravda*, August 6, 1988, 2; cited in *FBIS: Soviet Union*, August 8, 1988, 39.

20. Quoted in Bill Keller "Amid Rising Alarm, Gorbachev Urges a Purge of Party," *New York Times*, July 22, 1989, A4.

21. Army General V. Lobov, "Deputy's Opinion," *Sovetskaya Rossiya*, October 18, 1989, 2; cited in *FBIS: Soviet Union*, October 19, 1989, 101-102.

22. R.S. Bobovikov, speech at 25 April CPSU Central Committee Plenum in Moscow, *Pravda*, April 27, 1989, 3; cited in *FBIS: Soviet Union*, April 28, 1989, 35.

23. V. Dashkevich, "Careful! Paid for in Blood...About the Film `Pain' and Not Just About It," *Krasnaya Zvezda*, October 21, 1988, 2; cited in *FBIS: Soviet Union*, November 8, 1988, 23-24

24. Aleksandr Prokhanov, "Defense Consciousness and New Thinking," *Literaturnaya Rossiya*, May 6, 1988, 4-5; cited in *FBIS: Soviet Union*, June 9, 1988, 74-75.

25. General D.T. Yazov, "On the Basis of the New Thinking," *Krasnaya Zvezda*, April 13, 1989, 1-2; cited in *FBIS: Soviet Union*, April 13, 1989, 5.

26. A. Oliynik, "Society Must Display Concern," *Krasnaya Zvezda*, September 30, 1989, 6; cited in *FBIS: Soviet Union*, October 3, 1989, 90.

27. "Ostankino Radio Studio on the Line," Moscow Domestic Service, May 7, 1989; cited in *FBIS: Soviet Union*, May 8, 1989, 85-86.

28. "'Excerpt' of address by Major Ivan Ivanovich Mikulin," Moscow Television Service, July 5, 1990; cited in *FBIS: Soviet Union*, July 6, 1990, 10.

29. Lev Aksenov, TASS, July 5, 1990; cited in *FBIS: Soviet Union* July 6, 1990, 15.

30. Quoted in Dusko Doder and Louise Branson, *Gorbachev: Heretic in the Kremlin* (New York: Viking, 1990), 305.

31. Nina Andreyeva, "Socialism or Death," interview by Robert Bayrashev, *Sobesednik*, No. 25, June 25, 1990, 6; cited in FBIS: Soviet Union, August 14, 1990, 38, 39, 40.

32. I.K. Polozkov, "Our Choice Is at a Crossroads," Speech to the joint plenum of the CPSU Central Committee and Central Control Commission, January 31, 1991, *Sovetskaya Rossiya*, February 2, 1991, 2; cited in *FBIS: Soviet Union*, February 4, 1991, 29.

33. Yuri Belov, "A Party Worker's Stance:'Sobering Up'", *Sovetskaya Rossiya*, December 7, 1990, 1-2; cited in *FBIS: Soviet Union*, December 7, 1990, 51- 52.

34.N. Petrushenko, "On curtailed glasnost: Like Looking Into a Distorting Mirror," *Sovetskaya Rossiya,* January 22, 1991, 4; cited in *FBIS: Soviet Union,* January 24, 1991, 27-28.

35. Ye. K. Ligachev, "Today and Tomorrow," interview by N. Belan, *Sovetskaya Rossiya,* February 6, 1991, 3; cited in *FBIS: Soviet Union,* February 7, 1991, 28, 32.

36. "'Account' of speech delivered by A.N. Ilin," *Pravda,* July 27, 1991, 4; cited in *FBIS: Soviet Union,* August 1, 1991, 1.

37. Lieutenant Colonel V. Markushin, "Military-Political Review: Command of the Epoch," *Krasnaya Zvezda,* November 7, 1988, 3; cited in *FBIS: Soviet Union,* November 16, 1988, 11, 12.

38. "Perestroika, the 19th Party Conference and Foreign Policy," *International Affairs,* July 1988, 3-4.

39. Pavel Kuznetsov, "Outlook" radio program, August 2, 1988; cited in *FBIS: Soviet Union,* August 3, 1988, 13.

40. O.N. Bykov, "Viewpoint: Changes Are the Guarantee of Stability", interview by A. Kuvshinnikov, *Izvestiya,* March 29, 1989, 5; cited in *FBIS: Soviet Union,* March 30, 1989, 4.

41. Marshall Akhromeyev, "Restructuring Requires Action," *Rabotnichesko Delo,* December 6, 1988, 1, 4; cited in *FBIS: Soviet Union,* December 9, 1988, 1.

42. "The 19th All-Union CPSU Conference: Foreign Policy and Diplomacy," *International Affairs,* October 1988, 6.

43. Vadim Zagladin, "An Arduous But Necessary Path," *International Affairs,* September 1988, 34.

44. Ibid.

Chapter 5

1. Genrikh Tromfimenko, "Towards a New Quality of Soviet-American Relations," *International Affairs,* December, 1988, 22.

2. Vyacheslav Dashichev, "East-West: Quest for New Relations. On the Priorities of the Soviet States's Foregn Policy," *Literaturnaya Gazeta,* May 18, 1988, 14; cited in FBIS: Soviet Union, May 20, 1988, 5.

3. Interview with Professor V. Mikhaylov , by A. Khokhlov, "Third Generation Bomb," *Komsomolkskaya Pravda,* July 19, 1990, 2; cited in *FBIS: Soviet Union,* July 20, 1990, 2.

4. Alexei Pushkov, "Is an Ideological Concert Possible?" *International Affairs,* June 1990, 47.

5. Georgiy Pryakhin, interview by Dominique Lagarde, *Le Quotien De Paris,* July 4, 1989, 6; cited in *FBIS: Soviet Union,* July, 28, 1989, 93.

6. Alexander Chubaryan, "Historical Science, Foreign Policy and Perestroika," *International Affairs*, November 1988, 44.

7. Vadim Udalov, "Balance Of Power And Balance Of Interest," *International Affairs*, June 1990, 15.

8. Igor Malashenko, "Russia: The Earth's Heartland," *International Affairs*, July 1990, 47.

9. Vladimir Razuvayev, "Can Moscow Afford Being the Third Rome? Or Why the Soviet Union Has No National Interests," *New Times*, August 7-13, 1990, 16-17; cited in *FBIS: Soviet Union*, August 15, 1990, 37.

10. "Studio Nine," Moscow Television Service, March 9, 1990; cited in *FBIS: Soviet Union*, March 12, 1990, 69.

11. Igor Malashenko, "Hard Parting," *New Times*, March 28-April 3, 1989, 17.

12. Yuriy Tavrovskiy, "'IZVESTIYA Interview' with USSR First Deputy Foregn Minister V.F. Petrovsky," *Izvestiya*, August 14, 1991, 6; cited in *FBIS: Soviet Union*, August 14, 1991, 4.

13. Alexander Nikitin, "Alternative Futures for Soviet-American Relations: A Study of Soviet Experts' Opinion," unpublished manuscript. This study is also described in Andrei Melvil and Aleksander Nikitin, "The End of the Consensus that Never Was: The Future of Soviet-American Relations as Viewed by the Soviet Public" in Richard Smoke and Andrei Kortunov (eds.), *Mutual Security: A New Approach to Soviet-American Relations* (New York, St. Martin's Press, 1991).

14. Hans Rauscher, "We Are Now Learning To Know Our Limits," *Kurier*, September 22, 1988, 5; cited in *FBIS: Soviet Union*, September 22, 1988, 42.

15. "International Observers Roundtable," Moscow Television Service, September 18, 1988; cited in *FBIS: Soviet Union*, September 19, 1988, 9.

16. Andrei Kozyrev and Andrei Shumikhin, "East and West in the Third World," *International Affairs*, March 1989, 72.

17. V. Goldanskiy, "Could the USSR and the United States Become Allies?" interview by A. Ivanko, *Izvestiya*, June 17, 1990, 5; cited in *FBIS: Soviet Union*, June 20, 1990, 5.

18. Mikhail Gorbachev, address at USSR Supreme Soviet session at the Kremlin, Moscow Television Service, June 12, 1990; cited in *FBIS: Soviet Union*, June 13, 1990, 51.

19. P. Vorobyev, "Political Observer's Opinion:Candidate for the Role of Superpower. Why Did Iraq Decide To Take Such A Daring Step? Did the U.S. Invasion of Panama Set Iraq an Example?" *Trud*, August 11, 1990, 3; cited in *FBIS: Soviet Union*, August 13, 1990, 37.

20. Viktor Girshfield, "Superpowers or Superfools? - A Plea for Condominium," *Detente*, No. 13, November 1988, 4.

21. Yelena Arefyeva, "From Dogmas to Realism: Can Our Financial Burden Be Alleviated by Economizing on Aid to the Developing Countries?" interview

by V. Skosyrev, *Izvestiya*, July 11, 1989, 5; cited in *FBIS: Soviet Union*, July 24, 1989, 14-15.

22. "In Smolenskaya Square and Also in 122 Countries of the World," *International Affairs*, December 1989, 125.

23. Flemming Rose, "Will Fight for Power to the Last Drop of Blood," *Berlingske Tidende*, January 22, 1991, 7; cited in *FBIS: Soviet Union*, January 24, 1991, 25.

24. Moscow Radio Rossiya Network, December 26, 1990; cited in *FBIS: Soviet Union*, December 27, 1990, 26.

25. At the time of Shevardnadze's resignation Alksnis said: "Yes, I am in favor of the resignation of Foreign Minister Shevardnadze. But not because I oppose the foreign policy that is being pursued, no. I know that we must indeed leave East Europe, but I oppose the way this is being done at present." "Tape Recorder in Auditorium," *Komsomolskaya Pravda*, December 21, 1990, 3; cited in *FBIS: Soviet Union*, December 21, 1990, 12.

26. David Remnick, "The Hard-Liners' Bad Boy Challenges Gorbachev," *Washington Post*, February 8, 1991, A14-A15.

27. Stanislav Kondrashov, "Coachmen, Do Not Drive the Horses Too Fast," *Izvestiya*, January 3, 1991, 7; cited in FBIS: *Soviet Union*, January 3, 1991, 2.

28. Aleksandr Golts, "Will We Have Enough Parcels?" *Krasnaya Zvezda*, January 4, 1991, 3; cited in *FBIS*i: *Soviet Union*, January 4, 1991, 3.

29. B.I. Oleynik, "If the Hard Rain Falls," speech to the joint plenum of the CPSU Central Committee and Central Control Commission, January 31, 1991, *Sovetskaya Rossiya*, February 2, 1991, 2; cited in *FBIS: Soviet Union*, February 4, 1991, 32.

30. M. Loginov, "'Party of Freedom' and 'Party of Order'," *Literaturnaya Gazeta*, December 19, 1990, 1; cited in *FBIS: Soviet Union*, December 26, 1990, 49.

31. David Remnick, "Gorbachev Forges Odd Coalition with Russian Nationalists, Church," *Washington Post*, March 20, 1991, A27.

32. Michael Dobbs, "Gorbachev Appeals to Preserve Union: President Launches Campaign for Referendum, Hits Separatists" *Washington Post*, February 7, 1991, A1.

33. David Remnick, "Gorbachev Forges Odd Coalition with Russian Nationalists, Church," *Washington Post*, March 20, 1991, A27.

34. "Address to the People," *Selskaya Zhizn*, August 20, 1991, 1; cited in *FBIS: Soviet Union*, August 20, 1991, 23, 24.

35. David Remnick, "In New Commonwealth of 'Equals,' Russia Remains the Dominant Force," *Washington Post*, December 22, 1991, A39.

36. "Excerpts From Yeltsin Speech: Union Pact Ruthlessly Trampled Sovereignty," *New York Times*, December 13, 1991, A22.

Chapter 6

1. "Striving for Comprehensive Security. Speech by E.A. Shevardnadze, Head of the Soviet Delegation, at 43d UN General Assembly Session," *Pravda*, September 28, 1988, 4; cited in *FBIS: Soviet Union*, September 28, 1988, 6.

2. Mikhail Gorbachev, speech in Cuba to deputies of Cuba's National Assembly, TASS, April 5, 1989; cited in *FBIS: Soviet Union*, April 5, 1989, 46.

3. Bill Keller, "Moscow Says Afghan Role was Illegal and Immoral; Admits Breaking Arms Pact," *New York Times*, October 24, 1989, A4.

4. Aleksandr Dzasokhov, report on the decision to send troops into Afghanistan presented at the 24 December session of the Second Congress of USSR People's Deputies in the Kremlin, Moscow Television Service, December 24, 1989; cited in *FBIS: Soviet Union*, December 28, 1989, 72-73.

5. D. Volskiy, "Problems and Opinions: We and the 'Third World' Through the Prism of Modern Thinking," *Izvestiya*, December 22, 1988, 5; cited in *FBIS: Soviet Union*, December 23, 1988, 9.

6. N. Simoniya, "UN Speech: Boost for Quest and Action. Principle of Freedom of Choice," *Pravda*, January 18, 1989, 4; cited in *FBIS: Soviet Union*, January 27, 1989, 17.

7. Quentin Peel, "Soviets Take Hard Look at Their Foreign Policy," *San Jose Mercury News*, August 14, 1988, A1.

8. Aleksandr Bovin, "We Are Now Learning To Know Our Limits," interview by Hans Rauscher, *Kurier*, September 22, 1988, 5; cited in *FBIS: Soviet Union*, September 22, 1988, 42.

9. Eduard Shevardnadze, "Journey South of the Sahara," interview by APN correspondent, *Izvestiya*, March 18, 1990, 5; cited in *FBIS: Soviet Union*, March 19, 1990, 30.

10. Alexei Kiva, "Developing Countries, Socialism, Capitalism," *International Affairs*, March 1989, 57.

11. "Striving for Comprehensive Security. Speech by E.A. Shevardnadze, Head of the Soviet Delegation, at 43d UN General Assembly Session" *Pravda*, September 28, 1988, 4; cited in *FBIS: Soviet Union*, September 28, 1988, 6.

12. Gorbachev, *Perestroika*, 182-83.

13. Ye. Dolgopolov, "Regional Conflicts: Solutions and Impasses," *Krasnaya Zvezda*, November 10, 1989, 3; cited in *FBIS: Soviet Union*, November 17, 1989, 7.

14. A. Vasilyev, "The World and Us: Why Do We Need Africa?" *Izvestiya*, February 6, 1990, 5; cited in *FBIS: Soviet Union*, February 27, 1990, 24.

15. Andrey Kortunov, "Soviet Foreign Aid. Is It Always Put to Wisest Use?" *Moscow News*, December 3, 1989, 6; cited in *FBIS: Soviet Union*, December 15, 1989, 97.

16. A. Vasilyev, "The World and Us: Why Do We Need Africa?" *Izvestiya*,

February 6, 1990, 5; cited in *FBIS: Soviet Union*, February 27, 1990, 24.

17. Vladimir Petrovskiy, "New Internationalism," *Za Rubezhom*, No. 39, September 21-27, 1990, 9; cited in *FBIS: Soviet Union*, October 3, 1990, 12.

18. K. Brutents, "Brutents Discusses Regional Crises Policy," interview by Janiki Cingoli, *L'Unita*, February 16, 1989, 2; cited in *FBIS: Soviet Union*, February 28, 1989, 5.

19. "Primakov on Cooperation in Regional Conflicts," unattributed interview, August 23, 1988; cited in *FBIS: Soviet Union*, August 24, 1988, 9.

20. Proposal for Comprehensive System of International Peace and Security, 2, 4.

21. Ye. Dolgopolov, "Regional Conflicts: Solutions and Impasses," *Krasnaya Zvezda*, November 10, 1989, 3; cited in *FBIS: Soviet Union*, November 17, 1989, 7.

22. A. Bovin, "Panorama of International Events. A Political Observer's Opinion: Angola: A Glimmer of Hope," *Izvestiya*, June 27, 1989, 4; cited in *FBIS: Soviet Union*, July 6, 1989, 19.

23. TASS report, "E.A. Shevardnadze's Speech," *Pravda*, June 9, 1988, 4-5; cited in *FBIS: Soviet Union*, June 9, 1988, 7.

24. "Striving for Comprehensive Security. Speech by E.A. Shevardnadze, Head of the Soviet Delegation, at 43d UN General Assembly Session," *Pravda*, September 28, 1988, 4; cited in *FBIS: Soviet Union*, September 28, 1988, 7.

25. Andrey Kortunov, "Soviet Foreign Aid: Is It Always Put to Wisest Use?" *Moscow News*, December 3, 1989, 6; cited in *FBIS: Soviet Union*, December 15, 1989, 97.

26. E. Shevardnadze, speech to 45th UN General Assembly Session, TASS, September 25, 1990; cited in *FBIS: Soviet Union*, September 26, 1990, 4.

27. TASS report, "E.A. Shevardnadze's Speech," *Pravda*, June 9, 1988, 4-5; cited in *FBIS: Soviet Union*, June 9, 1988, 7.

28. "Striving for Comprehensive Security. Speech by E.A. Shevardnadze, Head of the Soviet Delegation, at 43d UN General Assembly Session," *Pravda*, September 28, 1988, 4; cited in *FBIS: Soviet Union*, September 28, 1988, 7.

29. "Primakov on Cooperation in Regional Conflicts," unattributed article, August 23, 1988; cited in *FBIS: Soviet Union*, August 24, 1988, 9.

30. Andrey Kortunov, "Soviet Foreign Aid: Is It Always Put to Wisest Use?" *Moscow News*, December 3, 1989, 6; cited in *FBIS: Soviet Union*, December 15, 1989, 97.

31. TASS, October 25, 1988; cited in *FBIS: Soviet Union*, October 26, 1988, 7.

32. Vladimir Petrovsky, October 18 News Conference at the U.N. Headquarters, TASS, October 18, 1988; cited in *FBIS: Soviet Union*, October 19, 1988, 5.

33. Ibid.

34. "Striving for Comprehensive Security. Speech by E.A. Shevardnadze, Head of the Soviet Delegation, at 43d UN General Assembly Session," *Pravda*,

September 28, 1988, 4; cited in *FBIS: Soviet Union*, September 28, 1988, 3.

35. "E.A. Shevardnadze Letter to UN Secretary General," *Izvestiya*, August 16, 1990, 4; cited in *FBIS: Soviet Union*, August 16, 1990, 7.

36. V. Makarevskiy, "The Threat From the South," *New Times*, August 21, 1990, 12; cited in *FBIS: Soviet Union*, August 29, 1990, 54.

37. E. Shevardnadze, speech to 45th UN General Assembly Session, TASS September 25, 1990; cited in *FBIS: Soviet Union*, September 26, 1990, 4.

38. Mikhail Gorbachev, Speech in Vladivostok, Moscow Television Service, July 28, 1986; cited in *FBIS: Soviet Union*, July 29, 1986, R16.

39. Mikhail Gorbachev, "The Reality and Guarantees of a Secure World," *Pravda*, September 17, 1987, 1-2; cited in *FBIS: Soviet Union*, September 17, 1987, 25.

40. TASS report, "E.A. Shevardnadze's Speech," *Pravda*, June 9, 1988, 4-5; cited in *FBIS: Soviet Union*, June 9, 1988, 4.

41. Ibid., 7-8.

42. "The Fate of the World Is Inseparable from the Fate of Our Perestroyka. Speech by E.A. Shevardnadze, Head of the Soviet Delegation, at the 44th UN General Assembly Session," *Pravda*, September 27, 1989, 4,5; cited in *FBIS: Soviet Union*, September 27, 1989, 12.

43. TASS report, "News Conference Statement," *Pravda*, October 6, 1989, 5; cited in *FBIS: Soviet Union*, October 6, 1989, 32.

44. "Plan to Bring All Troops Home," *New York Times*, December 16, 1989

45. Mikhail Gorbachev, speech in Vladivostok, Moscow Television Service, July 28, 1986; cited in *FBIS: Soviet Union*, July 29, 1986, R18.

46. TASS report, "Answers by M.S. Gorbachev to Questions from the Indonesian Newspaper MERDEKA," *Pravda*, July 23, 1987, 1-2; cited in *FBIS: Soviet Union*, July 23, 1987, C5.

47. TASS report, "E.A. Shevardnadze's Speech," *Pravda*, June 9, 1988, 4-5; cited in *FBIS: Soviet Union*, June 9, 1988, 7.

48. "Primakov on Cooperation in Regional Conflicts," unattributed article, August 23, 1988; cited in *FBIS: Soviet Union*, August 24, 1988, 9.

49. Vladimir Petrovsky, "Disarmament: U.S. Ambivalence," interview by Eduard Khamidulin, *Moscow News*, July 10, 1988, 6; cited in *FBIS: Soviet Union*, July 22, 1988, 5.

50. "Time for Action, Time for Practical Work. M.S. Gorbachev's Speech in Krasnoyarsk," *Pravda*, September 18, 1988, 1-3; cited in *FBIS: Soviet Union*, September 20, 1988, 39.

51. TASS, November 16, 1988; cited in *FBIS: Soviet Union*, November 17, 1988, 4.

52. I. Porshev, "Diplomatic Panorama," *Interfax*, May 24, 1991; cited in *FBIS: Soviet Union*, May 28, 1991, 19.

53. Clifford Kraus, "Mozambique Moves to Start Peace Talks with Rightist Rebels," *New York Times* , June 12, 1990, A8.

54. Mark A. Uhlig, "Soviets Reducing Arms for Nicaragua," *New York Times*, October 16, 1989, A13.

55. Thomas Friedman, "U.S. Issues Protest to Soviets on Arms to Salvador Rebels," *New York Times*, November 28, 1989, A8.

56. Al Kamen, "Soviets Reportedly Asked to Help Halt Arms Sales," *Washington Post*, March 3, 1991, A22.

57. Clifford Kraus, "U.S. and Soviets Press U.N. Role in Salvador Talks," *New York Times*, August 17, 1991, A3.

58. *New York Times* , March 16, 1989, A1.

59. "Diplomatic Panorama," *Interfax* 1638 GMT, September 20, 1991; cited in *FBIS: Soviet Union*, September 23, 1991, 14.

60. W. Raymond Duncan and Carolyn McGiffert Ekedahl, *Moscow and the Third World Under Gorbachev*, (Boulder: Westview Press, 1990), 120.

61. Yevgeniy Menkes, TASS, 0136 GMT, September 25, 1991; cited in *FBIS: Soviet Union*, September 25, 1991, 1.

62. TASS report on Shevardnadze news conference at UN in New York, NY, September 30, 1990; cited in *FBIS: Soviet Union*, October 1, 1990, 16.

63. "U.S. Military Presence in Asia-Pacific Criticized," Moscow Radio Peace and Progress, January 24, 1989; cited in *FBIS: Soviet Union*, February 2, 1989, 3.

64. TASS International Service, April 16, 1991; cited in *FBIS: Soviet Union*, April 17, 1991 1.

65. M. Moiseyev, "Sources of Tension: What Lies Behind the U.S. Plans in the Far East and Southeast Asia," *Pravda*, May 4, 1989, 4; cited in *FBIS: Soviet Union*, May 4, 1989, 6.

66. TASS report of E. Shevardnadze address in Vladivostok, September 4,1990; cited in *FBIS: Soviet Union*, September 5, 1990, 6.

67. Admiral I. Kapitanets, "Bringing It to Our Contemporaries and Preserving It for Our Descendents: Approaching the 300th Anniversary of the Foundation of the Navy," *Krasnaya Zvezda*, June 13, 1991; cited in *FBIS: Soviet Union*, June 17, 1991, 66.

68. "How the Soviet Navy Has Cut Back," *San Francisco Chronicle*, February 23, 1989, A22; "Statement of Rear Admiral Thomas A. Brooks, USN, Director of Naval Intelligence, Before the Seapower Strategic and Critical Materials Subcommittee of the House Armed Services Committee on Intelligence Issues," March 7, 1991, 18-30, 29.

69. Michael Ross, "Disarmament at Sea," *Foreign Policy* , No. 77, Winter 1989-1990, 104.

70."Statement of Rear Admiral Thomas A. Brooks, USN, Director of Naval Intelligence, Before the Seapower Strategic and Critical Materials Subcommittee of the House Armed Services Committee on Intelligence Issues" March 7, 1991, 18-30.

71. Richard Grimmett, *CRS Report for Congress: Conventional Arms Transfers to the Third World,* Congressional Research Service, August 2, 1991, CRS-46, CRS-47.

72. Rifat al-Najjar, *Abu Dhabi Al-Ittihan Al-usbu'i* September 19, 1991, 3; cited in *FBIS: Soviet Union,* September 23, 1991, 13.

73. Georgiy Shmelev, TASS, September 19, 1991; cited in *FBIS: Soviet Union,* September 23, 1991, 1.

74. Nikolay Kosukhin, recorded interview, Moscow Radio Broadcast, March 30, 1989; cited in *FBIS: Soviet Union,* April 4, 1989, 23.

75. Nikolay Kosukhin, recorded interview, Moscow Radio Broadcast, March 16, 1989; cited in *FBIS: Soviet Union,* March 21, 1989, 24.

76. Mikhail Kapitsa, interview by Kuwait News Agency (KUNA), KUNA, September 11, 1989; cited in *FBIS: Soviet Union,* September 13, 1989, 21.

77. Alexander Prokhanov, "Defense Consciousness and New Thinking," *Literaturnaya Rossiya,* May 6, 1988, 4-5; cited in *FBIS: Soviet Union,* June 9, 1988, 74.

78. Boris Kanevsky, Pyotr Shabardin, "The Correlation of Politics, War, and a Nuclear Catastrophe," *International Affairs,* February 1988, 100.

79. SAPA news release, Johannesburg, March 31, 1989; cited in *FBIS: Soviet Union,* April 3, 1989, 15.

80. TASS, April 1, 1989; cited in *FBIS: Soviet Union,* April 3, 1989, 15.

81. Colonel General Nikolay Chervov, recorded interview by Mikhail Kommissar, Moscow Radio Broadcast, February 10, 1989; cited in *FBIS: Soviet Union,* February 13, 1989, 34.

82. "International Program," Moscow Television Service, March 11, 1989; cited in *FBIS: Soviet Union,* March 13, 1989, 18-19.

83. Admiral K. Makarov, "Flying the Motherland's Ensign: 31 July Is Soviet Navy Day," interview by *TRUD* correspondent, *TRUD,* July 31, 1988, 3; cited in *FBIS: Soviet Union,* August 5, 1988, 58.

84. Sergei Blagavolin, "Military Power—How Much, What Kind, For What Reason?" unpublished paper

85. TASS, July 27, 1989; cited in *FBIS: Soviet Union,* July 28, 1989, 107.

86. Admiral K. Makarov, "Flying the Motherland's Ensign: 31 July Is Soviet Navy Day," interview by *TRUD* correspondent, *TRUD,* July 31, 1988, 3; cited in *FBIS: Soviet Union,* August 5, 1988, 58.

87. "PERESTROIKA, the 19th Party Conference and Foreign Policy," *International Affairs,* July 1988, 7.

88. Eduard Shevardnadze, "Foreign Policy and Perestroyka," speech, October 23, to plenary session of the USSR Supreme Soviet in Moscow, *Pravda,* October 24, 1989, 2-4; cited in *FBIS: Soviet Union,* October 24, 1989, 46.

89. D. Makarov, "E. Shevardnadze: The West Is Interested in the Stability of the USSR," *Argumenty I Faktiy*, October 1990, 4-5; cited in *FBIS: Soviet Union*, November 1, 1990, 3.

Chapter 7

1. Quoted in Charles Gati, *The Bloc That Failed: Soviet-East European Relations in Transition* (Bloomington, IN: Indiana University Press, 1990), 47.
2. M.S. Gorbachev, "The Reality and Guarantees of a Secure World," *Pravda*, September 17, 1987, Second Edition, 1-2; cited in *FBIS: Soviet Union*, September 17, 1987, 23-28.
3. Quoted in Milan Svec, "Soviet Think Tanks and Gorbachev's Foreign Policy—'New Thinking'" (Boston: Boston University's Program for the Study of Disinformation, 1989), 18.
4. "Press Club: From Balance of Forces to Balance of Interests," *Literaturnaya Gazeta*, June 29, 1988, 14; cited in *FBIS: Soviet Union*, June 30, 1988, 8.
5. Joerg R. Mettke and Fritjof Meyer, "Thus the Cart Stood Before the Horse," *Der Spiegel*, July 4, 1988, 123-127; cited in *FBIS: Soviet Union*, July 8, 1988, 20-21.
6. "International Observers Roundtable," Moscow Domestic Service in Russian; cited in *FBIS: Soviet Union*, July 12, 1988, 9.
7. "Meeting at the Polish Sejm: Speech by M.S. Gorbachev," *Pravda*, July 12, 1988, 2; cited in *FBIS: Soviet Union*, July 12, 1988, 42.
8. "In Honor of the Lofty Guest": "Speech by M.S. Gorbachev," *Pravda*, July 12, 1988, 4; cited in *FBIS: Soviet Union*, July 12, 1988, 50.
9. "Soviet-Polish Joint Statement," *Pravda*, July 15, 1988, 1, 2; cited in *FBIS: Soviet Union*, July 15, 1988, 47.
10. L.S. Yagodovskiy, "Czechoslovakia: August 1968," *Argumenty I Fakty*, August 13-19, 1988, 4-5; cited in *FBIS: Soviet Union*, August 15, 1988, 42.
11. Ibid.
12. Bernard Guetta, Report on interview with Nikolay Shishlin, *Le Monde*, September 7, 1988, 1,4; cited in *FBIS: Soviet Union*, September 8, 1988, 31.
13. "Korniyenko Dismisses Brezhnev Doctrine," Rome ANSA, September 16, 1988; cited in *FBIS: Soviet Union*, September 19, 1988, 76.
14. "Panorama," Budapest Television Service, August 19, 1988; cited in *FBIS: Soviet Union*, August 22, 1988, 45-47.
15. Aleksandr Kondrashov, "About the Anti-Czechoslovak Campaign in the West," *Izvestiya*, August 22, 1988, Morning Edition, 3; cited in *FBIS: Soviet Union*, August 23, 1988, 20.
16. Yevgeniy Ambartsumov, "Imre Nagy's Sacrifice," *Moscow News*, July 2,

1989, 7; cited in *FBIS: Soviet Union*, July 5, 1989, 17.

17. Yevgeniy Tikhonovich Grachev, "The International Situation—Questions and Answers," Moscow Domestic Service, July 1, 1989; cited in *FBIS: Soviet Union*, July 5, 1989, 18.

18. "Budapest Radio Highlights Remarks," Budapest Domestic Service, February 8, 1989; cited in *FBIS: Soviet Union*, February 9, 1989, 34.

19. "Hungary's Membership Discussed," Budapest Domestic Service, February 20, 1989; cited in *FBIS: Soviet Union*, February 23, 1989, 4.

20. Josef Kirchengast, "Defense Forces at Lowest Level," *Der Standard*, May 11, 1989, 3; cited in *FBIS: Soviet Union*, May 12, 1989, 5.

21. Stanislav Polzikov, "Interview with Aleksandr Yakovlev," *Trud*; cited in *FBIS: Soviet Union*, July 3, 1989, 1.

22. "New Times Interviews Walesa on Solidarity," Moscow World Service, February 9, 1989; cited in *FBIS: Soviet Union*, February 10, 1989, 37.

23. Paris AFP, July 4, 1989; cited in *FBIS: Soviet Union*, July 5, 1989, 19.

24. Janiki Cingoli, "Interview with Deputy Chief Karen Brutents," *L'Unita*, February 16, 1989, 2; cited in *FBIS: Soviet Union*, February 28, 1989, 5.

25. "Brochure on Restructuring Appears in CSSR," Moscow Domestic Service, March 15, 1989; cited in *FBIS: Soviet Union*, March 21, 1989, 27. Gerasimov, "April 4 Is Hungarian Liberation Day. Time of Hope." *Pravda*, April 3, 1989; cited in *FBIS: Soviet Union*, April 13, 1989, 30.

26. "Hears Gorbachev on Multiple Parties," Budapest MTI, March 3, 1989; cited in *FBIS: Soviet Union*, March 3, 1989, 29.

27. Mikhail Gorbachev, news conference with Francois Mitterrand, Moscow Domestic Service, July 5, 1989; cited in *FBIS: Soviet Union*, July 6, 1989, 34.

28. Mikhail Gorbachev, "Address to the Council of Europe Parliamentary Assembly," July 6, 1989; cited in *FBIS: Soviet Union*, July 6, 1989, 29.

29. TASS report: "M.S. Gorbachev's Answers to Questions From Representatives of the French Intelligentsia," *Pravda*, July 6, 1989, Second Edition, p 2; cited in *FBIS: Soviet Union*, July 10, 1989, 40.

30. Interview of the Agrarian Policy Commission Yegor Ligachev, "Panorama," Budapest Television Service, July 17, 1989; cited in *FBIS: Soviet Union*, July 19, 1989, 82-83.

31. Aleksandr Kondrashov, "About the Anti-Czechoslovak Campaign in the West", *Izvestiya*, August 22, 1988, 3; cited in *FBIS: Soviet Union*, August 23, 1988, 20-21. TASS report, "In the Working People's Interests. *Rude Pravo* on the 20th Anniversary of the Rendering of International Assistance," *Pravda*, August 20, 1988, 4; cited in *FBIS: Soviet Union*, August 23, 1988, 21-22.

32. Interviews of participants in CSSR 1968 events, TASS, August 19, 1989; cited in *FBIS: Soviet Union*, August 21, 1989, 35.

33. Interview with Kiril Mazurov, "Panorama," Budapest Television Service,

September 4, 1989; cited in *FBIS: Soviet Union*, September 7, 1989, 27.

34. Excerpt, TASS, August 21, 1989; cited in *FBIS: Soviet Union*, August 22, 1989, 5.

35. "E.A. Shevardnadze Comments on 1968, CSSR, Poland," Prague Domestic Service, October 27, 1989; cited in *FBIS: Soviet Union*, October 30, 1989, 27.

36. Interview with Kiril Mazurov, "Panorama," Budapest Television Service, September 4, 1989; cited in *FBIS: Soviet Union*, September 7, 1989, 27.

37. Bill Keller, "Warsaw Pact Condemns '68 Prague Invasion," *New York Times*, December 5, 1989 A1.

38. Gennady Gerasimov, "Friendship Fest Speech," ANSA, September 8, 1989; cited in *FBIS: Soviet Union*, September 8, 1989, 24.

39. Viktor Sheynis, "The World and We: August Harvest," *Izvestiya*, October 14, 1989; cited in *FBIS: Soviet Union*, October 18, 1989, 100.

40. D.D. Biryukov, "Political Tribune," Interview With Yevgeniy Maksimovich Primakov, *Moscow Television Service*, cited in *FBIS: Soviet Union*, November 12, 1989, 8.

41. Ye. Korolev, "The Lessons of 13 August," *Izvestiya*, August 14, 1989; cited in *FBIS: Soviet Union*, August 15, 1989, 5.

42. M. Podklyuchnikov, "It Has Defended Peace," *Pravda*, August 13, 1989; cited in *FBIS: Soviet Union*, August 16, 1989, 24.

43. V. Shutkevich, "Firecrackers on the Other Side of the Fence," *Komosomolskaya Pravda*, September 24, 1989, p 3; cited in *FBIS: Soviet Union*, October 4, 1989, 43.

44. "A.J." report, "The Whole World Is Changing,"*Le Monde*, October 8-9, 1989; cited in *FBIS: Soviet Union*, October 11, 1989, 21.

45."P.H." report, "Perestroyka Will Affect All the European Socialist Countries," *Paris Liberation*, October 7-6, 1989; cited in *FBIS: Soviet Union*, October 11, 1989, 22.

46. Francis X. Clines, "Gorbachev Calls, Then Polish Party Drops Its Demands," *New York Times*, August 23, 1989.

47. Scott Sullivan, "Now It's the Czechs," *Newsweek*, November 27, 1989, 9.

48. Bill Keller, "In Soviet Speeches, 2 Nightmares: Europe's Ideologies, or Its Armies," *New York Times*, February 7, 1990, A8.

49. "Further on Lukyanov Meeting," TASS, October 13, 1989; cited in *FBIS: Soviet Union*, October 18, 1989, 90.

50. "More on Primakov, Shishlin Comments," Budapest Television Service, October 30, 1989; cited in *FBIS: Soviet Union*, October 31, 1989, 19.

51. "Yakovlev Says Reunification Up to Germans," *Kyodo*, November 15, 1989; cited in *FBIS: Soviet Union*, November 15, 1989, 24.

52. "Panorama," interview with Gennadiy Gerasimov by David Dimbleby, London BBC Network, November 13, 1989; cited in *FBIS: Soviet Union*, Novem-

ber 15, 1989, 27.

53. "Gorbachev's Remarks on a United Germany" *New York Times*, February 21, 1990, A9.

54. Gennadiy Gerasimov, "International Panorama," Moscow Television Service, November 12, 1989; cited in *FBIS: Soviet_Union*, November 13, 1989, 32.

55. "'Military Force' Not Ruled Out in German Issue," Montreal International Service, February 16, 1990; cited in *FBIS: Soviet Union*, February 20, 1990, 11.

56. Serge Schmemann, "Soviets Unyielding on a New Germany in Western Orbit" *New York Times*, May 6, 1990, A8.

57. Thomas Friedman, "Wide Differences Over Germany Are Still Said to Divide the Superpowers," *New York Times*, June 2, 1990, A7.

58. "Shevardnadze's *Pravda* Article Criticized," Commentary by Mikhail Mayorov, Moscow World Service, June 27, 1990; cited in *FBIS: Soviet Union*, June 28, 1990, 3.

59. E.A. Shevardnadze, "On Foreign Policy," *Pravda*, June 26, 1990; cited in *FBIS: Soviet Union*, June 26, 1990, 3.

60. Moscow Domestic Service, July 3, 1990, cited in *FBIS: Soviet Union*, July 3, 1990 (Supplement), 39.

61. "Excerpts From Kohl-Gorbachev News Conference," *New York Times*, July 17, 1990, A6.

62. Eduard Shevardnadze, *The Future Belongs to Freedom* (New York: Free Press, 1991), 134.

63. "S. Akhromeyev: Warsaw Pact 'Alliance of Interests,'" Voice of GDR Domestic Service, October 23, 1989; cited in *FBIS: Soviet Union*, October 24, 1989, 21.

64. Marshall Sergey Akhromeyev, interview by Ezio Mauro, Rome *La Repubblica* (Rome), November 22, 1989, 11; cited in *FBIS: Soviet Union*, November 30, 1989, 105.

65. *Liberation*, June 30-July 1, 1990, 14; cited in *FBIS: Soviet Union*, July 3, 1990, 56.

66. Interview with General Geli Viktorovich Batenin, "Moscow Will Regard NATO as a Partner Against Threats by Third Parties," *Die Welt*, July 25, 1990, 5; cited in *FBIS: Soviet Union*, July 26, 1990, 2.

67. Steven Greenhouse, "Death Knell Sounds in Prague for the Warsaw Pact," *New York Times*, July 2, 1991, A7.

68. Mikhail Kozhokin, "Kremlin Demands Too Much from Former Allies," *Moscow News*, June 16, 1991, 12; cited in *FBIS: Soviet Union*, July 2, 1991, 7.

69. Gorbachev, *Perestroika*, 197-198.

70. M.S. Gorbachev, speech at gala marking the fortieth anniversary of the founding of the GDR, Moscow, *Pravda*, October 7, 1989; cited in *FBIS: Soviet*

Union, October 10, 1989, 31.

71. Gorbachev, *Perestroika,* 195.

72. Ibid.

73. TASS report, Gorbachev speech to Council of Europe, Paris, July 6, 1989; cited in *FBIS: Soviet Union,* July 7, 1989, 33, 34.

74. As spoken on "Studio 9," Moscow Television Service, July 30, 1988; cited in *FBIS: Soviet Union,* August 2, 1988, 14-15.

75. TASS, May 10. 1989; cited in *FBIS: Soviet Union,* May 10, 1989, 5.

76. Manki Ponomarev, "Looking for an Opportunity," *Krasnaya Zvezda,* May 12, 1989, 3; cited in *FBIS: Soviet Union,* May 15, 1989, 21.

77. TASS August 11, 1989; cited in *FBIS: Soviet Union,* August 11, 1989, 3.

78. "Dialogue: European Horizons," *Izvestiya,* November 24, 1989, 5; cited in *FBIS: Soviet Union,* December 4, 1989, 11.

79. Soviet Foreign Ministry press briefing, Moscow TASS, October 30, 1989; cited in *FBIS: Soviet Union,* October 31, 1989, 6.

80. Charles Lambroschini, "Interview with USSR Deputy Foreign Minister Vladimir Petrovskiy," *Le Figaro,* December 2-3, 1989; cited in *FBIS: Soviet Union,* December 8, 1989, 3.

81. TASS, December 15, 1989; cited in *FBIS: Soviet Union,* December 18, 1989, 4.

82. Moiseyev, M., "Dialogues at NATO Headquarters," *Krasnaya Zvezda,* November 6, 1990; cited in *FBIS: Soviet Union,* November 8, 1990, 4.

83. Shevardnadze, Eduard, "Europe—From Division to Unity," *Izvestiya,* January 19, 1990; cited in *FBIS: Soviet Union,* January 19, 1990, 13-14.

84. Bjarne Stenquist dispatch: "Warning Against Excessive Faith in CSCE," *Dagens Nyheter* (Stockholm), June 28, 1990; cited in *FBIS: Soviet Union,* July 5, 1990, 8.

85. "Speech by Mikhail Gorbachev at the CSCE summit in Paris," Moscow Domestic Service, November 19, 1990; cited in *FBIS: Soviet Union,* November 20, 1990, 2.

86. Quoted in V. Boykov, "One Continent—Common Security," *Trud,* February 28, 1990; cited in *FBIS: Soviet Union,* March 6, 1990, 7.

87. Moscow Television Service, March 5, 1990; cited in *FBIS: Soviet Union,* March 6, 1990, 9-10.

88. Aleksandr Prokhanov, "The Tragedy of Centralism", *Literaturnaya Rossiya,* January 1990; cited in *FBIS: Soviet Union,* May 1, 1990, 44.

89. Thomas Friedman, "Wide Differences Over Germany Are Still Said to Divide the Superpowers," *New York Times,* June 2, 1990, A7.

90. Official text of the USSR Foreign Ministry statement circulated on March 13, 1990; cited in *FBIS: Soviet Union,* March 2, 1990, 2.

91. Moscow, Moscow Television Service, July 12, 1990; cited in *FBIS: Soviet*

Union, July 13, 1990, 5.

92. AFP, November 18, 1990; cited in *FBIS: Soviet Union,* November 20, 1990, 8.

93. Text of Shevardnadze's speech, Moscow, TASS, June 5, 1990; cited in *FBIS: Soviet Union,* June 6, 1990, 7.

94. Interview with Yu.S. Deryabin by Izvestiya correspondent G. Stepanov, "The Human Dimension, or What Will Be Discussed in Copenhagen," June 5, 1990; cited in *FBIS: Soviet Union,* June 6, 1990, 11.

95. "Shevardnadze Outlines Arms Cuts," Moscow TASS, June 5, 1990; cited in *FBIS: Soviet Union,* June 6, 1990, 8.

96. Ibid.

97. Interview with USSR Deputy Minister of Foreign Affairs Yuriy Deryabin by A. Sychev, "A State of Emergency and Human Rights," *Izvestiya,* September 20, 1991, 6; cited in *FBIS: Soviet Union,* September 26, 1991, 7.

98. S. Pankratov, interview with Yu.S. Deryabin, "Man in the New Europe," *Trud,* November 24, 1990; cited in *FBIS: Soviet Union,* December 7, 1990, 9.

99. "Shevardnadze Outlines Arms Cuts," Moscow TASS, June 5, 1990; cited in *FBIS: Soviet Union,* June 6, 1990, 8.

100. Address by Mikhail Sergeyevich Gorbachev to the CEPA (Council of Europe Parliamentary Assembly) in Strasbourg on July 6, Moscow Television Service, July 6, 1989; cited in *FBIS: Soviet Union,* July 7, 1989, 33.

101. "Boris Yeltsin's Concluding News Conference Took Place in Rome," TASS, December 21, 1991; cited in *FBIS: Soviet Union,* December 23, 1991, 53.

102. AFP, December 20, 1991; cited in *FBIS: Soviet Union,* December 20, 1991, 40. TASS, December 20, 1991; cited in *FBIS: Soviet Union,* December 23, 1991, 49.

Chapter 8

1. Narkomindel Reply to the Invitation to Attend the League of Nations Conference on Naval Disarmament, 15 March 1923, in Jane Degras, *Soviet Documents on Foreign Policy,* Volume 1, (London: Oxford University Press, 1953), 381.

2. Jane Degras, *Soviet Documents,* Volume 3, p. 45.

3. John Lewis Gaddis, *Strategies of Containment* (Oxford: Oxford University Press, 1982) 56.

4. Quoted in David Holloway, *The Soviet Union and the Arms Race* (New Haven, Conn.: Yale University Press, 1983), 31.

5. Quoted in Albert L. Weeks and William C. Bodie, *War and Peace:: Soviet Russia Speaks* (New York: National Strategy Information Center, 1983), 6.

6. Quoted in Harriet F. Scott and William F. Scott, *The Soviet Art of War: Doctrine, Strategy and Tactics* (Boulder, Colo.: Westview Press, 1982), 175.

7. Quoted in Edward L. Warner III, *The Military in Contemporary Soviet Politics: An Institutional Analysis* (New York: Praeger, 1977), 252.

8. Rear Admiral V. V. Shelyaga, "Two World Outlooks—Two Views on War," *Red Star* (*Krasnaya Zvezda*), February 7, 1974, 2-3; cited in *FBIS: Soviet Union*, February 12, 1974, A4.

9. Quoted in James M. McConnell, "Shifts in Soviet Views on the Proper Focus of Military Development," *World Politics*, 37.3, Spring 1985, 338-39.

10. "Striving for Comprehensive Security. Speech by E.A. Shevardnadze, Head of the Soviet Delegation, at 43d UN General Assembly Session," *Pravda*, September 28, 1988 (Second Edition), 4; cited in *FBIS: Soviet Union*, September 28, 1988, 4.

11. "M.S. Gorbachev's Speech at the UN Organization," *Pravda*, December 8, 1988 (Second Edition), 1,2; cited in *FBIS: Soviet Union*, December 8, 1988, 11-19.

12. "God—or History," *Time*, December 19, 1988, 20.

13. Eduard Shevardnadze, *The Future Belongs to Freedom*, (New York: Free Press, 1991), 107.

14. Paul Lewis, "US and Russians Agree to Bigger World Court Role," *New York Times*, August 7, 1989, A1.

15. "Ours About Us: Opinion for Export,"*Pravda*, May 20, 1991, 5; cited in *FBIS: Soviet Union*, May 21, 1991, 35.

16. *Interfax*, August 23, 1991; cited in *FBIS: Soviet Union*, August 26, 1991, 1.

17. Interview with USSR Deputy Minister of Foreign Affairs Yuriy Deryabin by A. Sychev, "A State of Emergency and Human Rights," *Izvestiya*, September 20, 1991, 6; cited in *FBIS: Soviet Union*, September 26, 1991, 7.

18. Interview with Soviet Foreign Minister Boris Pankin by Vladimir Markov, "We Have to Ask our Neighbors for Advice from Time to Time," *Die Presse*, September 5, 1991; cited in *FBIS: Soviet Union*, September 6, 1991, 39.

19. "Transcript of President's Address to U.N. General Assembly," *New York Times*, October 2, 1990, A12.

20. President Bush, "Operation Desert Storm Launched, "Address to the nation broadcast from the White House at 9:00 P.M. (EST) on January 16, 1991, U.S. Department of State *Dispatch* ,Vol., 2, N0. 3, January 21, 1991, 38.

21. President Bush, "The World After the Persian Gulf War," Address Before Joint Session of Congress, March 6, 1991, U.S. Department of State *Dispatch*, Vol. 2, No. 10, March 11, 1991, 162.

22. "Transcript of President's Address to U.N. General Assembly," *New York Times*, October 2, 1990, A12.

23. President Bush, "The World After the Persian Gulf War," Address before Joint Session of Congress, March 6, 1991, U.S. Department of State *Dispatch*, Vol.

2, No. 10, March 11, 1991, 162.

24. John E. Yang, "Bush Defends Non-Intervention in Iraq," *Washington Post*, April, 14, 1991, A27.

25. Dan Balz and Ann Devroy, "Bush Keeps Earlier Vow to Set Terms," *Washington Post*, February 23, 1991, A10.

About the Book and Author

For decades U.S. foreign policy was focused on battling the menace of Soviet communism; then, seemingly overnight, the implacable foe collapsed. How did this extraordinary event come about? Political psychologist Steven Kull argues that only a revolution in the thinking of the country's top leaders can explain the swiftness and comparative peacefulness of the recent political transformation. His analysis, based on probing interviews with Soviet policymakers and on a careful reading of the public record, reveals the painful process by which they came to accept the failure of Leninism and to forge an alternative ideology dubbed "new thinking." Kull assesses the influence of new thinking and other streams of thought on post-Soviet foreign policy and behavior and describes the new challenges they present to Western nations.

Steven Kull is currently a senior visiting scholar at the Center for International Security Studies, University of Maryland, and senior research associate at Global Outlook, Palo Alto, California.

Index